AIMÉ CÉSAIRE

Black Lives series

Elvira Basevich, *W. E. B. Du Bois*
Nigel C. Gibson, *Frantz Fanon*
Jane Hiddleston, *Aimé Césaire*
Denise Lynn, *Claudia Jones*
Utz McKnight, *Frances E. W. Harper*
Joshua Myers, *Cedric Robinson*
Sherrow O. Pinder, *David Walker*

Aimé Césaire

Inventor of Souls

Jane Hiddleston

polity

Copyright © Jane Hiddleston 2025

The right of Jane Hiddleston to be identified as Author of this Work has been asserted in accordance with the UK Copyright, Designs and Patents Act 1988.

First published in 2025 by Polity Press

Polity Press
65 Bridge Street
Cambridge CB2 1UR, UK

Polity Press
111 River Street
Hoboken, NJ 07030, USA

All rights reserved. Except for the quotation of short passages for the purpose of criticism and review, no part of this publication may be reproduced, stored in a retrieval system or transmitted, in any form or by any means, electronic, mechanical, photocopying, recording or otherwise, without the prior permission of the publisher.

ISBN-13: 978-1-5095-4977-1
ISBN-13: 978-1-5095-4978-8(pb)

A catalogue record for this book is available from the British Library.

Library of Congress Control Number: 2024940613

Typeset in 10.5pt on 14pt Janson by
Cheshire Typesetting Ltd, Cuddington, Cheshire
Printed and bound in Great Britain by CPI Group (UK) Ltd, Croydon

The publisher has used its best endeavours to ensure that the URLs for external websites referred to in this book are correct and active at the time of going to press. However, the publisher has no responsibility for the websites and can make no guarantee that a site will remain live or that the content is or will remain appropriate.

Every effort has been made to trace all copyright holders, but if any have been overlooked the publisher will be pleased to include any necessary credits in any subsequent reprint or edition.

For further information on Polity, visit our website:
politybooks.com

Contents

Acknowledgements vi

Introduction 1

1 1930s Paris and the *Cahier d'un retour au pays natal*:
'It is beautiful and good and legitimate to be nègre' 23

2 Wartime Martinique, *Tropiques*, and *Les Armes miraculeuses*:
'Open the windows. Air. Air' 58

3 Departmentalisation, *Soleil cou coupé* and *Corps perdu*:
'I shall command the islands to exist' 100

4 The Political Upheavals of the 1950s:
'History I tell of the awakening of Africa' 133

5 The Theatre of Decolonisation:
'One does not invent a tree, one plants it' 173

6 Political and Poetic Disillusionment:
'I inhabit a sacred wound' 214

Afterword 241

Notes 249
Bibliography 276
Index 283

Acknowledgements

George Owers at Polity Press contacted me in August 2020, in the wake of the brutal murder of George Floyd, to ask me to write this book on Aimé Césaire for the new Black Lives series. The press wanted to develop the series to explore the history of black activism behind the contemporary protests, to offer the long view of antiracist thought and recognise the contributions of a range of key antiracist figures. Having taught Césaire's poetry and thought for at least fifteen years and having written on various aspects of his work in several publications, I was delighted to have this opportunity to produce a full analysis of his long and productive career and his copious writing. The project has given me the opportunity to immerse myself in his many political essays, poems and plays to discover a rich, complex and multifaceted œuvre. I am immensely grateful to Polity for offering me this opportunity to contribute to the Black Lives series by working on this important and enriching thinker. Julia Davies and Helena Heaton have been encouraging and flexible editors, whose efficiency has helped enormously in bringing the book to fruition.

I am grateful to the Rector and Fellows of Exeter College Oxford for granting me two terms of sabbatical in 2023, during which I was able to work on the book. I am particularly grateful to the librarian Joanna Bowring for purchasing the 1978 edition of *Tropiques* and allowing me to keep the volumes on my desk throughout this project. Nick Hearn at the Taylor Institution also kindly bought many crucial volumes, including all the *Écrits politiques*, which have been central to the book. I am also grateful to the many students with whom I've discussed Césaire, from the first years who studied the *Cahier* to the final-year and graduate students who chose courses on race and negritude and kept me revisiting Césaire. This book has also benefited greatly from dialogues I've had with several colleagues and friends. James Arnold has been a supportive advisor from the start, offering helpful suggestions along the way and perceptive comments on the manuscript in its final stages. Clare Finburgh-Delijani has been a most lively and energising interlocutor on Césaire and negritude for the last couple of years, giving me lucid pointers on some of my writing but also many inspiring conversations on race, anticolonialism, ecopoetics and much more. Cécile Bishop has read some of my related work, and it has been great to share ideas with her over the last few years. Many other colleagues have contributed through debates at conferences and seminars or through informal conversations, and I am indebted to them all. Colin and Natasha have been my constant companions and patient listeners, their love and support makes me what I am. The book is dedicated to my sister Anna, my longest ally. I'm so thrilled that, alongside everything else, we came to share this interest in Césaire.

Jane Hiddleston, Exeter College Oxford, July 2024.

Introduction

On 22 May 2020, the 172nd anniversary of the abolition of slavery in the French colonies, activists in Martinique tore down two statues of the French abolitionist Victor Schoelcher. Schoelcher had been writing and lobbying against slavery since 1833, and was responsible for the decree finally passed by the Second Republic on 27 April 1848 that definitively abolished slavery in all French colonies. Schoelcher condemned slavery in all its forms, dismissed attempts at a protracted transition, and insisted that an end to slavery was both an ethical and an economic imperative. Yet whilst Schoelcher's influence on abolition was crucial, he did not fight this battle alone. Abolition was the consequence of years of revolts by enslaved people in the French Caribbean, notably those led by Toussaint Louverture in Haiti (that finally led to independence in 1804) and by Louis Delgrès in Guadeloupe in 1802 (that was violently quashed). In Martinique, the activists who destroyed the statues of Schoelcher in 2020 acted in the name of those who revolted after the 27th April decree but before news of the decree had reached Martinique. Insisting that 'Schoelcher is not our saviour', they sought to commemorate not the great French benefactor but workers at the Habitation Duchamp in Sainte Philomène, who caused an uprising in Saint Pierre that led to the authorisation of the treaty that

2 INTRODUCTION

outlawed slavery in Martinique on 23 May. The celebration of Schoelcher's memory through the statues was regarded as a misrepresentative veneration of French benevolence and, even more, as a symbol in defence of the colonial project, at the same time as it eclipsed the agency of Martinicans in claiming their own freedom.

As a great spokesman for the freedom and equality of black people, Aimé Césaire may, if he had lived to see the destruction of the statues, have had some sympathy with the activists' cause. But if we consider the work of Césaire in relation to contemporary activism, it is striking that his response to Schoelcher is radically different. In fighting tirelessly for equal rights for Martinicans, Césaire situates his work as part of the ongoing legacy of that of his great forebears, Toussaint Louverture and Victor Schoelcher. He refers repeatedly to Schoelcher as an exemplary figure, and notably wrote the introduction to Schoelcher's *Esclavage et colonisation* on the centenary of abolition in 1948. In a speech celebrating Schoelcher delivered on 21 July 1945, Césaire speaks in impassioned tones of Schoelcher's honesty, courage, conscience, audacity and generosity, and indeed characterises his own eulogy as 'a statue made in sound'.[1] He evidently does not shy away from the form of monumentalisation to which the 2020 activists objected. In the same speech, Césaire notes that Schoelcher reminded his opponents, who tried to argue that black people were not seeking their own freedom, of the multiple slave revolts precisely demanding liberation. In the 1948 preface to Schoelcher's book referenced above, Césaire goes on to affirm that his legacy goes beyond abolitionism, characterising him as a revolutionary. Charting the abortive attempts of some of Schoelcher's predecessors as well as the hypocritical, racist discourse of his detractors, Césaire lauds Schoelcher's categorical calls for immediate and definitive abolition. He also notes Schoelcher's continued endeavour, following abolition, to promote the economic and political emancipation of black people, and to pursue assimilation and federation, principles for which Césaire

INTRODUCTION 3

himself would fight throughout his own career a century later.

The distance between Césaire's adulatory rhetoric and the denunciation of Schoelcher by the protestors who removed his statues tells us something about Césaire's own form of activism. His critique of colonialism was voiced not on the streets but at the Assemblée Nationale, where he was Deputy for Martinique for forty-eight years between 1945 and 1993. His legacy is a model not so much for grassroots activism as for exemplary, inspiring, but considered leadership. It is also an extraordinarily prolific corpus of political, cultural and poetic writing, in which the contemporary reader can find careful analyses as well as incendiary rhetoric. In praising Schoelcher, moreover, Césaire distinguishes himself as a careful reader of his work, attentive to its detail and to its time. He repeatedly evokes the contemporary relevance of the abolitionist's vision and conceives his own work as imbued with the spirit of Schoelcher. And yet Césaire also reads him in his historical context and is able to identify the nuances that would no longer be appropriate in the twentieth century. In a speech delivered in 1958, for example, he evokes Schoelcher's lack of reference to class, his conception of the people as 'that great undifferentiated entity', and recommends a more nuanced awareness of social antagonism in the contemporary context. Schoelcher, then, is an ongoing interlocutor for Césaire, but his ideas 'bear the mark of his time'.[2] We might remark on his achievements, but we must adapt his pursuit of liberation to suit the demands of the present: 'to bear homage to 1848 is good, but it is better to keep in step with 1958'.[3] If Césaire is able to read Schoelcher in his own time, this book seeks to understand his resonance by reading Césaire in his. Césaire maintains Schoelcher's revolutionary spirit rather than dismissing his inevitable association with French colonialism, as the 2020 activists did. He models an understanding of history that we must endeavour to preserve as we make our way through his own complex, evolving and multifaceted trajectory.

Closer scrutiny of the Schoelcher statues is revealing. Two statues of Schoelcher were destroyed, but the statues were not identical. One depicts Schoelcher with his arm around a young slave boy, who looks up at him with admiration. This one sat in front of the Palais de Justice in Fort-de-France, the capital of Martinique, with the inscription 'no French land shall any longer bear slaves'. It was made by a Frenchman, Anatole Marquet de Vasselot, in 1904. The other statue, situated in the town named Schoelcher, was by the Martinican Marie-Thérèse Julien Lung Fou, who was also a pioneer for writing and cultural production in Creole. Lung Fou's Schoelcher stood alone, seemed to gaze into the distance, and took a much more minimalist form than that of Vasselot. If the first statue conveys French dominance, the second does so markedly less. If Césaire recognised the beauty of Vasselot's Schoelcher, moreover, he also noted that it was sculpted by a white man. And in 1971, he celebrated the construction of a further statue by the Martinican artist Joseph Sainte Croix René Corail, known as Khokho René Corail, this time not of Schoelcher but taking the abstract form of a woman clutching her dead child while brandishing a weapon. The statue is conceived as a 'Homage to the struggles of the Martinican people' and symbolises the 22nd May slave revolt that finally triggered the treaty for abolition. It serves as a fitting rejoinder to the monuments devoted to Schoelcher, and Césaire is keen to underline its resonance. Whereas the Schoelcher statues depict freedom being bestowed upon Martinicans by a Frenchman, that of René Corail portrays a black woman seizing her own freedom. Césaire's understanding of Schoelcher's contribution to abolition may have meant that he would not have seen it fitting to tear down his statue, but his recognition of the importance of René Corail's work suggests that he was keenly aware of the thorny politics of memorialisation. Yet his activism is one of well-informed but dynamic reading, of dialogue and creativity: René Corail with Schoelcher rather than against, but with a sceptical eye towards the mythologisation of the past.

INTRODUCTION 5

The Inventor of Souls

This book takes Césaire's vision of writers and artists as 'inventors of souls' as a starting point for the conceptualisation of this unique mode of contestation expressed both through politics and through literature. Whilst Césaire's activism was above all that of an intellectual – a man of culture who sought change from within the corridors of power – it was nonetheless incendiary. He was a visionary in both his political and his poetic ambition. His explosive address at the *Deuxième congrès des écrivains et artistes noirs* held in Rome in 1959 captures this visionary ambition in its virulent denunciation of colonialism and its call for the wholesale reinvention of culture as integral to complete decolonisation, as he invokes his colleagues: 'we are *propagators of souls*, multipliers of souls, even *inventors of souls*'.[4] Césaire secured the status of a French department for Martinique in 1946, but he was soon disillusioned by the failed promises of that law, and by 1959 was yet more damning in his critique of colonialism and more rebellious in seeking autonomy for his country. The speech at the *Deuxième Congrès* reflects this anger and sense of betrayal, but also articulates a close connection between culture and politics. With literary and artistic creation, he intones, 'unexpected physical resources rise up which contribute to the re-establishment of the social body that was shaken by the shock of colonialism through its ability to resist and vocation to take action'.[5] The phrase 'inventor of souls' bears traces of Césaire's Marxism, but replaces Joseph Stalin's reference to writers as 'engineers of the soul' in his speech at the First Congress of the Union of Soviet Writers in 1932 with the more experimental, improvised notion of invention. Césaire left the French Communist Party in 1956, criticising both its association with Stalinism and its failure to consider the effects of colonialism and racism, yet the notion of the 'inventor of souls' suggests a renewed vision for democratic socialism through art. In the letter probably written by Suzanne Césaire and signed by

6 INTRODUCTION

Aimé Césaire and his colleagues in response to the censorship of the avant-garde journal *Tropiques* in Martinique in 1943, the contributors are also 'poisoners of the soul'. Whilst Césaire blended his poetry with his politics explicitly only from the mid-1950s, this early riposte indicates the strong contestatory effect he sought for the literary journal even before his political career was launched.[6]

Césaire's visionary call to the 'inventors of souls' in 1959 crystallises his growing belief in the complicity, if not the resemblance, between culture and politics. His best-known work, the epic poem *Cahier d'un retour au pays natal* [*Notebook of a Return to the Native Land*], was first published in 1939 in the journal *Volontés*, and in its initial incarnation took the form of a spiritual quest, a journey of self-transformation that was not yet explicitly political. When the final version of the poem was published by Présence Africaine in 1956, however, Césaire's visionary blend of aesthetic and political revolt became clearly visible in the poem's vocabulary of defiance. Césaire's 1959 address at the *Deuxième Congrès* was also a continuation of his speech 'Culture et colonisation' delivered at the *Premier Congrès des intellectuels et artistes noirs* held in Paris in 1956, where he outlines the devastating effect of colonialism on local cultures and summons his colleagues to strive for the regeneration of black culture.[7] The point is reinforced in his address at the *Festival mondial des arts nègres* in Dakar in 1966, where he argues that African art is crucial to the restoration of the dignity and humanity of the people as they free themselves from oppressive colonial regimes. Decolonisation in Africa sharpened Césaire's denunciation of French colonialism in the Caribbean, and the 1950s and 60s saw both a radicalisation in Césaire's literary writing and an intensification in his demand for political autonomy in Martinique.

The vocabulary of invention that stands out in the 1959 speech is at the same time an apt signifier of the explosive language characteristic of Césaire's poetry, as well as of his political speeches and essays. Césaire's unique activist power lies in his unrivalled linguistic mastery, in the unprecedented aesthetic

INTRODUCTION 7

experimentation of his poetry and theatre, and in the rhetorical force of his political interventions. He was the producer of 'incandescent speech', a lexical and formal inventiveness that makes his poetry revolutionary in both content and form, and that makes his political speeches boldly hard-hitting in their retort to the seat of power. His lasting significance stems no doubt from the inspiring power of this visionary language, his sharp excoriation of the evils of colonial history as well as of ongoing racism, and his vision of renewal on both a cultural and a political level. Volcanic imagery runs through many of Césaire's poetic volumes and represents this explosive linguistic energy. The massive eruption of Mount Pelée in 1902 that devastated the city of Saint Pierre is remembered as a catastrophe in Martinican history, but it also repeatedly returns in Césaire's poems as a figure for incendiary revolt, for a force capable of sweeping away cultural and political stagnation in favour of renewal. Linking the prevalence of the volcano in Césaire's poetic imaginary with his inflammatory style throughout his writing, the Guadeloupean writer Daniel Maximin aptly dubs him 'brother volcano'.[8]

The eruptive challenge of Césaire's poetry can be read as a fierce expression of visceral revolt in a language he could not use in the political arena. Yet his political speeches also intensify their rhetorical impact through their linguistic crafting. At the Assemblée Nationale, his proposal for departmentalisation and, soon after and for much of his career, his calls to the French government to fulfil the promises offered in that status, do not hold back in conjuring the difficult living conditions endured in Martinique, and his demands both for specific rights and eventually for autonomy are articulated with force and erudition. Yet Césaire's unique achievements originate in part in his ability to think and to speak on different levels, to produce the most inventive poetry whilst taking on the role of a practical negotiator. While he was criticised by later Caribbean thinkers for pushing for departmentalisation rather than independence, Césaire was an anticolonial throughout; he conceived departmentalisation as a means of securing equality for Martinicans when he believed that full independence was, at least for the time being, economically unrealistic. With departmentalisation, Césaire worked with Republican ideology and drew on the rhetoric of the rights of man to demand that the Republic adhere more faithfully to its own principles. For Thomas Hale and Kora Véron, departmentalisation was 'the art of the possible'; Césaire knew how to envision revolution but sought departmental status for Martinique in order to address quickly problems such as food shortages and the high cost of living in Martinique.[9] Césaire nevertheless always thought of himself as a rebel, a marginal figure or interloper even in his interactions with the establishment.[10] Césaire's ability to play the two roles of the visionary and the negotiator at once makes him an exemplary figure for contemporary antiracist cultural innovation and political action, and it is his linguistic agility in both fields that lends his work its exceptional power. His powers of persuasion as a poet and as a politician offer a singular model of both cultural and political activism.

Césaire's early years provide the starting point for this unusual trajectory. He was born in 1913 at the Habitation Eyma in North-East Martinique. His father Fernand was a tax inspector, and his mother Eleanor Hermine was a dressmaker. His father's role meant that the family belonged to the petit bourgeoisie while remaining close to the working class, and the young Aimé would have been well aware of the difficulties of life on the plantations. The family valued education especially highly as a conduit to success, and Fernand used to read French classics to his children in the evenings. Aimé Césaire's grandfather Nicolas Fernand Césaire was the first Martinican to go to the prestigious *École normale supérieure* in Paris, though he died young, at the age of 28. His grandmother Eugénie Macni was also a significant figure in his childhood: she had excellent French and taught Aimé to read at a young age. French was very much privileged as the language of education, with the result that Césaire never considered writing in Creole – a decision for which he was later criticised, even

INTRODUCTION 9

though his attitude was reflective of the culture of his time.[11] He also grew up with an awareness of the history of enslavement, and it appears that one of his ancestors was involved in a slave revolt in December 1833 and condemned to death by Louis-Philippe. Césaire's biographer Georges Ngal notes that the young Aimé was particularly affected by this story of a rebel slave with the name Césaire, though it is not certain that the condemned man was actually related to Aimé Césaire's family.[12] In 1924, Césaire obtained a scholarship to the Collège Schoelcher in Fort-de-France, and the family moved to the city, though he missed the rural landscape where he was born. Here he met Léon Gontron Damas, later a co-founder of the negritude movement, but his studious attitude meant he was often isolated.

In September 1931, Césaire won a scholarship to study in France, and made the two-week journey by boat to enrol at the Lycée Louis-le-Grand in Paris. He was then successful in the tough competition for entry into the prestigious Ecole normale supérieure, where he continued his studies from 1935. His years in Paris were a turning point in his life, the significance of which it is difficult to overestimate. Soon after arriving he met the writers (and later politicians) Léopold Sédar Senghor and Ousmane Socé, both from Senegal. They quickly befriended him, and he started to discover Africa. This discovery provided the seeds for what was to become the negritude movement and convinced him of the significance of Africa as the original source of Caribbean identity before its decimation by the slave trade. Césaire developed this conviction also through reading the work of European ethnographers, such as Leo Frobenius's *Histoire de la civilisation africaine* and Maurice Delafosse's *Les Nègres*.

The years that he spent in Paris were not easy: he struggled with his health and with a sense of alienation, studied hard but was often isolated. Senghor not only offered friendship but a sense of racial identity, the conviction that black people shared their origins in Africa and that a reconnection with their roots could serve as a catalyst for cultural regeneration. Paris during the 1930s was a vibrant site of black internationalism, with pan-Africanist movements gathering in the city to debate and share ideas. It was here that Césaire discovered the work of the Nardal sisters, Paulette and Jane, whose salons and journal, the *Revue du monde noir*, formed a meeting point for francophone Africans and Caribbeans as well as for African American writers such as Claude McKay, Alan Locke and Langston Hughes. Césaire would also have been aware of *Légitime Défense*, a journal whose single issue published in 1932 was also preoccupied with the question of race, combined with a commitment to Marxism and a surrealist aesthetic. Césaire nevertheless kept a guarded distance from both journals and from the salons, seeing them as rather too bourgeois and assimilationist, but edited and contributed to *L'Étudiant noir* in 1934–5 with his first reflections on black identity and culture. Césaire's *Cahier* was also born during this period, with early drafts originating in 1935 before the first version was published in 1939, the same year that Césaire returned to Martinique.

Césaire took a post as a teacher at the Lycée Schoelcher in Fort-de-France soon after his return. But Martinique during the 1940s was a place of oppression and the poet's return to his homeland was one of disillusionment. The island was under the control of the Vichy government, represented by Admiral Robert whose regime was racist and divisive. Together with his wife Suzanne, René Ménil and several other colleagues, Césaire founded the avant-garde journal *Tropiques*, which set out to celebrate the local culture and landscape and to resist the stultification of the Vichy regime. The journal was closed down for a period during 1943 until the Free French took control of the island, however, since although its focus was literary rather than political, Lieutenant de Vaisseau Bayle (the Chief of Information Services for the government) denounced its revolutionary tenor. In 1945 Césaire, having hitherto not seen himself as a political figure, was elected Mayor of Fort-de-France, as well as Deputy for Martinique representing the Communist Party, at the Assemblée Nationale. With the end of the war, Césaire sought a fresh start for Martinique with

INTRODUCTION 11

the departmentalisation bill, with which he argued that whilst Martinique and Guadeloupe were fully assimilated with the metropole on an administrative and political level, this had not been translated into the domain of social justice. The cost of living was as high as in France, but salaries were low and there were no benefits for maternity, sickness, unemployment or retirement.[13] After the hierarchy and misery of the Vichy regime, Césaire called for 'France d'outre-mer' to represent a genuine fraternity, part of a united but diverse Republic that would relinquish the old master–slave relationship and usher in fresh hope.[14] Departmentalisation was in this sense an anticolonial move for Césaire, in that it was to terminate Martinique's subordinate status.

Departmentalisation was passed unanimously in March 1946, but Césaire's optimism was short-lived. Although he, as well as the Martinican people, had hoped that liberation from the Nazis and the transformation of Martinique and Guadeloupe into overseas departments would bring the end of racial discrimination, this was far from the case. In an incendiary article published in *Justice* in September 1949, Césaire spoke out 'against the sabotage of assimilation'.[15] The administration of Martinique was in the hands of the colonialist Préfet Trouillé, who extended the property rights of the 'békés' (or white landowners) and failed to put in place social security for black workers. Césaire warned that if the situation did not improve, then the Martinican people would demand a rethinking of their status.[16] This disillusionment grew into a sense of angry betrayal, as Césaire continued through the 1950s to draw attention at the Assemblée Nationale to ongoing discrimination, low salaries, the lack of social security and insufficient investment.

This period brought a renewed revolutionary fervour into Césaire's writing. His explosive critique of colonialism, *Discours sur le colonialisme* [*Discourse on Colonialism*], was published by Présence Africaine in 1955, though parts of the text were published as 'L'impossible contact' in *Chemins du monde* as far back as 1948. The text starkly equates colonialism with

12 INTRODUCTION

Nazism and argues that Europe's dehumanising colonial enterprise finally unfolded on its own territory with the horrors of National Socialism. At the same time, the surrealist visions of Césaire's earlier poetry, such as *Les Armes miraculeuses* [*The Miraculous Weapons*] of 1946 and *Soleil cou coupé* [*Solar Throat Slashed*] of 1948, are dampened and interwoven in *Ferrements* [*Ferraments*], published in 1960, with overt political critique. It is also in the late 1950s that Césaire started work on his tragedies of decolonisation, turning to the theatre to address a broader audience more directly. Whilst *Et les chiens se taisaient* [*And the dogs were silent*], first published as part of *Les Armes miraculeuses* [*The Miraculous Weapons*] in 1946, portrays the murder of the slave master by the slave in a timeless, universalised form indebted to Greek tragedy, *La Tragédie du Roi Christophe* [*The Tragedy of King Christophe*] of 1963 and *Une Saison au Congo* [*A Season in the Congo*] of 1966 are historical studies of the troubled aftermath of decolonisation in Haiti and the Congo. *Une Tempête* [*A Tempest*], published in 1969, follows the tragedies of decolonisation with a riposte to Shakespeare's classic placing the slave Caliban's revolt centre stage while also incorporating African and Voodoo references.

The most widely known aspect of this first part of Césaire's career is his invention of negritude, the cultural movement that first sought defiantly to reinvent black identity in robust defiance of colonial and racist discourse. Whilst negritude was a provocative and controversial term, its role in the development of antiracism was decisive. The regime of enslavement in the French Caribbean may have ended with abolition in 1848, but exploitation and inequality continued in a society that remained brutally hierarchical. A pigmentocracy persisted, which situated those ethnic groups with the palest skin at the top of the hierarchy, with those with the darkest skin at the bottom. Negritude was a concerted movement to overturn that hierarchy, to affirm the value of black culture and to reinvigorate its origins in Africa. If contemporary movements such as Black Lives Matter are founded on the affirmation

INTRODUCTION 13

of the value of black lives, culture and history, and on resistance to ongoing oppression, such endeavours clearly find their roots in the cultural and political energy of negritude as it emerged in the 1930s. Together with Léopold Sédar Senghor and Léon Gontran Damas, and with the influence of the effervescent black internationalism of 1930s Paris, Césaire coined the term 'negritude' at the very start of his career. His continuing championing of black culture and black rights over the first decades of his career can be construed, despite its tensions, under its banner.

Negritude started with *L'Étudiant noir*, the journal of the Association des Étudiants Martiniquais edited by Césaire and Senghor, in 1935. In an article printed in the third issue, 'Nègreries: Conscience raciale et évolution sociale', Césaire announces the precondition for revolution: 'to break with the mechanistic identification of races, to destroy superficial values, to seize within us the unmediated nègre, to plant our negritude like a beautiful tree until it bears its most authentic fruit'.[17] Negritude is here a refusal of racism and a quest for authenticity, calling for the embrace of lived experience as well as a new cultural productivity. It heralds the inauguration of a long-term commitment to establishing connections between black people across the world through the celebration of African culture and history. Despite his lack of personal knowledge of Africa and his reliance on Senghor and Frobenius, Césaire associated the affirmation of negritude with a renewed connection with Africa as the originary home of black culture and identity. Yet if he goes on to use the term several times in the *Cahier*, Césaire keeps its meaning dynamic. Negritude is not, despite the objections of many critics, the affirmation of particular characteristics, and it is not the name for a pre-established, static identity. It is used in the *Cahier* to describe the first uprising of slaves in Haiti, under Toussaint Louverture, and is associated with protest rather than identity. It describes not a state of being but an action or process, a reintegration with the land in defiance of a history of alienation:

Ma négritude n'est pas une pierre, sa surdité ruée
contre la clameur du jour
ma négritude n'est pas une taie d'eau morte sur l'œil
mort de la terre
ma négritude n'est ni une tour ni une cathédrale
elle plonge dans la chair rouge du sol
elle plonge dans la chair ardente du ciel
elle troue l'accablement opaque de sa droite patience

[My negritude is not a stone, its deafness hurled against the
   clamor of day
my negritude is not a leukoma of dead liquid over the
   earth's dead eye
my negritude is neither tower nor cathedral
it takes root in the red flesh of the soil
it takes root in the ardent flesh of the sky
it breaks through the opaque prostration with its upright
   presence.][18]

Negritude for Césaire is dynamic, and serves as a starting point for revolt rather than as an essentialising definition of black identity. It is also a cultural movement and does not uphold biological conceptions of race. In this, it differs from the negritude celebrated by Léopold Sédar Senghor, who at least early in his career sought to celebrate the particular characteristics that make up the black soul. Senghor's early evocations of negritude foreground sensuality, the close connection between mind and body, and contrast what he sees as the black man's affectivity with the rationality of European culture: 'emotion is negro just as reason is Greek'.[19] Senghor's early use of biological essentialism was clearly highly problematic and met with intense criticism, although it is often ignored that negritude shifts in meaning through his writing, and later becomes both more cultural and more dynamic. Yet Césaire's version was always cultural and always dynamic, and the risk of essentialism was one of which he was evidently aware. In the 1966 speech at the Dakar *Festival mondial des arts nègres*, he expresses with hindsight his unease towards the term and regrets its history of creating tension between antiracist thinkers.[20] Yet importantly, despite its difficulties, Césaire insists on the significance of the term in responding to the history of brutality against black people. It fuelled the burgeoning of black culture in the 1930s, established solidarity between black people in different parts of the world, and in turn gave strength to the African independence movements of the 1960s.

Negritude is crucial to Césaire's contribution to antiracist thought, but this book seeks to demonstrate its shifting and multifaceted meaning, which is crucial to its relevance to contemporary activism. Césaire retains the term, despite his discomfort, precisely because it offered the first great challenge to racist dehumanisation. It redefined and reinvigorated black culture when white discourse had tried to reduce it to a caricature. It responded to a specific history of black suffering but was also a form of universal humanism in its affirmation of freedom and emancipation: *'if Negritude is a rooting in the particular, it also transcends this and blossoms into the universal'*.[21] At the same time, negritude is a catalyst for fraternity or solidarity, and in this it can be seen to anticipate the foundation of more recent movements such as Black Lives Matter, which too crafts itself as 'an inclusive and spacious movement' that seeks to restore and affirm black people's humanity.[22]

Critical responses to negritude nevertheless vary, with many detractors rejecting what they see as its essentialism. The Nigerian writer Wole Soyinka famously dismissed it, mocking the term with the remark that 'the tiger does not proclaim its tigritude'.[23] The Africanist literary scholar Francis Abiola Irele claims in his substantial introduction to the *Cahier* that Césaire's form of negritude there *is* associated with racial endowment and can be seen as 'hyperromanticism'.[24] These claims seem not to take into account both the dynamic imagery surrounding negritude in Césaire's writing or his own explicit theorisation of it as lived experience, as 'refusal' and 'combat'.[25] Jean Khalfa's recent interpretation seems more apt:

> this is not a racial category, the claim of an essential difference or another border. In fact, it denotes the refusal of a specific ontological attitude, the exclusively instrumental stance of those who can only think in terms of mastery, that is, in terms of the separation of the self from the other, and the rediscovery of another stance.[26]

A study of the association of Césaire's work with negritude should nevertheless do justice to the diversity of his intellectual and political universe rather than reducing it to anything resembling a single programme. His early poetry is more personal than political, and although the *Cahier* was composed during Césaire's period in Paris surrounded by the black internationalism of the 1930s, the 1939 version is more of a spiritual quest for transformation than a collective, activist endeavour. This early *Cahier* shows evidence of his reading of Frobenius not only in its references to African culture, but also in its vision of spiritual transformation. It is also clearly influenced by Frobenius's conception of Ethiopian civilisation, where man is seen to be tightly implicated in the environment through the concept of the 'homme-plante', celebrated by Suzanne Césaire.

Césaire's *Cahier* – and, indeed, all his poetry – closely links the human with the ecological, with both specific forms of local vegetation and with the larger forces of the elements. *Tropiques* is devoted to exploring Martinican culture as intricately immersed in its flora and fauna. In the essay 'Poésie et connaissance', published in 1945, Césaire imagines the poet containing within him the dynamic life of the nonhuman world around him. The humanism championed in Césaire's negritude is importantly not a sovereign humanism but one that understands the relationship between human and nonhuman in ways that challenge the history of environmental destruction in the Caribbean and that can speak to the contemporary climate crisis.

INTRODUCTION 17

At the same time, the quest for liberation and transformation initiated by negritude during this period is coupled with or enriched by Césaire's engagement with surrealism. Césaire's poetry particularly during his earlier years challenges the putatively rational underpinnings of colonial and racial theory by drawing on the surrealist affirmation of the irrational. The 1939 *Cahier*'s quest for spiritual transformation is also a personal journey into the unconscious, where liberation is evoked using startling erotic imagery and aesthetic experimentation more pervasively than with imagery of political revolt. Césaire was closely connected with surrealism at this point, as is testified by the first publication of the *Cahier* in *Volontés*, a literary magazine for the avant-garde. He met André Breton during the latter's visit to Martinique in 1941; Breton then wrote the preface for the revised, bilingual version of the *Cahier* published in New York by Brentano's in 1947, and that revised version was perhaps the most linguistically explosive in its deployment of surrealist imagery. With Breton, Césaire pursued freedom from a history of oppression but also from normative social structures and aesthetic tradition. Cultural freedom had to involve the unfettered liberation of the imagination and a disruption of existing forms of versification, of familiar lexis and syntax. With its surrealist influences, negritude has also been as a form of modernism, a challenge to the existing literary order and an attempt to disrupt the limits of meaning.[27]

Beyond negritude, ecology and surrealism, however, Césaire became in the late 1950s and 1960s more focused on decolonisation, its implications in Africa and the form it might take in the French Caribbean. The politicisation of his poetry, with *Ferrements* [*Ferraments*] and the tragedies of decolonisation mentioned above, coincided with a new turn in Césaire's politics, in that he started to push for political autonomy in Martinique. A decisive turn came in 1956, when he broke with the French Communist Party, though he remained committed to Marxist principles in his conception of a more egalitarian political system for Martinique. In 1958 he founded the Parti

Progressiste Martiniquais, which sought a degree of autonomy for the island, articulated as somewhere between assimilation and full autonomy, but within a larger federal state.[28] This would confer upon Martinique the power to manage its own affairs but would not require national state sovereignty; rather, federalism would maintain the connection with France that the island required economically while assuring self-government. This conception of autonomy continued to evolve over the next decade, as the notion of a federal union became less realistic and less appealing and he became more convinced of the need for Martinique to attain the status of a state, governing its own affairs within a federal Republic. At the same time, however, Césaire's literary output slowed, as his energies were devoted to the political cause. The late volume of poetry, *moi, laminaire. . . [i, laminaria. . .]* published in 1982, also marks a shift in its move away from political activism. The collection's tone is far more humble than that of his earlier works, as the vision of the poet as spokesman has disappeared and the poetic self is no longer at the centre. Rather, the poems invoke the Martinican landscape, the traces of the history of enslavement and the vast cosmic forces that remind us of our human frailty.

Yet Césaire is unique in his vibrant, original and prolonged double life as poet and politician. His combination of poetry and politics is rarely seen in our present historical moment, where culture may be politically motivated but is rarely imbricated in the political arena in the way that it was for Césaire, and where literature is too often driven by market forces. Césaire understood that there was a leap between his poetic and political work and the modes of thinking that accompanied them, and he recognised the difference between his ideal vision of revolutionary change and the immediate demands of the concrete sphere. In an interview with Jacqueline Sieger in 1961, he admits that, 'I've never wanted to separate dream from action. But there is always a deep hiatus'.[29] The postcolonial critic Mireille Rosello analyses the two strains in Césaire's thought in her article 'The Césaire Effect', noting that major critics such as Lilyan Kesteloot conceive these as

INTRODUCTION   19

paradoxical, characterising Césaire as a 'homo duplex'.[30] And certainly Césaire became a controversial figure in Martinique from the late 50s, when he failed to fight for independence and his continuing belief in the importance of the connection with France was seen to betray the more revolutionary tenor of his poetry at that stage. Nevertheless, Rosello concludes that Césaire's political and poetic visions are not so distinct; in both he is committed to an understanding of reinvention that is not necessarily violent but that is radical. Furthermore, Césaire scholars Thomas Hale and Kora Véron answer in the affirmative the question 'is there unity in the writings of Aimé Césaire?', and examine moments in his career when particular political struggles were obliquely though still identifiably reflected in poems written at the same time.[31] Césaire himself articulates the complicity between poetry and politics with a commitment to creativity: 'creating a poem and creating a city are to some extent the same thing. What animates me is the will to create, the will to do, to build in the present and in the future'.[32]

There are, however, clearly many ways to paint Césaire, many dimensions to his thought, and many interpretations of his diverse writings. This study seeks to capture this dynamism and to identify the complex interweaving of currents and threads through his politics and poetry without reducing him to a particular stance or movement. As we saw at the beginning in his response to Schoelcher and René Corail, he maintained a dialogue between France and Martinique, between negotiation and activism, and between the visionary and the pragmatic. His thought shifted and evolved through his long career, with emancipation as a constant goal but with many languages conceived in its name. This singular trajectory was, moreover, one of constant tension. Euzhan Palcy's documentary films portray him as a figure of conflict and contradiction, and biographers and friends note a sense of isolation as he tried to work on multiple levels when other critics and commentators chose more specific cultural or political approaches.[33] If he was on some level a father figure for successive generations of Caribbean writers, moreover, their memory of him contains tensions, as is testified most extensively by Raphaël Confiant in his acerbic study *Aimé Césaire, une traversée paradoxale du siècle*. The popular Guadeloupean writer Maryse Condé asserts that, despite his contradictions, Césaire's devotion to Martinique makes him an exemplary cultural figure for the Caribbean: unlike some of the other major francophone Caribbean writers, he lived in his native land for most of his life.[34] Yet despite her own attention to the intersection between race and gender, Condé does not mention here another of Césaire's difficulties; that is, his failure to consider the distinct position of black women. Césaire's poetic rhetoric was at times androcentric, using the imagery of virility to conjure revolution and containing scant reference to women's experiences of racial oppression. It is surprising, moreover, that in celebrating the René Corail statue, Césaire evokes the agency of the black subject but says nothing about the fact that the statue is in this case a woman.

Despite his difficulties, Césaire was an impressive embodiment of a particular form of intellectual activism along the lines of that of major French thinkers such as Jean-Paul Sartre, Albert Camus, André Malraux or Simone de Beauvoir. He can be associated with a twentieth-century French model of political engagement in that he conceived literature as a project that must pursue freedom. Sartre and his colleagues responded to the Nazi Occupation of France by writing literature that theorised both the ontological and the political freedom of the subject, and indeed for Sartre this evolved into an impassioned call during the 1950s for the decolonisation of Algeria. Césaire went further: his literary writing voiced and performed first subjective and then collective revolt, but his political engagement was not just that of a commentator. Rather, it was that of a determined negotiator and actor. His achievements as an intellectual are unique in that he was the first black man in the French-speaking world to play that role with such scope and such success, and he also used his skills not just to critique the establishment from the outside, but to effect change from

INTRODUCTION 21

within in his position at the Assemblée Nationale. Césaire dissects and rewrites black history in his poetry and theatre while using his powers of analysis and expression to advocate for the rights of Martinicans. He embodies a model of engagement that is highly unusual in our contemporary era but that serves as a resonant example in its combination of cultural activism with political influence and power. He can be seen, according to one of his biographers, Romuald Fonkoua, as the last of a generation of French intellectuals to ally literature and politics and to rise to the challenge of both. His example shows how cultural movements, such as negritude, can parallel practical politics and how crucially important the awareness they bring can be in fuelling political change.

Césaire was an inspirational leader. Known as the 'founding father' of negritude, he remains (despite the ambivalent paternalism implied by that status) a crucial source of inspiration to subsequent Caribbean writers such as Patrick Chamoiseau and Daniel Maximin, who repeatedly affirm his importance to their work. At the same time, he serves as a model for considered, dignified, reasoned political leadership; he addressed a predominantly white administration from within, as have negotiators such as Barack Obama and Kamala Harris. All aspects of his work provide, according to political scientist Fred Constant, 'lessons in leadership', which Constant argues comprise mastery of language, abstract principles, a commitment to the avant-garde while communicating with the people, a belief in the universal as well as in the importance of identity, an indefatigable will, responsibility and empathy.[35] Césaire knew well the difficulties associated with the position of the leader, as he demonstrates most clearly in charting the errors of Christophe in newly independent Haiti in *La Tragédie du roi Christophe* or in portraying Patrice Lumumba's solipsism in the Belgian Congo after decolonisation in *Une Saison au Congo*. In his own career, however, despite his intermittent isolation, he sought to combine the role of spokesman with listening and dialogue at once with his own people and with the French establishment.

A need for black leadership was aptly articulated much more recently by Patrisse Cullors, co-founder of the Black Lives Matter movement. In a 2017 interview, Cullors envisions the movement's next step as an increase in black people's participation in government: 'one of the biggest places that I see us will be in local and national government. I think you'll see not just black people, but black folks and our allies really pushing to be part of local government, city government and national government – to move to be mayor, county board of supervisors, to be on boards'.[36] Black Lives Matter has insisted on its loose, decentralised structure, its focus on local rather than national levels of organisation. Cullors clearly imagines not a hierarchical mode of leadership but a collaborative one, with black leader figures working with local and national government as well as with grassroots organisations. Césaire's model of leadership inevitably situates him in an elite role, but his position at the Assemblée Nationale at the same time as his work as Mayor of Fort-de-France shows how leadership can work on different levels at once. His political writings attest to his commitment to wider forms of empowerment, and his efforts were addressed both to local communities and to the French imperialist centre. He may, in the view of his critics, have struggled to address these different levels at once, but he was a skilled politician who worked for the emancipation of his people both by focusing on local issues and by addressing the highest levels of power. He was also an inspirational writer who led the creation of a modernist French Caribbean culture with his invention of a singular new poetic language and form.

1

1930s Paris and the *Cahier d'un retour au pays natal*

'It is beautiful and good and legitimate to be nègre'

In the 1935 article 'Nègreries: Conscience raciale et révolution sociale', where he first coins the term 'négritude', Césaire makes the following statement about the importance not just of political revolt but of black consciousness: 'they therefore forgot the main thing, those who tell the black man that he should revolt without becoming conscious of himself, without telling him that it is beautiful and good and legitimate to be nègre'.[1] The French term 'nègre' has a complex history, which will be discussed shortly, but which is distinct from corresponding English terms, so this term is retained here in my use of English translations in an effort to capture the meaning of Césaire's powerful redeployment of this derogatory term. Césaire's simple but hard-hitting affirmation is repeated in the *Cahier*, at the end of which Césaire reclaims 'la danse saute-prison / la danse il-est-beau-et-bon-et-légitime-d'être nègre' ['the prison-spring dance / the it-is-beautiful-good-and-legitimate-to-be-nègre dance'], as if the proud assertion of black identity here becomes a dance, the liberated self-expression of the body.[2] The reprisal of the phrase demonstrates how Césaire's thinking migrates between genres, between the essay and the poem, in ways that this book will continue to explore. It also reinforces his fundamental insistence on the value of black identity and the importance of the black subject's reclaiming of a sense of self and of racial consciousness. This direct and lucid assertion is later cited by the Martinican psychiatrist and antiracist thinker Frantz Fanon. Fanon was both compelled by and ambivalent towards Césaire's thought, but nevertheless notes the significance of his being the first to say to Caribbean society 'that it is fine and good to be nègre'.[3] Written before the establishment of Césaire's political career, during his restless years as a student in Paris struggling to make sense of his identity as a black intellectual, the statement is decisive, and captures the impetus of this early period of cultural creativity and activism in Césaire's career. This is the decade of the birth of negritude, of effervescent black internationalism in Paris, and marks a crucial foundation for successive movements of black solidarity across the globe.

Césaire was 18 years old when he arrived in Paris to study at the Lycée Louis-le-Grand in 1931. The eight years he spent in the city before returning to Martinique in 1939 were a period of introspection, fuelled by the cultural movements and journals alive at the time and in which he also participated. This early form of activism was much more cultural than political – Césaire's political career did not begin until 1945 – yet it serves as a compelling example of the power of cultural innovation in generating energy and changing attitudes. The assertion that 'it is beautiful and good and legitimate to be nègre' announces the principle of self-affirmation that lies at the heart of that movement of innovation, and its echoes resonate beyond that initial moment.

In January 1962, for example, photographer and journalist Kwame Brathwaite's photographs of the 'Naturally '62' fashion show held at Purple Manor nightclub in Harlem helped popularise the movement known by the slogan 'Black is Beautiful'. The show was for black models only and eschewed Western notions of beauty in favour of clothes influenced by African styles. This was part of a movement to condemn the internalisation of negative imagery of black bodies and to combat the use of skin-lightening products. The origins of the movement can be found in negritude and indeed in Césaire's assertion of the beauty and value of black men and women. It also serves as a bridge between 1930s negritude and subsequent black activist movements such as Black Lives Matter, which is more explicitly political than both negritude and 'Black is Beautiful', with its primary goal to combat police brutality and social injustice. Black Lives Matter is less explicitly concerned with the history of colonialism and slavery than negritude, and yet its insistence on black humanity and creativity can also be associated with the self-affirmation championed by these earlier movements. Black Lives Matter at the same time promotes the 'legitimacy' of black identity before the law in ways that play out Césaire's punchy assertion.

Césaire's insistence that it is beautiful and good and legitimate to be 'un nègre' is at the heart of his first article in the inaugural issue of *L'Étudiant noir* and summarises his early critique of cultural assimilation. The article again anticipates the 'Black is Beautiful' movement in its derision of European styles of dress. It opens with the image of a black man proudly seizing and donning a white man's tie and bowler hat, a practice he ridicules and describes as an attempt at a kind of self-destruction. It should not be forgotten that Césaire himself was very much an assimilated intellectual, and his derisory portrait of the black man dressed as a white man could also have reflected his own position. Nevertheless, while struggling with his own self-image as a black man studying at an elite institution in Paris, Césaire is acerbic in his critique of the aesthetics of assimilation and passionate in his call to black people to shed the costumes and performances that mask their own culture. This emphasis on the image and particularly the clothing of the black man in the metropole picks up on similar references made by some of his contemporaries. Césaire would have been aware, for example, of the work of the Nardal sisters, Jane and Paulette, whose salons were dynamic spaces in 1930s Paris for gatherings of black and mixed-race people seeking to explore and affirm black culture. Paulette Nardal had already denounced assimilation in an article entitled

'L'internationalisme noir', published in *La Dépêche Africaine* in February 1928. She also published 'Guignol Ouolof' alongside Césaire's 'Nègreries' in the first issue of *L'Étudiant noir*, another vilification of the black man's use of costume, this time a ridiculously decorated military outfit:

> An immense black man. The costume of a general in an operetta. A black sheet on which there seem to erupt imposing brandebourgs, epaulettes, the flat helmet of a German officer with gold and red tassels, and – an even more unexpected detail – a monocle on a black string, fitted into the arch of his left brow.[4]

This fantastical portrait is created, according to Nardal, for the benefit of 'white consumers' and serves only to fuel racist stereotypes of the black man's appearance as comical and grotesque. A more sober questioning of the black man's image and clothing can equally be found in a piece by Louis-Thomas Achille in the highly influential *Revue du monde noir* in 1932. If the *Revue* set out specifically to explore and give voice to black culture in Paris, here Achille wonders, 'how should black people living in France dress?'[5] These anxious tropes of clothing and performance clearly fuel Césaire's insistence on the beauty, goodness and legitimacy of blackness.

These early reflections on image and clothing demonstrate the emergence of negritude out of the critique of assimilation. Césaire's first coining of the term 'négritude' followed a burgeoning culture of black self-affirmation that had been growing since the 1920s and was animated by both francophone and American writers and intellectuals in Paris's lively cultural arena. Césaire draws on works by writers of the Harlem Renaissance, such as Alain Locke, Langston Hughes and Claude McKay, who were engaged in dialogue with the Nardal sisters as well as with other contributors to the francophone negritude movement such as Léopold Sédar Senghor and Léon Gontran Damas. Locke had already in 1925 heralded the invention of the 'New Negro' in his volume of that name, which brought together writings by major figures such as Hughes and McKay, as well as W. E. B. Du Bois, Countee Cullen and Zora Neale Hurston. In his foreword, Locke announces, 'we have, as the heralding sign, an unusual outburst of creative expression. There is a renewed race-spirit that consciously and proudly sets itself apart'.[6] The concept of the 'New Negro' was a clear rejection of 'old' stereotypes around black identity and a call for self-creation that would resonate with Césaire. Indeed Césaire's announcement in the *Cahier* that 'la vieille négritude progressivement se cadavérise' ['the old negritude progressively cadavers itself'] could be read as a subtle reference to Locke's work.[7] Jane Nardal had translated parts of Locke's volume into French, and Locke's own introductory essay was translated by Louis and Renée Guilloux in *Europe* in 1931, so Césaire would have had access to these, even though a full translation never appeared in French (Césaire's English was excellent).[8] Nevertheless, this was the start of an ongoing exchange of ideas and concepts redefining racial identities.

The term 'nègre' is contentious and evolving, and its usage in French should perhaps be glossed for an anglophone audience. Whilst 'negro' in English was not at the time necessarily pejorative and indeed conveyed a certain respectability, there can be little doubt about the negative connotations of 'nègre' in French. It is therefore perhaps surprising to see the term used proactively by negritude writers. With its history of pejorative use, it is redeployed in the 1930s, however, in an affirmative gesture of reappropriation and as a signifier of the 'New Negro' recreating himself. As Brent Hayes Edwards notes, in France during the 1920s and 30s, 'nègre' was the most offensive term for 'black' and was used to signify those at the bottom of the hierarchy. Its use initially emerged in the context of the institutionalisation of slavery with the 'Code Noir' of 1685, where Edwards argues that it came to represent 'a specific alterity'.[9] While the term 'noir' was still used, for example, by abolitionists critical of the mistreatment of slaves, 'nègre' served to conflate all black Africans with slaves.

As a result, 'noir' would have been the term that black French citizens used to describe themselves in the early twentieth century, whilst 'homme de couleur' was associated with the elite. This highly pejorative use of the word 'nègre' is analysed by Lamine Senghor (a Senegalese Marxist thinker who fought for the French during the First World War and who went on to found the Comité de la Race Nègre when he was living in Paris in 1926) in an incendiary article entitled 'Le mot nègre' published in *La Voix des Nègres* in 1927. Senghor argues that the different terms 'homme de couleur', 'noir' and 'nègre' serve only to undermine the unity of black people. In response, he calls for a rehabilitation of the term 'nègre' as a rallying cry for black solidarity, throwing the divisive rhetoric back in the coloniser's face:

> Yes, gentlemen, you have wanted to use this word as a divisive watchword. But we use it as a rallying cry: a banner. We do ourselves honor and glory by calling ourselves *Nègres*, with a capital *N* at the head. We wish to guide our 'nègre' race on the path of its total liberation from the yoke of enslavement that it now bears. We wish to impose the respect that is due our race, as well as its equality with all the other races of the world: this is its right and our duty; and we call ourselves *Nègres!*[10]

The reappropriation of the term 'nègre' by writers such as Césaire, then, is a deliberate attempt to acknowledge its history of brutality while investing it with new meaning. Later on, in the article 'Antillais et Africains', Fanon too noted the different usages of 'noir' and 'nègre', this time suggesting that the former was used for Caribbean people, assumed to be more assimilated, and the latter was for Africans.[11] Fanon too vilifies this divisive logic.

The emergence of negritude can be linked back to Lamine Senghor's analysis of the term 'nègre' back in 1927, but the flourishing of black culture and thought associated with negritude was then fuelled by the development of successive cultural journals and magazines through the 1930s, all devoted to the celebration of black history and creativity in various forms. The first and perhaps most significant of these was the *Revue du monde noir*, which ran for just two years, before censorship and financial difficulties forced the editors to suspend publication, but it nevertheless played an indispensable role in the history of the emergence of negritude. Its appearance coincided with the huge *Exposition coloniale internationale* in Paris in 1931, which exhibited the cultural diversity of France's colonies with the aim of celebrating French colonial beneficence, though it would also have attracted black writers and activists at the time seeking to find a voice in the métropole. Once again, the *Revue* set out to puncture the myth of assimilation and to establish a space for an authentic and unified black culture. Louis-Thomas Achille's preface to the series refers again to Locke's 'new Negro', and goes on to describe the role of the journal in creating a cultural hub for black people from different parts of the world: 'not a black people or *nation*, but a culture, a soul, a black humanism, a *black World*, both diverse and open to all men and women who want to enrich themselves in it or simply to discover it'.[12] In her biography of Césaire, Kora Véron also shows how the *Revue* asked a series of questions about the unity and diversity of black identity, the idea of the black soul, and the place of 'métissage' in black culture.[13] Black solidarity did not necessarily promise harmony or homogeneity, as Claude McKay had shown in his lively depiction of black people of diverse origins in the port of Marseilles in the novel *Banjo*, published in 1929. It did nevertheless promise effervescent and creative cultural dialogue between black people seeking a place in the European capital.

If Césaire read the *Revue du monde noir*, however, he also kept his distance from the journal, considering it to be rather too elitist, representing mulattoes rather than black people. And indeed, the editorial of the first issue clearly addresses black intellectuals rather than the wider black population. The editors state their aim at the outset to 'give the intellectual elite of the black Race and to the friends of Black people a mouthpiece where they can publish their artistic, literary and scientific works', and also to, 'create between Blacks across the whole world, with no distinction in nationality, an intellectual and moral link that allows them to know themselves better, to love one another fraternally, to defend more effectively their collective interests and to illustrate their Race, this is the triple goal of the REVIEW OF THE BLACK WORLD'.[14] Césaire was uncomfortable with this explicit address to the elite, which lacked the radical vision for change that he was seeking, even if the journal was crucial in introducing him to the writers of the Harlem Renaissance as well as the German ethnologist Leo Frobenius. The *Revue du monde noir* was at the same time the public voice for the discussions that unfolded at the Nardal salons, which too were spaces for reflection on colonialism and racism, and for music and poetry by black artists and writers. In the preface quoted above, Achille compares these salons to those of the French *ancien régime*, where conversation was celebrated as an art, though Césaire was perhaps alienated by the elitism inherent in this sort of comparison. In an interview with Françoise Vergès, he claims to have attended only once or twice, noting nevertheless that it was there that he met American writers such as Langston Hughes and Claude McKay.[15] Kora Véron tells us that, according to his friend Pierre Aliker, he was in fact there more often than he admits, but either way, it is clear that the salons and the *Revue* were influential in their contribution to black cultural activity at the time, even if Césaire was keen not to affiliate himself too closely with the bourgeois elite they represented.[16]

Whilst the *Revue du monde noir* was for Césaire too elitist, in June 1932 another group of Martinican students published a single issue of a much more radical journal, *Légitime Défense*, with which Césaire would have been familiar but to which he again did not contribute. Several of those behind *Légitime Défense* had also been involved with the *Revue*, but here they set out to pursue an explicitly Marxist and Surrealist agenda, led this time by Étienne Léro together with René Ménil and Jules Monnerot. The title was taken from an article written in

1926 by André Breton, in which he defended surrealism against accusations of idealism and demonstrated that the movement was concerned with the proletariat seeking power at the same time as with internal psychic experience. *Légitime Défense* promoted both class struggle and creative experimentation, and in its opening editorial made clear its triple engagement with Marxism, Surrealism and Freudian psychoanalysis. Several of its contributors, including René Ménil and Étienne Léro, lamented the failings of existing forms of Caribbean literature, which they considered to remain steeped in white culture and lacking in originality: 'stuffed full to bursting with white morals, white culture, white education and white prejudice, Caribbeans display in these publications a puffed up image of themselves'.[17] Indeed Ménil suggested in his introduction to the re-edition of the journal in 1978 that the *Cahier* was precisely the form of literature that the journal's participants had been soliciting.[18]

Nevertheless, Césaire was not involved in *Légitime Défense*, as he felt that not enough attention was paid to the question of blackness. This disaffiliation at the same time had in the background the recent dispute surrounding the 'Affaire Aragon' in 1932, involving the condemnation of poet Louis Aragon's involvement with supposedly anarchist propaganda and for glorifying the Soviet Union in a poem whose imagery was thought to be excessively violent. The editors of *Légitime Défense* seemed not to be aware that the 'Affaire Aragon' had introduced a split within the surrealist movement, as Breton ultimately criticised Aragon's subordination of poetic form to Communist doxa. Césaire was keen not to sacrifice poetic art in the name of class struggle, and though he supported the journal's call for a renewal of Caribbean culture, he remained preoccupied with the discovery of his own lyric voice. Whilst he was later a member of the Communist Party at the time of the inauguration of his political career in 1945, he was not yet affiliated during this period in Paris.

Césaire was nevertheless becoming increasingly culturally active and was elected President of the Association des

Étudiants Martiniquais in 1934. Another journal, *L'Étudiant martiniquais*, had also been running since 1932 with the aim of promoting the establishment of a specifically Martinican cultural voice. In 1935, together with his friend Léopold Sédar Senghor, Césaire took over *L'Étudiant martiniquais*, renamed it *L'Étudiant noir*, and set out a plan for dramatic cultural renovation. He clearly wanted to relinquish the specific focus on Martinique and to 'l'élargir au monde entier' ['broaden it to the whole world'], and it is here that he began his concerted effort not just to reinvent Caribbean culture but to create the dynamic new black culture that would become negritude.[19] Césaire had been reading the writers of the Harlem Renaissance with enthusiasm, and would go on to write his thesis on the theme of the South in black American poetry. With *L'Étudiant noir*, he would inaugurate his own search for a 'new Negro' culture. Shaking off the shackles of assimilation, Césaire calls for assertive creative action:

> Young black people want to act and create. They want to create their own poets and novelists, who will speak to them of their own misfortunes and their own greatnesses; they want to contribute to universal life, to the humanisation of humanity; and for that, once again, it is necessary to conserve or rediscover oneself; it is the primacy of the self.[20]

It is in the third issue of 'Nègreries' that Césaire, as we saw in the Introduction, first coined the term 'négritude', and it is evident here that the rhetoric celebrating black self-invention steadily gains fervour. The affirmation of blackness is here evoked as a step towards revolution, as he concludes decisively: 'let us work at being nègre, in the certainty that this is working for the Revolution, for he will create the Revolution with his strength, and will find his strength is his true character'.[21]

Césaire's invention of the idea of negritude in *L'Étudiant noir* took the existing debates and activity around black culture to a new level. His vocabulary was more radical and provocative than that of the *Revue du monde noir*, and his imagery more devoted to black identity and culture than that of *Légitime Défense*, where (as Ménil explains in the introductory essay cited above) black values were explicitly addressed only within the Marxist framework of social transformation. It was Césaire who above all equated the reinvention of black culture and identity with revolution and who suggested that cultural activity is able to command extraordinary powers of contestation. Césaire was also working with Léopold Sédar Senghor on *L'Étudiant noir*, however, and though the young men were mutually supportive of one another (and, indeed, considered each other close allies throughout their careers), Senghor's rhetoric in the journal was already less militant. Alongside Césaire's 'Nègreries' in issue one, Senghor wrote an article on René Maran, a writer originally from Martinique best known for publishing the first 'roman nègre', *Batouala*, in 1921. Senghor praises Maran's illustration of black humanism, conceived as the result of a fusion between black culture and European culture. Senghor glosses it as 'a cultural movement that has the black man as its aim, and Western reason and the black soul as the instruments of its research'.[22] At the same time, Senghor demonstrates his belief in an authentic 'black soul' in terms that are rather more essentialising than Césaire's call for action and creation. The distinctiveness of Césaire's negritude also stands out in comparison with the lengthy piece by Gilbert Gratiant in the same issue, 'Mulâtres: pour le bien et le mal', in which Gratiant affirms his blackness but insists that this is just one part of him, and that he also embraces Creole culture and his status as a 'Martinican mulatto'.[23] Césaire, on the contrary, was not interested in a specific métis identity but insisted on the importance of the term 'nègre' as an identity linking all Caribbeans with their origins in Africa. This stance can be seen to be supported by the poems 'I have seen Black Hands' by Richard Wright and 'Strong Men' by Sterling Brown, evoking the oppression and resistance of black men, that Césaire translated for the same volume.

Césaire's relationship with Senghor was instrumental in his invention of negritude and his own coming to voice. The story of their meeting has been told multiple times in interviews and biographies, with some subtle variation, though in each case the men's immediate affection for one another is evident. Ngal cites an interview held in 1967, where Césaire tells of how they met by the Lycée Louis-le-Grand, as he himself was entering and Senghor was leaving.[24] Véron notes that Senghor was no longer studying at the Lycée but had moved on to the Sorbonne, so that it would not have been possible for them to meet in the corridors of the school as is often assumed, though the version cited by Ngal still seems plausible.[25] Nevertheless, Césaire's fondness for telling the anecdote of their meeting helps emphasise its significance for him. Newly arrived in Paris, Césaire was disoriented and alienated, and Senghor took him under his wing. Most importantly, it was through Senghor that Césaire became fascinated by Africa, a sentimental and idealised vision of Africa that nevertheless served as a counter to metropolitan culture and provided a sense of a shared heritage – one which for Césaire was bound up in a myth of precolonial origin. Senghor's knowledge of Africa was a fantasy for Césaire, as Véron suggests: 'Césaire's Africa, which nourished his thinking, his dreams and his hopes, is an Africa glorified by the tales Senghor told him about it and to which the odes of *kim* or *Chants d'ombre* testify'.[26] It was also with Senghor that Césaire read Frobenius and Delafosse, whose descriptions of African civilisation worked both to correct colonial stereotypes of primitivism and to provide the young Césaire with a broader culture to which he could feel he belonged. Frobenius corrected the assumption that Egypt was the only source of civilisation in Africa, mapped out the stages of African civilisation, and explored how its rich production of art testifies to its complex development.[27]

I have already noted the difference between Césaire's and Senghor's versions of negritude, however, with Senghor's idea of the black soul tipping closer to essentialism than Césaire's vision for cultural revolution. Negritude would evolve through the careers of both thinkers, and in the 1930s Césaire had coined the term but the concept was not yet developed.

Yet although Césaire speaks of authenticity in 'Nègreries', he also insists on negritude as a 'cultural task' and black identity is already something to be created rather than discovered. Senghor's most sustained reflection on negritude during this early period can be found in the 1939 essay 'Ce que l'homme noir apporte', where his notorious comment on black emotion versus Greek reason, cited in my Introduction, originates. Senghor reflects extensively on the nature of the black soul, on the connection between contemporary black communities and their ancestral histories, for example. He notably also discusses black culture and art, and his analysis of the use of rhythm (often taken as a sign of Senghor's essentialism) is clearly intended as a reflection on a particular artistic technique.[28] Césaire's differences from Senghor are only made explicit later; Césaire, too, refines his understanding of negritude as his thinking develops, as we shall see over the course of this book. During the 1930s, however, Césaire's vocabulary is already very different from that of Senghor, and despite his fascination with Africa, there is no imagery of an originary identity or black soul to be found there, as there is in Senghor. While Senghor describes certain traits and dispositions in black people, Césaire evokes action and creativity, and would later reflect on the dangers of constructing 'a black essence': 'if you do that, you fall into reverse Gobinism'.[29] Césaire is vilifying here the racial hierarchy promulgated by Joseph Arthur de Gobineau in his 1855 *Essai sur l'inégalité des races humaines*, and warning against using negritude simply to reverse the hierarchy rather than to abolish the system of racial thinking entirely.

Césaire's early evocation of negritude in 'Nègreries' is couched, then, in revolutionary terminology and is evidently ambitious in its critique of colonial thinking. Yet he was not yet politically active, and indeed was often introverted and withdrawn. The 1930s were a period of political tension in Paris, with the rise of fascism and the outbreak of the Second World War in the same year as the publication of the *Cahier*. As the political far right gained traction in France, socialist and Communist groups were mobilised against the fascist threat. Antifascist movements also helped to spark the anticolonial movements that were growing at the same time. Césaire did not engage directly in these in the 1930s, but he would have been affected when André Aliker, the brother of his friend Pierre, was assassinated in 1934 after investigating a case of tax fraud in Martinique, for which the guilty party was wrongly exonerated. Césaire was struggling with his health at the time and did not sign the call for justice printed in *L'Étudiant martiniquais* in May 1934, but he would have been aware of the riots and their brutal suppression that followed.[30]

It was during this period, moreover, that Césaire underwent a sort of crisis. Césaire had always been a more anxious and alienated figure than the more worldly Senghor and his more gregarious colleague and friend, Léon Gontran Damas. He suspended his studies between February 1934 and January 1935 for health reasons, though he then succeeded in the competition for entry to the prestigious *École normale supérieure* in 1935 on his third attempt. Between 1935 and 1939, however, Césaire was largely silent, and he struggled to relate his studies to his lived experience: 'all the classical study I was doing seemed so far from life, so far from what I wanted to do'.[31] His mental state improved when he met the beautiful young student Suzanne Roussi, also from Martinique, was smitten, and married her on 10 July 1937.

Césaire started work on the *Cahier* in the mid-1930s, and he was preoccupied by it during this period of crisis. The origins of the work can be traced back to a holiday in Croatia, where he was invited to spend the summer by his friend Petar Guberina in the hope that it would provide him with the solace and refreshment he needed. Several critics date the trip to the summer of 1935, though Véron argues that it must have been 1936.[32] The landscape at the coast where Césaire was staying reminded him of Martinique, and indeed he was thrilled when he discovered that the group of islands he could see from the shore were called 'Martinska', as if to echo his native Martinique. His response was to start writing the *Cahier:* 'I come to a country that is not mine, which I'm told is called Martinique. "Give me a piece of paper!": that's how I started the *Notebook*'.[33]

The production of this first and most extensive poetic work was nevertheless prolonged and arduous for Césaire, a process that Senghor called 'giving birth in suffering'.[34] He was writing during a period of intense anxiety, and the poem itself is testimony to his resolute departure from familiar modes of writing and thought. The *Cahier* makes a decisive break with French poetic form, shedding an artifice that would have been inauthentic for him, just like the tie and hat ridiculed at the opening of that first 'Nègreries' article. It also abandoned the flat and uninspired form of Caribbean literature, previously denounced in *Légitime Défense*, in a bold process of experimentation that was both spiritual and aesthetic. Describing his thinking during this period of composition, Césaire reflects, 'at the start it was necessary to break everything, to create a Caribbean literature from scratch. This required a cannibalistic violence'.[35] This poetic innovation was also influenced by the American poetry Césaire had been reading, and which he subsequently describes in an article published in 1941 in *Tropiques* after his return to Martinique. Relinquishing the grandeur of French lyric, this was rather 'a direct outpouring, rapid like a mountain stream', an evocation that risks implying that this poetry is lacking in sophistication.[36] Nevertheless, one can intermittently see this directness in the punchy verse sections of the *Cahier*, whilst the torrent might describe some of the more profusive prose. Césaire's spiritual crisis generated a revolution in poetry that can now be seen to dramatise the restlessness and energy of negritude.

The 1939 Edition of *Cahier d'un retour au pays natal*

Césaire's *Cahier d'un retour au pays natal* is an unrivalled poetic masterpiece. It reflects a period of intense personal and spiritual change; it defiantly breaks with all expectations surrounding the form of French verse and dramatises the reinvention of black consciousness. Césaire himself called it an 'anti-poem', as if it were a revolt not just against racism and colonial oppression but also against traditional poetic form.[37] Its insurrectionary energy has been described in manifold different ways by critics and readers. In the early 1940s, the French surrealist writer André Breton described the life-giving force of Césaire's lyric voice as 'nascent oxygen', and on reading the *Cahier* he evoked, 'that all-pervasive movement, that gushing exuberance, that ability to turn inside out the world of emotions'.[38] In his famous essay on negritude poetry, 'Orphée noir', published in 1948, Jean-Paul Sartre used imagery of cosmic energy in his evocation of Césaire's poetry as an explosive attack on European colonisation: 'a poem by Césaire ... bursts and wheels around like a rocket; suns turning and exploding into new suns, come out of it; it is a perpetual going-beyond'.[39] These evocations all seek to capture the poem's astonishing power, its aesthetic novelty testified by its lexical diversity and inventiveness, its juxtaposition of prose and verse forms that exploit a variety of rhythmic patterns, and its astonishingly rich, varied, and sometimes jarring imagery capturing the dynamic history and geography of black resistance.

Yet it must be recognised that these readers and critics are commenting on the successive versions of the *Cahier* that followed at various stages its first publication in 1939. Césaire's great epic was not a static magnum opus but a dynamic, living being to which he repeatedly returned and which he altered, reshaped and honed in successive versions. The first version was published in the little-known avant-garde journal *Volontés* in 1939. Césaire had tried to send it to another journal, it is not known which one, but it was rejected.[40] One of his teachers suggested that he send the text to the editor Georges Pelorson at *Volontés*. Pelorson was intrigued by the manuscript, suggested a number of improvements including a more conclusive ending, and agreed to print it. Whilst

Césaire's interaction with black culture in Paris during the 1930s was highly influential, then, this first version would have been addressing not so much black writers in France and the Caribbean as an eclectic international group of writers interested in various forms of modernism and literary experimentation. The editors and readers would have been interested in the poem's linguistic inventiveness, and would not necessarily have been steeped in the racial tensions that Césaire was also recording.

Césaire continued rethinking the work during the 1940s, printing a sequence of a few pages entitled 'En guise de manifeste littéraire' in *Tropiques* in 1942, and also reworking and adding to the 1939 text as a result of his interaction with André Breton and French surrealism. A version heavily imbued with surrealism was published by Brentano's in New York in 1947, together with Breton's preface and an English translation by Ivan Goll and Lionel Abel, though this version reflects work carried out during the early 1940s. Also in 1947, a further version was published by Bordas in Paris, including the addition and rearranging of passages in such a way as to highlight the ideological, anticolonial thrust of the poem. In 1956, Présence Africaine published what has been seen as the definitive edition, where the imprint of the writer's interest in the African decolonisation movements becomes apparent and where the poet seems to be making a more militant political call for anticolonial resistance. James Arnold has carefully documented these successive versions in his monumental edition of Césaire's writings and has disputed the critical privileging of the Présence Africaine edition. Arnold conceives the 1947 Brentano's version as the 'centrepiece' in his analysis of the poem's evolution, though he has also, together with Clayton Eshleman, translated and commented on the 1939 version, highlighting above all its spiritual dimension as opposed to its more politicised reincarnation in 1956.[41] Arnold insists that the 1939 version is a quite different work, a more personal and quasi-religious quest that is wrongly eclipsed by the critical focus on 1956.

40   1930S PARIS

Arnold's work editing and analysing the successive versions of the *Cahier* is indispensable, but his insistence that the 1956 version obscures the spiritual resonances of 1939, and on some level subordinates the original text's poetry to politics, should not be taken to mean that there is a clear rupture between them. The *Cahier* should be read as a continual process, a living work that its author reinvigorated to varying ends, but the changes are part of a continuum and the poem gained resonances and shifted emphases as it developed rather than losing its original meaning. Césaire returned to this story of return over a period of nearly twenty years and that process performs the activity of return precisely as an ongoing journey. The poem itself depicts not a rerooting from an original point of departure, but multiple returns, to Martinique and to Africa, as well as new departures, with references to black culture and experience in the US and to other forces of oppression around the world. Similarly, Césaire returns to his work to keep it moving on its continual journey, as all the elements of the 1939 version remain in 1956, but parts of it are rearranged and insertions are made to reveal the development of the poet's thinking in different directions. Moreover, if in the present Introduction it was argued that throughout his career Césaire continually worked on, and blended, poetry and politics, the journey of the text of the *Cahier* traces the evolution of both in his thinking rather than a move from one to the other. The 1939 text certainly precedes the concretisation of Césaire's political motivations during the 1950s, but it is highly assertive in its denunciation of the history of enslavement and oppression and in its call for revolt. It still provides the substance of the 1956 version and the foundation for Césaire's ensuing political work, even if later works introduce a new political impetus and vocabulary not present in the introspective vision of 1939.

The rest of this chapter offers a reading of the 1939 version as an insight into Césaire's thinking during the 1930s. I will return to the *Cahier* intermittently later in the book to reflect on the changes that were made during different periods but will confine the analysis here to that first version in order to preserve the chronology of Césaire's thought. The 1939 version of the *Cahier* can be read as the culmination of his experiences during the 1930s, developing the thoughts with which he experimented in *L'Étudiant noir*, and inventing and exploring the idea of negritude. The poem depicts a return first to Martinique and then, only tentatively in this version, to Africa as a means of capturing the identity of the poet and his people, but rather than finding either selfhood or black culture already established in either, these returns trigger a process of recreation and revolt. The poem does not yet have a clear anticolonial agenda, and yet it certainly excoriates a history of violence against black people. It denounces the dehumanising practice of enslavement and its legacies and traces the transformation of the poetic self as he calls for revolt. In this sense it can be seen to perform the invention of negritude, as the poet plays with the term at various junctures through the poem to different effects and dramatises the action and creativity heralded in the two 'Nègreries' articles. Africanist scholar Christopher Miller insists on the centrality of negritude throughout the publishing history of the *Cahier*, regarding this concept as one in which the poet's lyrical and political aspirations are both at play, with the result that, 'the *Cahier* has always been the epic of negritude'.[42] Arnold, too, links the poem with negritude, in the sense that he reads it as working through the various stages of revolt charted when Césaire originally coined the term, though for him this remains a spiritual process.

As we saw in the Introduction, Césaire spoke in 'Nègreries', of the need to 'break with the mechanistic identification of races, destroy superficial values', each of which can be associated with the poem's first endeavour to overturn both racism and assimilation. He then calls his readers to 'seize within us the unmediated nègre', to embrace black lived experience, and then to 'plant our negritude like a beautiful tree', to create and give full expression to a new and continually growing black consciousness.[43] These stages, though neither here nor in the

1939 *Cahier* couched in terms of a political endeavour, enact a process of resistance and recreation that will also remain foundational when Césaire's language becomes more militant. This process forges the creation of a 'new Negro', a new self, addressed to a people also renewing itself, and it is crucial to its ethics that it is continually ongoing, as black identity evolves through the poem, through the different versions, and on through the manifold black cultural movements that have succeeded this dramatisation.

The 1939 *Cahier* is roughly divided into four parts, comprising first the poet's return to Martinique and his disillusionment, followed by a renewed call for departure and reflection on his own alienation, the invention of negritude in light of the memory of the suffering of black people, and finally an assertion of renewal.[44] Whilst the first part is mostly formed of long and convoluted prose sentences, the subsequent sections are in free verse that takes a variety of rhythms and forms, by turns lyrical or declamatory, lexically obscure or defiantly direct. The poem opens with a disturbing evocation of the Martinique to which the poet has returned, and which he finds hungry, diseased, desolate and inert.[45] If Césaire insisted, as we have seen, that it is beautiful and good to be nègre, his writing nevertheless conjures the vile conditions of black people's lives both past and present. Successive bundles of images are introduced by the refrain 'au bout du petit matin' ['at the end of first light'], as if the poet is at once capturing the awakening that comes with dawn and portraying that moment of awakening as already spent.[46] Long prose sentences pile images of sickness, putrefaction and apathy on top of one another, often with rich, obscure and sonorous vocabulary detailing the people's hideous deformation with unusual diseases: 'ici la parade des risibles et scrofuleux bubons, les poutures de microbes très étranges, les poisons sans alexitère connu, les sanies des plaies bien antiques, les fermentations imprévisibles d'espèces putrescibles' ['right here the parade of laughable and scrofulous buboes, the forced feeding of very strange microbes, the poisons without known alexins, the

1930S PARIS

43

sanies of really ancient sores, the unforeseeable fermentations of putrescible species'].[47] At the same time, the people are depicted as an anonymous mass, without culture or agency. The speaker himself is not yet present; rather, he laments the inertia of the undifferentiated crowd: 'cette foule qui ne sait pas faire foule, cette foule, on s'en rend compte, si parfaitement seule sous ce soleil' ['this throng that does not know how to throng, this throng, one realises, so perfectly alone under the sun'].[48] Césaire regrets here the absence of solidarity but also the lack of self-assertion, as if, as he noted also in 'Nègreries', the black man here has no sense of self but rather suffers from 'une peur de soi-même' ['a fear of himself'].[49]

The later part of this section introduces the speaker's subjective voice, as the depiction of poverty in Martinique now includes his childhood, 'une autre petite maison qui sent très mauvais dans une rue très étroite, une maison minuscule qui abrite en ses entrailles de bois pourri des dizaines de rats et la turbulence de mes six frères et sœurs' ['another little house very bad-smelling in a very narrow street, a minuscule house that harbours in its guts of rotten wood dozens of rats and the turbulence of my brothers and sisters'].[50] The poet conjures his father's bouts of melancholy and his mother's endless sewing as she strove to earn more money for the family. It is at this point that the lyric voice emerges and introduces the subjective quest that will drive the rest of the work. It is also here that the poet first conjures the black race as a whole. If so far the poem takes the form of an impersonal description, here the poet establishes a subjective voice but also suggests that out of his own dilapidated home emerges the beginnings of racial consciousness: 'le lit de planches d'où s'est levée ma race, tout entière ma race de ce lit de planches' ['the bed of boards from which my race arose, my whole entire race from this bed of boards'].[51] The chiasmatic structure of the line and association between the uprising of black people and the poet's poor living conditions serves intriguingly to heighten the connection between the emergence of racial consciousness and this history of poverty. At this moment in the text the black race is still passive, and the people's powerlessness is emphasised through reference to the landscape in turn wielding its force against the downtrodden population. But it is important that this first section introduces this idea of the whole race, as if to anticipate the emergence of black consciousness out of the history of subjugation and stultification.

Césaire's reference to race at the end of this first section could be read as a catalyst for the abrupt shift that marks the start of the second section. The disastrous return to Martinique is cut off with the sudden invocation, 'partir' ['to leave'], as if the poet needs to leave and return afresh if he is to disrupt the people's state of apathetic entrapment. This is a moment where the 'je' suddenly takes centre stage, bonding once again with his native land, and even more, imagining setting himself up as a spokesman for the people. Addressing his country, he seems confidently to claim: "'ma bouche sera la bouche des malheurs qui n'ont point de bouche, ma voix, la liberté de celles qui s'affaissent au cachot du désespoir'" ["'my mouth shall be the mouth of those calamities that have no mouth, my voice the freedom of those who break down in the prison holes of despair'"].[52] Critics have tended not to draw attention to the quotation marks here, but these suggest that the poet is experimenting with the idea of speaking for the people rather than assuming that position unproblematically. He is exploring the potentialities of his role as poet, and indeed the emphasis on action, the warning against maintaining the sterile position of a spectator, echoes the call to 'agir et créer' in 'Nègreries'. The poet would himself be a source of creation, almost a godlike figure, as he sees himself as 'moi homme d'ainsi bouleverser la création' ['I a man to so overturn creation']. Later passages also make it clear that this moment of apparent poetic hubris is a stance with which Césaire is toying in his creation of negritude, but the text does not allow him to play out this role in an unreflective manner.

These apparently hubristic lines are followed by passages recalling the history of suffering of black people across the world, the legacy of enslavement and the violent quashing of slave revolts. The poetic 'je' at first takes on a proprietorial stance, evoking the horrors of enslavement but prefacing these ghastly images with the affirmative 'ce qui est à moi' ['what is mine'].[53] It is as if the speaker wants to identify with his people, and to acknowledge this history of brutality, as integral to the process of revolt. Yet revolt at this stage is conjured in the context of the history of its brutal suppression, a history recaptured out of a web of metaphors of entrapment and containment woven through the evocation of Martinique, the Caribbean and the Americas. It is here that Césaire uses the term negritude for the first time in the poem, as he describes the Haitian Revolution as the inauguration of black resistance: 'Haïti où la négritude se mit debout pour la première fois et dit qu'elle croyait à son humanité' ['Haiti where negritude rose for the first time and stated that it believes in its humanity'].[54] Negritude is not so much concerned with cultural identity as with anticolonial resistance, with the political demand for independence and the end of enslavement. This shift in the meaning of negritude indicates already the plasticity of the term for Césaire as his thinking migrates and evolves between the essays of *L'Étudiant noir* and the *Cahier*. The poet follows this image with references to slave revolts in the Southern states of America, 'Virginie. Tennessee. Géorgie. Alabama', the staccato structure of the line contrasting with the rambling prose of the preceding lines and indeed of the first section of the poem, its thirteen syllables stubbornly refusing to fit into the twelve syllables of an alexandrine, the classical unit of French poetry. Yet this time resistance only brings more brutality: 'putréfactions monstrueuses de révoltes inopérantes / marais de sang putrides / trompettes absurdement bouchées' ['monstrous putrefactions of revolts stymied, / marshes of putrid blood / trumpets absurdly muted']. The echo of 'putréfactions' with 'putrides' makes the rotting seem all-pervasive and serves as an apt example of Césaire's technique of weaving images together through subtle echoes in sound. Next the poet remembers the death of Toussaint Louverture, who led the slave revolt in Haiti, and figures the attempt to silence him

46   1930S PARIS

with imagery of obliteration in the white snow, by the white coloniser, imprisoned in the French Jura mountains. The repetition of 'blanc' captures the oppressive force of whiteness, the term itself trapping Toussaint within the poetic structure, whilst the ensuing anaphora, where the term 'la mort' is repeated at the beginning of several lines, presents a series of images of violent death that capture the devastating consequences of past revolts.

The term negritude first appears in the *Cahier* at this point, then, but the poet uses it to remind his reader of the horrors of slavery and of the quashing of the revolts of enslaved people. The poetic 'je', moreover, still seems unable to believe in the role of spokesman, but instead figures himself as trapped by, shifting around between, a series of ridiculous and obscene racist stereotypes: 'je tourne, inapaisée pouliche' ['I circle about, an unappeased filly'], and 'je sais le tracking, le Lindy-hop et les claquettes' ['I can boogie-woogie, do the Lindy-hop and tap dance'], and then 'ma dignité / se vautre dans les dégobillements' ['my dignity wallows in puke'].[55] At the same time, if he might have hoped to recover a sense of origin, a foundation for negritude, in Africa, he stresses that he cannot identify with African figures of nobility ('non, nous n'avons jamais été amazones du roi de Dahomey . . .' ['no, we've never been Amazons of the king of Dahomey . . .']); rather his origin lies in the slave ship.[56] The following passage forms one of the most devastating moments in the *Cahier*, as it is where the speaker most shockingly demonstrates his alienation from the people for whom he might have claimed to speak. It is here that the poet reaches the lowest point in his crisis of confidence, admitting his hypocrisy and his inability to play the role of leader. He describes a moment on the tram, when he sees a 'nègre' horrifically ravaged by 'la Misère' ['Poverty'], and conjures him in a hideous image of downtrodden suffering, 'sa négritude même se décolorait sous l'action d'une inlassable mégie' ['even his negritude discolored as a result of untiring tawing'].[57] Negritude on this occasion is pathetically faded, connoting here not cultural affirmation but the loss of identity, as if blackness itself has lost its meaning. The man's voice is evoked as muted by alcohol and poverty, his eyes are hollowed out and his back is bent in the posture of an enslaved man. His appearance is so pathetic that the women sitting behind laugh at him, yet most disturbingly, the poet too finds himself complicit with those women, momentarily wanting to make it clear that this man is not like him. He calls him 'COMIQUE ET LAID', the capital letters reminding us that this phrase originates in Baudelaire's poem 'L'Albatros', where the once majestic bird (a figure for the poet himself) becomes cumbersome and ugly when it tries to walk on land. The image again serves to ridicule the man, but reinforces the poet's complicity in elite European culture, with the result that his ambition to speak up for suffering black people is betrayed: 'mon héroïsme, quelle farce!' ['my heroism, what a farce!'].[58]

If this marks the lowest moment in the poet's crisis of self-doubt, it is from here that he starts to move towards a more affirmative conception of negritude. Negritude has so far represented first the Haitian Revolution and then the suffering man on the tram, but here it is figured with a series of dynamic, active verbs. It remains less a specific cultural identity than an action, again responding to the call to 'agir et créer' in 'Nègreries'. As we saw in the Introduction, it is not a fixed and opaque object, 'une pierre' ['a stone'] or 'une taie d'eau morte' ['a leukoma of dead liquid'], nor is it a proud but fixed monument, 'ni une tour ni une cathédrale' ['neither a tower nor a cathedral'];[59] it is rather a dynamic rooting in the soil at the same time as an aspirational projection into the ether. Brent Hayes Edwards reads the structure of negativity followed by positivity here as revelatory of a sort of overcoming, not so much a strict opposition as an assumption and transcendence. Above all, negritude represents dignity and rejects the humiliating posture of enslavement, 'elle troue l'accablement opaque de sa droite patience' ['it breaks through opaque prostration with its upright patience']. The anaphoric structure, repeating 'ma négritude', both offers rhythmic emphasis and also highlights the distinct and diverse imagery that follows the repeated term, as if to dramatise its flexibility. The use of anaphora is associated, according to Arnold, with the work of the French Catholic poet Charles Péguy, whom Arnold argues was highly influential to Césaire, though Edwards links it rather with Sterling Brown's 'Strong Men', a poem Césaire had translated for *L'Étudiant noir*, and in this case Edwards suggests it is a figure that highlights not just reiteration but transformation.[60] The poet then goes on to celebrate with negritude a more integrated relationship with the earth in a statement of resistance against colonial attempts to master and domesticate the land. With the exclamation 'Eia pour le Kaïlcédrat royal!' ['Eia for the royal Cailcedra!'], he uses the celebratory 'Eia' found in Greek tragedy and Latin missal to confer solemnity, and evokes the African mahogany tree in order to root negritude in the African landscape.[61] The following passage testifies to Césaire's interest in Frobenius and his conception of the 'homme-plante', later developed by Suzanne Césaire in *Tropiques*, as it conjures up those who live immersed in the natural world rather than seeking mastery:

Eia pour ceux qui n'ont jamais rien inventé
pour ceux qui n'ont jamais rien exploré
pour ceux qui n'ont jamais rien dompté

mais ils s'abandonnent, saisis, à l'essence de toutes choses
ignorants des surfaces mais saisis par le mouvement de
    toutes choses
insoucieux de dompter, mais jouant le jeu du monde
véritablement les fils aînés du monde

[Eia for those who never invented anything
for those who never explored anything
for those who never conquered anything

but who yield, seized, to the essence of all things
ignorant of surfaces but captivated by the motion of all
    things

indifferent to conquering, but playing the game of the
world
truly the eldest sons of the world].[62]

This passage is significant in elaborating what Césaire seeks
as he asserts a new form of black culture and identity. The
poet on some level seeks to return to an authentic, fundamental mode of existence, but this is not expressed as a particular
set of traditions but rather as a relationship with the environment, a refusal to dominate and a search for integration in the
ecological world. The poet celebrates not facile and material-
istic achievements, acquired at the expense of the land and of
others, but a sensory harmony with the living world: 'poreux
à tous les souffles du monde' ['porous to all the breathing of
the world']. The vocabulary here is also reminiscent of the
call to 'seize within us the unmediated nègre' that prefaced
the introduction of negritude in 'Nègreries'. The repetition
of 'saisir' implies understanding but also a dynamic action or
embrace, an ability to live with the movement of the world
rather than to seek a position of control, as the coloniser did.
The immersion in the land at the same time dramatises the
action to 'plant our negritude' heralded in that first usage
of the term. This return to and embedding within the land
is deeply imbued with the philosophy of African civilisation
promoted by the German ethnographer Leo Frobenius. But
if Césaire's vision is associated with a return to Africa here,
this is to recapture a dynamic relationship with the land rather
than a static tradition.

The assertion of negritude for those who do not seek to
conquer again leads the poet to consider his capacity to speak
for them. The anaphoric repetition of 'pour ceux' ['for those']
evidently raises this question of what he is to do for them,
what the status of his work as poet might be. The poet's
answer at this point reintroduces the poem's spiritual resonance, as now he adopts the language of a prayer and uses a
biblical lexicon to evoke his role as a father figure: 'et de moi,
mon cœur, ne faites ni un père ni un frère, / ni un fils, mais

le père mais le frère, mais le fils / ni un mari, mais l'amant de cet unique peuple' ['and as for me, my heart, make me not into a father or a brother, / nor a son, but into the father, the brother, the son, / nor a husband, but the lover of this unique people'].[63] This passage confirms the journey of the *Cahier* as a kind of spiritual quest, yet it is significant that the poet does not seem to be appealing to God here, but rather to his own heart. He summons his own energies to fulfil the role of poet as father, as a leader figure for all peoples, and as prophet. The language here at the same time seems less bound up with black specificity than with humanism. If the poet sets himself up as the 'bêcheur de cette unique race' ['digger for this unique race'], then nevertheless 'ce que je veux / c'est pour la faim universelle / pour la soif universelle' ['what I want / is for universal hunger / for universal thirst'].[64] Negritude is now not only concerned with black history but with human suffering and human emancipation on a universal scale. Like Christ, the poet aspires to serve as a figurehead for the downtrodden and not just for a particular culture.

Césaire seeks for negritude a universal resonance, but it is also at this point that he moves to an assertion of revolt against the specific history of enslavement. There follows a passage that details the worst excesses of the regime of enslavement as it was sanctioned by the Code Noir of 1685, as the poet tracks the punishments recorded in the Code as legitimate. Here as elsewhere in the poem, he makes use of anaphora, giving emphasis by repeating introductory phrases ('j'accepte' ['I accept'], 'ma race' ['my race'], 'ma reine' ['my queen'] and simply 'et'), followed by sequences of horrific images of disease and punishment that capture the brutality of the regime in telegraphic form.[65] Arnold discusses the biblical references at play in the imagery, noting that African literature scholar Lilyan Kesteloot has perceived in the repetition of 'j'accepte' the echo of Christ's address to God from the cross.[66] Yet at the same time, the poet's revolt here takes the form of a clear denunciation of violence against black people in a way that can be seen to anticipate the Black Lives Matter protests specifically vilifying gratuitous brutality by the authorities. The historical focus of the passage is emphasised by the citation of the names of particular slave owners, followed by a curt list of single terms isolated in lines on their own that serve as indexes for the horrific regime: 'et le pian / le molosse / le suicide / la promiscuité / le brodequin / le cep / le chevalet / le cippe / le frontal' ['and the yaws / the mastiff / the suicide / the promiscuity / the bootkin / the shackles / the rack / the cippus / the headscrew'].[67] All these practices are bound up in the formation of negritude, which Césaire specifies here has no biological significance, as racial theorists such as the Comte de Gobineau would have had it, but names a shared history of suffering: 'la négritude, non plus un indice céphalique, ou un plasma, ou un soma, mais mesurée au compas de la souffrance' ['negritude, no longer a cephalic index, or plasma, or soma, but measured by the compass of suffering'].[68]

This descent into the horrors of enslavement works as a catalyst for the poet in establishing his voice as the leader of revolt. If he conjures 'merveilleusement couché le corps de mon pays dans le désespoir de mes bras' ['the body of my country miraculously laid in the despair of my arms'] like a pietà, he then summons his strength in a striking image of fertilisation and resuscitation.[69] The surging forth of poetic energy is captured in sexual terms with the figure of Onan, taken from Genesis, who spills his seed on the soil like the speaker here, who imagines inseminating and rebirthing the land: 'et voici soudain que force et vie m'assaillent comme un taureau et je renouvelle ONAN qui confia son sperme à la terre féconde' ['suddenly now strength and life assail me like a bull and I revive ONAN who entrusted his sperm to the fecund earth'].[70] This image is excluded from the 1956 version, but here serves to blend the poet's assertion of lyric power with both sexuality and spirituality. The sequence also conjures the explosive energy of the volcano, as this rebirthing invigorates the land with a 'gigantesque pouls sismique' ['gigantic seismic pulse']. Here and intermittently through the rest of the poem, the poet figures his own poetic enterprise as

52 1930S PARIS

bound up with the life of the elements, forces that he conjures like Shakespeare's Prospero but which also inject their capacious energy into his incantatory words and remind him of what humans cannot domesticate and control.

In the last few pages of the poem, the poet defiantly moves away from the old stereotypes of the black man, as 'la vieille négritude' gives way to this assertive stance. The climax of this process is represented by the image of enslaved people standing up and taking control of the ship, though here this is evoked as 'elle est debout la négraille' ['the négraille is on its feet'] and not 'la négritude', as it was when Haiti 'se mit debout' for the first time.[71] Arnold translates 'négraille' using the 'n' word to capture the derogatory connotations of the term, and it is noteworthy that the revolt is not just a re-assumption of black identity through negritude but also a reappropriation of this brutal negativity. If negritude is a process of mining black history and reinventing black consciousness, 'la négraille' is a defiant reclaiming of the language of racial stereotype at the very moment when the master is overthrown through the slave's seizing of the control of the ship. Once again Césaire uses anaphora here:

et la voici:
Plus inattendument debout
debout dans les cordages
debout à la barre
debout à la boussole
debout à la carte
debout sous les étoiles
    debout
      et
        libre

[and there it is:
most unexpectedly standing
standing in the rigging
standing at the tiller

standing at the compass
standing at the map
standing under the stars
   standing
      and
         free].[72]

Whilst the repetition of 'debout' provides rhythmic consistency, the various images that follow chart a movement or process of transformation, as 'la négraille' gradually assumes the position of the master, before seizing his freedom alongside the forces of the cosmos.

The culmination of this evolution of negritude is in this way not any putative solidification of black identity but the claim to power by 'la négraille'. The 1939 version concludes soon after this climactic moment, with the poet once again claiming as his the negative imagery of the 'danses de mauvais nègre', before celebrating, as I noted at the beginning of this chapter, the free, expressive dance 'il-est-beau-et-bon-et-légitime-d'etre-nègre' ['it-is-beautiful-good-and-legitimate-to-be-nègre'].[73] The poetic 'je' adopts a position of assertion here, as if to leave behind the doubt he felt on the tram and appealing to the wind to sweep away the remnants of the enslaved past, though it remains unclear if he commands the elements or whether the elements carry him through their own autonomous and overwhelming force. This last passage at the same time seems to transcend any notion of a specific black culture in its conjuring of 'nos multicolores puretés' ['our multicoloured purities'], and in its vision of the binding of humanity with the earth. There follows an image of uprising, 'monte, Colombe / monte / monte / monte' ['rise, Dove / rise / rise / rise'], signifying the journey towards freedom.[74] This image of upwards movement also, perhaps, anticipates the much more recent poem by Amanda Gorman 'The Hill We Climb', read at US President Joe Biden's inauguration and acknowledging a history of oppression while calling for a more egalitarian future.

Césaire's concluding lines have generated much critical debate, particularly around the neologism 'verrition', about which interpretations vary. For Arnold, 'son immobile verrition' implies the paradox of a fixed process of movement, influenced by Breton's 'explosante fixe', as 'verrition' connotes a turning motion. The term is also associated with the Latin 'verri', 'to sweep', and in this way suggests the tabula rasa brought about by the volcano, but also, as Noland explores, the sweeping of the tongue around the mouth, as if 'la langue maléfique de la nuit' ['the malevolent tongue of the night'] invents a new language while also gaining nourishment.[75] The semantic richness of the line is an apt reminder of the interpretive challenge of Césaire's poetry and of his notion of negritude, as here too meaning shifts and evolves, and opens up new possibilities in new readers. Either way, it seems that the poet concludes again by relinquishing the 'grand trou noir' ['great black hole'] of slave history and racial prejudice to summon at once a continual turning movement and a clear break from the past.

This final figure of movement captures the dynamism of the *Cahier* itself as it kept evolving over the next twenty years. The text of 1939 remains almost entirely in the successive versions, but lines are added, moved and reframed. Rather than a definitive statement, the work should be read as an ongoing experiment, part of the process of inventing negritude and an indication of its provisionality, as Césaire's thinking evolved with the history of the Martinique to which he would return. If this early text is not explicitly political, moreover, its evolution in tandem with the political situation of Martinique ultimately testifies to that continual dialogue between poetry and politics that defined Césaire's career. The emergence and continuing development of negritude resonates with Césaire's future political work and his increasingly virulent critique of colonial oppression in the present as well as in the past. The explosive denunciation of colonial history and call for renewal, articulated at the same time with extraordinary lexical and formal inventiveness, is undoubtedly the foundation for Césaire's ongoing, shifting but tireless commitment to the critique of racism and to the quest for equality as he articulates these through both political activity and literary writing.

I will return to the *Cahier* during the course of this study in order to consider the changes made in later versions. We might note briefly here, however, that if the text shifted through successive incarnations, so too did critical responses to it. I have already mentioned the controversy surrounding the concept of negritude and have tried to show that Césaire's usage of the term here is far more eclectic and dynamic than some critics allow. The denunciation of the term's putative essentialism by thinkers such as Stanislas Adotevi and Wole Soyinka overlooks this plasticity and experimentalism. Yet if the 1939 *Cahier* clearly rejects racial essentialism, some readers might notice that the depiction of gender in this version could be construed to be troublingly reductive. Certainly, there is no reference to the experiences of black women, either past or present, or to the particular challenges brought on by their double subjugation by both colonialism and patriarchy. Césaire's assertion of negritude is also often couched in highly masculine and, indeed, virile terminology. Most strikingly, the reference to Onan and the poet spreading his seed on the land, which as noted above was cut from later versions, associates resistance with virility in ways that make the place of women in the assertion of revolt seem uneasy. The poet's role as spokesman is also conflated with that of the father, with its connotations of patriarchy, as we saw in the lines quoted above that depict the speaker as a godlike paternal figure. The poem also more than once portrays solidarity with the metaphor of fraternity, notably in the closing section, 'lie, lie-moi, fraternité âpre' ['bind, bind me, bitter brotherhood'], in ways that again risk excluding black women.[76] In addition, in exploring the representation of gender in the poem, the critic Hedy Kalikoff has shown that, when femininity is fleetingly mentioned, it often has negative connotations, such as when the inert city is portrayed as thoughtless in a way that is compared with the behaviour of a woman.[77]

56 1930S PARIS

Kalikoff is reading the 1956 version, but the issue is worth signalling here because of the explicit sexuality of the 1939 version. Yet, as Kalikoff also argues, whilst there is no doubt that Césaire uses imagery of heroism and virility, the poet's outlook and vocabulary are changeable and eclectic enough that the poem should not be seen as a simple reflection of gender stereotypes. The speaker is plagued, as we have seen, with self-doubt, and the imagery of revolt throughout is too complex to be simply heroic. Mireille Rosello may be correct when, in her introduction to her translation of the 1956 *Cahier*, she suggests that the rhetoric of virility and the assumptions Césaire makes elsewhere about the association between femininity, irrationality and poetry, are 'theoretically and politically unsound'.[78] But the speaker's clear abandonment of the role of the hero, and the protean imagery conjuring the process of revolt, indicate that Césaire's text should not be seen unproblematically to perpetuate gender stereotypes. Black femininity is no doubt not something that Césaire explored in the *Cahier*, but the dynamism of negritude and of the poet's self-questioning suggest that his conception of gender identity, too, should not be essentialised. Gendered imagery is used here as a critical strategy, but it remains one strategy among many, and is attenuated by the poem's privileging of dynamic self-creation. Moreover, the poet may frequently use the term 'man' to assert his humanity, but this is a continual project of self-invention, and 'homme' represents humanity rather than a specifically gendered identity. The imagery of masculinity in the *Cahier* no doubt reminds us of the need for female black voices to articulate their resistance in their own language, as many subsequent writers in the francophone Caribbean have done, most notably perhaps Maryse Condé. But Césaire's early version of the *Cahier* should be remembered as a complex and open-ended work, one where black identity, either masculine or feminine, is never static and where the voice of the poet and his invention of negritude remain open to change.

The publication of this first version of the *Cahier* should be read as the first stage in a process of experimentation that would continue through to 1956 and beyond as Césaire's poetry developed during the later stages of his career. This early text expresses the poet's insecurity with black culture and identity at the end of his years in Paris, and records his first prolonged exploration of negritude, the meaning of which is not clearly defined and which comprises various connotations and strategies. It is the product of years of alienation – as well as of camaraderie and discovery – in the diverse black community of 1930s Paris, and it combines a depiction of suffering with a call for revolt as if to record those two sides of the poet's experience. Although it was composed while Césaire was living in Paris, however, its publication coincided with his return to Martinique in August 1939, where he would take up a teaching post at the Lycée Schoelcher in Fort-de-France. The uncertain, disillusioned and ultimately diasporic journey of the *Cahier* was succeeded, then, by the poet's actual return to his homeland. Nevertheless, if the 'return' of the poem, like the negritude the poet wanted to claim as his own, was never completed but rather formed a starting point for self-questioning, Césaire's return to Martinique, too, would trigger a new series of questions about Martinican culture, about its relationship with France, and about the language of resistance against ongoing and shifting forms of oppression.

2

Wartime Martinique, *Tropiques*, and *Les Armes miraculeuses*

'Open the windows. Air. Air'

Césaire travelled back to Martinique on board the *Bretagne*, together with Suzanne and their first child, Jacques, in August 1939, just before war broke out between France and Germany. The next few years would be difficult for Martinique. Admiral Georges Robert arrived on the island in September and assumed the role of High Commissioner of the Republic to the Antilles and Guiana. Although he claimed a neutral position towards the Vichy government after the armistice in 1940, he was closely affiliated with Maréchal Pétain. His role was to maintain a peaceful relationship between the French Antilles and the US, who were effectively overseeing the islands, and he negotiated with the Americans that they be allowed to station naval fleets around Martinique and Guadeloupe and to keep an eye on gold stored around the islands in exchange for keeping them well provided with food and fuel. The atmosphere was extremely tense, as Robert promoted Vichy culture and values, removing the Mayor of Fort-de-France and dissolving city councils to ensure the island was governed by whites. French naval officers stationed on the island with little to do were guilty of racist attitudes and behaviour, giving rise to an oppressive cultural and political atmosphere. Increasing tensions with the US led to naval blockades and food shortages, until the situation reached a crisis point in 1943, and protests against the regime forced Admiral Robert's departure and the assumption of control of the island by the Free French in July of that year.[1]

Césaire describes the situation in wartime Martinique as suffocating, as the stultifying racist regime created a sense of entrapment and placed restrictions on freedom of expression. In February 1944, just after the fall of Robert's regime, he evokes the 'révolution refoulée' ['repressed revolution'] of Martinique, the stifled revolt of a people living under a regime that foreclosed questioning by means of censorship.[2] This repression is described with metaphors of breath and asphyxiation: 'the Martinican Revolution will be carried out in the name of bread, of course, but also in the name of air and poetry (which amount to the same thing). I say that we are suffocating. The principle of a healthy Antillean politics is to open the windows. Air. Air'.[3] In the wake of the oppressive Vichy influence in Martinique, Césaire insists that the people need to breathe, as if poetry, too, is a vital life force. The oppressive racist regime and its restrictions on freedom of expression are experienced as hindrances to both creativity and breathing, as the need for free speech and creativity is related, through the notion of inspiration, to unrestricted breath. This association between freedom, expression and respiration was already present in the *Cahier*, where Césaire celebrated black people's embrace of the earth by conjuring their complicity with the movement of the elements, here the wind, 'poreux à tous les souffles du monde / aire fraternelle de tous les souffles du monde' ['porous to all the breathing of the world / fraternal locus for all the breathing of the world'].[4] The metaphor of unrestricted breathing is then taken up later on in 1952 by Frantz Fanon, who gives it perhaps more urgency when he insists that revolt occurs not just as a result of the discovery of one's own culture but also as a result of this unbearable suffocation: 'it is not because the Indo-Chinese discovered a culture of their own that they revolted. Quite simply this was because it became impossible for them to breathe'.[5] Political and cultural oppression cut off the breath,

60   WARTIME MARTINIQUE

and revolt is therefore the necessary demand for air, for the preservation of life.

This association between oppression and suffocation has of course come sharply into focus with the Black Lives Matter movement calling for an end to gratuitous police brutality. In 2014, a 43-year-old African American man named Eric Garner was approached by the police, who suspected him of selling single cigarettes without tax stamps. Although he denied the accusations, a police officer held him in a choke-hold while attempting to arrest him. Garner repeatedly said the words 'I can't breathe', but he lost consciousness and died in hospital an hour later. The horrific video footage of Garner's murder provoked a massive outcry among activists, fuelled by the uncanny echoing of Garner's words in those of Fanon, and the phrase 'I can't breathe' went viral on social media and on banners and placards at protests across the US. Garner's asphyxiation became a figure for a history of stifling and oppression of black people, as Fanon's metaphor of suffocation was hideously literalised by this act of police violence.

In 2020, and after multiple further instances of murder of black people by US police officers, the 46-year-old African American George Floyd was stopped by police officer Derek Chauvin for allegedly using a counterfeit 20-dollar bill. Chauvin knelt on his neck for nine minutes, during which Floyd, too, protested that he couldn't breathe. Despite Floyd's distress, and even though he became unconscious, Chauvin did not remove his knee and Floyd died at the scene. Once again, the phrase 'I can't breathe' became a slogan for Black Lives Matter protests against the unceasing use of violence against black people in the US and across the world. The echoing of Fanon's phrase would have been familiar to some but certainly not all activists, yet the resonance in this context of Césaire's even earlier demand for air in the stultifying political climate of 1940s Martinique has passed unnoticed. It is revealing that so many years previously, racist oppression was already figured as a form of asphyxiation, and it is chilling that Césaire's metaphor should be so brutally made real in the twenty-first century. Césaire's phrase was not paraded in the streets, as was Black Lives Matter's 'I can't breathe', and yet his language resonates with ongoing protests because he too conceived racism as cutting off the life force of the breath. For Césaire, this suffocation also represented the crushing of cultural and literary creativity, yet the imagery used in his damning diagnosis of oppression in wartime Martinique is obscenely extended and concretised by these twenty-first-century scenes of racial murder.

If Césaire's vocabulary bears this sombre prescience, his activism was not like that of grassroots movements, however, and consisted in the early 1940s in the demand for cultural renewal issued by the journal *Tropiques* that he ran between 1941 and 1945 together with Suzanne Césaire, René Ménil, Georges Gratiant and Aristide Maugée. Césaire's rallying cry was expressed not through demonstrations but through this collaborative intellectual forum, read mostly by students and by the pupils that Césaire taught at the Lycée Schoelcher. At the heart of the journal was a demand for the cultural liberation of Martinique. The explicit appeal for political change would follow for Césaire only after 1945, when he became Mayor of Fort-de-France and Deputy at the French National Assembly. With *Tropiques*, however, Césaire and his colleagues responded to the oppressiveness of Admiral Robert's regime with calls for free self-expression and poetic innovation, and with a celebration of the Martinican landscape to recapture the vitality of the land that was portrayed in the early pages of the *Cahier* as stagnant and rotting.

In its intellectual background, *Tropiques* was a sort of synthesis of *Légitime défense* and *L'Étudiant noir*, combining the surrealism and Marxist thinking of the former with the exploration of African history and culture championed in the latter.[6] Césaire and his colleagues experimented with surrealism in order to throw off the constraints of imposed discourses, supposedly backed up by Western 'reason', with the aim of accessing the unconscious as well as unfettered forms of creativity in ways that reflected and were later fuelled by the thinking of French surrealists such as André Breton. At the same time, they sought to give expression to the local environment and ecology, as if to rescue the island, too, from its history of management by colonial forces and to access its rich diversity. This was celebrated in dialogue with visions of African culture, often filtered through the philosophy of Frobenius, who conceptualised the African or specifically Ethiopian mode of being as a better integration between the human and the plant world. These strands worked together to perform and promote liberation from the stifling environment of wartime Martinique, not at this point through political action but through at times incendiary visions for cultural reinvention. While *Tropiques* was in no way a political manifesto, it was a vital source of cultural inspiration and crucial precursor to Césaire's later political endeavours.

Freedom from racial oppression remains a central focus for *Tropiques* and for Césaire's poetry during the early 1940s, yet the term negritude is not explicitly theorised here, perhaps because it would have contributed to the risk of censorship. Certainly, negritude was a concept with which Césaire experimented in *L'Étudiant noir* and the *Cahier*, but he does not go on during this period to solidify it as a theory, even if its concerns are very much still present. Rather, he continues to denounce racism whilst exploring further the dynamism of Martinican culture and of the black subject, maintaining the emphasis on reinvention while refraining from allowing these interests to coalesce into a unified notion of black identity. Reflecting on negritude in a 1978 interview with Jacqueline Leiner, in which he looks back on *Tropiques*, Césaire suggests that negritude should only be affirmed as a signifier of shared oppression: 'if black people had not been conquered so to speak, had not been an unfortunate, humiliated people etc, we had to overturn History, make them into conquerors, I think from my point of view that there would be no negritude. I would not claim negritude, that would seem intolerable to me'.[7] Césaire conserves negritude only insofar as it represents 'a community of suffering', and certainly his writing during this period is concerned with suffering, and with freedom through revolt and creativity, rather than with the assertion of identity.[8] At the same time, the object of Césaire's critique in the early 1940s is in part, again, the history of enslavement, as we saw with the *Cahier*, but it is also more immediately and more directly the stultifying climate of contemporary Martinique under Admiral Robert. Since the regime did not tolerate dissent (indeed, the publication of the journal was suspended for a period in 1943 because of its supposedly revolutionary implications), this critique is often veiled and covert, with the result that *Tropiques* did not make a political statement but promoted active and varied forms of cultural liberation in response to oppression and to the stifling of freedom of expression. This emphasis on culture rather than politics in no way reduces the power of the resistance voiced by *Tropiques*, however, as Césaire insists in the same interview with Leiner on the incendiary force of poetic invention: '*true* poetry is an *upheaval*'.[9] The journal inherits from Césaire's experimentation with negritude in the 1930s this belief in the creative energy of poetry, harnessed not in the service of identity politics but in the name of a more explosive, inventive and dynamic expression of cultural freedom.

Césaire's opening article in the first issue of *Tropiques*, published in April 1941, announces the journal's focus on Martinique and its stagnation, and voices a veiled critique of the stultifying regime. Reminiscent of the opening pages of the *Cahier* with their devastating portrait of poverty and stagnation, the article evokes a 'mute and sterile land', where the poet finds 'the monstrous atrophy of the voice, age-old despondency, prodigious mutism'.[10] Silencing is here associated not so much with asphyxiation as with wilting and depression, but the atrophy implies a comparable sapping of life force. Oppression causes bodily suffering and sickness, a physical weakening, of which breathlessness is evidently one of many symptoms. The cause of this devastation is not explicitly named here, as indeed René Ménil notes of *Tropiques* in general, 'Pétain and his regime are denounced but are not named. They are present, but in an act of writing that excludes them systematically from the texts and leaves their place empty'.[11] Rather, Césaire identifies merely the darkness that causes the oppression of the Martinican people, and asserts his defiance not to the regime but to this culture of obliteration: 'we are those who say no to the shadow'.[12] The condemnation of the Vichy regime is uncompromising, then, but it is expressed through imagery of silencing and obscurity so as to avoid censorship. The article clearly uses this critique, moreover, to issue the journal's call for cultural insurrection, as Césaire repeats a line from the *Cahier* announcing the black man's girding of strength: 'the time has come to gird one's loins like a brave man'.[13] This reference to the participation of the body in the process of critique again suggests that oppression is experienced as a physical affliction or attack, and resistance might come from the free expression of bodily agency.

Whilst the articles and poems in successive volumes of *Tropiques* were highly eclectic, mixing poetry and cultural theory, the critical thrust of the journal is once again expressed powerfully in issue four, published in January 1942, in Césaire and Ménil's ironic 'Introduction au folklore martiniquais'. Césaire and Ménil refuse to evoke a local folkloric tradition that would be cosy or exoticising for white readers, and rather display the poverty and dejection of Martinicans in terms that resonate with negritude and its assumption of shared suffering: 'there was once upon a time, a time of poverty and shame, a black man clinging to our black land'.[14] The imagery here is once again reminiscent of the *Cahier*, this time recalling the scene of the black man on the tram ravaged by 'la Misère'. Martinican folk tales, suggest Césaire and Ménil, always tell this story of poverty and above all of hunger, and although this is portrayed as a product of the regime of enslavement, they would also have been thinking here of the impact of food shortages in the contemporary period. In addition to hunger, folk culture also tells stories of fear, fear of the slave master and of punishment, and ultimately defeat. The trio of hunger, fear and defeat at the same time clearly dominate in the contemporary climate, even if Césaire and Ménil do not reference this directly. It is perhaps somewhat problematic that the examples that follow this introduction are either written by the European Lafcadio Hearn or edited and translated by their colleague Georges Gratiant, suggesting they did not have intimate knowledge of local culture. Nevertheless, their preface serves as a clear critique of the oppression of the people of Martinique.

This acerbic critique, printed in 1942, is complemented and developed, moreover, by that of Suzanne Césaire in her incendiary essay 'Le Grand camouflage', printed as the last article in issue 13–14 in 1945. Here, she suggests that despite the liberation of the island in 1943, 'refined forms of slavery still run rampant', so that the critique of past forms of oppression is now more pointedly directed at the present.[15] The 'camouflage' of her title refers to the surface beauty of the island, its ecological richness, which nevertheless covers up its past and present inequality, exploitation and suffering. Evoking the integrated relationship between the people and the land, she also anticipates the overturning of the system of exploitation through the surging of 'an invisible vegetation of desires' that would inevitably lead to revolution.[16]

The new culture to be forged in *Tropiques* in the wake of this oppression is multifarious, eclectic and wide-ranging, and indeed this multiplicity is crucial to the principle of freedom that the journal sought to promote. Césaire always intended negritude to connote a dynamic and ongoing process of invention, and the collaborative and evolving form of *Tropiques* demonstrates even more expansively the protean form of negritude and its reincarnations. Several cultural influences can be found in the journal's pages, revealing its participants' eclectic, dialogic creativity as it evolves by harnessing exchanges with various precursors and contemporaries. One of the prominent threads woven through the reimagination of Martinican culture is its connection with African civilisation, theorised by both Aimé and Suzanne Césaire through Frobenius – not to promote an African identity but to champion an integrated relationship with the earth that eschews the colonial drive to mastery. African civilisation is preserved and celebrated in the reinvention of Martinique sketched by *Tropiques*, but in such a way as to refuse essentialised notions of racial identity and to promote instead the conservation as well as the dynamic growth of both landscape and people. This African mode of civilisation provides both a mythical connection with a history that precedes slavery, and a celebration of free organic growth as opposed to the rigid colonial system that sought to manage and control both humanity and the environment. It is Frobenius's *Histoire de la civilisation africaine* that provides the foundation for this ethical position, and the text weaves through the writing of both Aimé and Suzanne Césaire to provide a renewed ethics as much as a cultural vision.

Most importantly, the Césaires take from Frobenius his conception of the 'homme-plante', an expansive and dialogic mode of living with the plant world and the ecological environment, one that contests the colonial assumption of human sovereignty over the land. In 'Léo Frobénius et le problème des civilisations' in the first issue of *Tropiques*, Suzanne Césaire celebrates Frobenius's concept of the Païdeuma, a term describing the organic evolution and growth of living things, manifested in different ways by Hamitic and Ethiopian civilisations. It is Ethiopian civilisation that embraces this organic development along with the plant world, in contrast with the Hamitic mode, which is associated with the animal and which conceives its survival as dependent on conquest. In Suzanne Césaire's terms:

> Ethiopian civilization is tied to the plant, to the vegetative cycle. It is dreamy, drawn inward upon itself, mystical. The Ethiopian does not seek to understand phenomena – to grasp and dominate facts outside of himself. He lives and lets live, in a life identical to that of the plant, confident in the continuity of life: to germinate, grow, flower, bear fruit, and the cycle starts all over again.[17]

Suzanne Césaire's use of Frobenius in no way intended to associate this 'vegetative' life with the negative connotations that the term might retain in current English, but works to celebrate an alternative mode of being to that dominated by rationality and science in the service of conquest and mastery. In 'Malaise d'une civilisation', Suzanne Césaire goes on to use this concept of the 'plant-human' to celebrate Martinicans' integration with the environment, to denounce the 'pseudomorphosis' that subjugated them and forced them to live according to the colonial system, and ultimately she champions a reinvigorated fusion with the soil: 'it is exhilarating to imagine on these tropical shores, finally restored to their inner truth, the long-lasting and fruitful harmony between humankind and soil. Under the sign of plantlife'.[18] The same issue of *Tropiques* contains an extract from Frobenius's work celebrating the rich vibrancy of African civilisation.

The use of Frobenius in this evocation of African culture may appear problematic, in that it rests on an opposition between modes of civilisation that is perhaps ultimately somewhat schematic. Indeed, Frobenius's work has long been discredited, and though it was used creatively by the Césaires in the 1940s, its troubling implications should be acknowledged. The notion of 'vegetative' existence and the emphasis on passivity in Ethiopian and Martinican civilisation risks being taken to sound pejorative, even though for the Césaires these notions were at once enriching and anticolonial. It is important, however, that Africa is referenced in these articles for its association not with an essentialised set of origins or a determinate identity but with an ethical relationship with the environment. Although, as Donna Jones puts it, essentialism or biologism can be seen to 'haunt' Césaire's work, and it is true that at times his rhetoric is suggestive of a desire for a fundamental and originary black authenticity, the African mode of existence represents for Césaire not a static tradition or identity but a refusal of the European science that founded colonialism.[19] It names less a specified culture than a mode of being that promotes growth and change in humanity along with ecology, and that rejects colonialism not only for its racist discourse but also for its programme of both human and environmental conquest. This mode of thinking was evidently already very much present in the *Cahier*, as we saw towards the end of the text the rehabilitation of the colonised through the embrace of landscape and through the summoning of the elements to sweep away the follies of colonial mastery.

Césaire theorises this ethical stance, and even more, associates it with poetic endeavour, in the essay 'Poésie et connaissance', originally a speech made in Haiti in 1944 and reprinted in a slightly reduced form in *Tropiques* in January 1945. Here, Césaire contrasts scientific knowledge with poetic knowledge and associates the latter with 'an astonishing mobilisation of all human and cosmic forces'.[20] Steeped in Frobenius, and drawing on Bergson's idea of the 'vital force' as well as on Nietzsche, Césaire's vision embraces the creativity of the life force of the world, but also conceives the poet as the figure most attuned to that force. It is the poet, insists Césaire, who best understands and captures the rhythms of the earth: 'like trees and animals, he has abandoned himself to the primary form of life, he has said yes, has assented to this great life that transcends him. He has rooted himself in the earth, he has stretched out his arms, he has played with the sun, he has become a tree: he has blossomed, he has sung'.[21] Poetry is from this point of view not so much the redefinition of racial identity, but a much more expansive embrace of vital energy, of the interconnectivity of life forms, and of human evolution in dialogue with ecology and with the cosmos. The denunciation of racial oppression is expressed here not only as a refusal of the mistreatment of human beings but also of the mismanagement of the land. The poet's intensified sensitivity to the environment affirms the integration of humanity with ecology as both grow and change in organic ways.

If Frobenius is one of the Césaires' most significant interlocutors in their affirmation of an African presence in *Tropiques*, however, they also draw on a range of French poets in whose work they find other forms of cultural liberation.

Poetic revolt is in this way conceptualised not as a rejection of French poetry, but as a continuation and development of a history of innovation, highlighted by figures such as Arthur Rimbaud, Stéphane Mallarmé, Charles Péguy and André Breton. Notably, Aimé Césaire quotes Rimbaud's assertion of the visionary power of poetry as the epigraph to 'Fragments d'un poème', an early draft of the poem 'Les pur-sang' that would figure in *Les Armes miraculeuses*, printed in the first issue of *Tropiques*: 'I say one must be a seer, one must make oneself a visionary'.[22] Rimbaud's 'voyant' is conceived as a force for transformation, the producer of radical new visions of the world, where images are juxtaposed in striking and unforeseen ways. Rimbaud's poetry brings about the 'long, boundless and systematised disorganisation of all the senses', the upending at once of meaning, of the senses and of direction, in an attempt to liberate the mind from familiar patterns of perception and understanding.[23] Césaire's citation of Rimbaud, and the references to him that recur in his essays and interviews, reinforce his own project to invent a poetry capable of liberating and transforming the mindset of oppressed Martinicans.

This affirmation of the poet as rebel and visionary is intensified, moreover, in Césaire's 'Maintenir la poésie', published in issue 8–9 in 1943, and where Rimbaud is cited alongside Baudelaire, Breton and Valéry. Poetry here is once again a vitalist expression of life force, an affirmation of freedom, conceived also in visceral terms as the liberated voice of the suffering body: 'like an ulcer, a panic, images of catastrophe and freedom, of fall and deliverance, ceaselessly devouring the liver of the world'.[24] Alongside nineteenth-century poets such as Rimbaud, moreover, Césaire lauds the humanism of Charles Péguy, a socialist French poet killed in battle in 1914, and whose combination of spirituality with political commitment also informs his own aesthetics. Péguy's use of anaphora in his poetry also clearly influenced Césaire, as we saw in the *Cahier*, where anaphora was used as a structuring feature in the poet's calls for change.

The poet with whom Césaire was most closely involved during this period was the French surrealist André Breton. Césaire had already been experimenting with his own form of surrealism before he met Breton. Breton arrived in Martinique in April 1941 as a refugee from the Vichy regime in France; he had travelled by boat together with André Masson and Wifredo Lam, and he happened upon the first issue of *Tropiques* in a haberdashery shop that turned out to be that of René Ménil's sister, a moment that would provide the starting point for an extensive dialogue between surrealism and Caribbean culture.[25] Before Césaire and Breton met, Ménil would have helped introduce Césaire to surrealism through *Légitime Défense*. In issue three of *Tropiques*, published in October 1941, Ménil's 'Introduction au merveilleux' would demonstrate how surrealist principles, such as those of the liberation of the imagination and exploration of dream life, already infused and indeed could be seen to characterise local Caribbean culture. Césaire's meeting with Breton was nevertheless pivotal, as he stresses in the interview with Leiner cited earlier. As with Senghor, the encounter with Breton marked a new start, and was in Césaire's words nothing less than extraordinary.[26]

It is Suzanne Césaire, however, who theorises the significance of Breton and of surrealism most explicitly in *Tropiques*. In issue three, she produced an article on 'André Breton, poète', in which she lauds the affirmation of the 'liberty to do and undo', citing Breton's joyful affirmation of emotion, sensation and the unconscious in the pursuit of freedom in ways that complement the journal's covert denunciation of the oppressive contemporary political regime.[27] In 1943, she goes further in her celebration of the surrealist project to promote liberation from false and reductive forms of rationality, and links it more clearly with resistance to fascism at that time: 'but when freedom found itself threatened throughout the world in 1943, surrealism, which never for a single instant ceased to stand in service to the greatest emancipation of humankind, wanted to sum up the entirety of all its efforts in one magic word: freedom'.[28]

This combination of the surrealist liberation of the imagination with resistance to fascism and to all forms of oppression is expressed in pointed ways by Césaire in his 'En guise de manifeste littéraire', printed in 1942 in issue five of *Tropiques*, and integrated into later versions of the *Cahier*. The text comprises a few pages of free verse with some short passages of prose, which serve at once to amplify Césaire's revolt against oppression and to reformulate the antiracist critique of the 1939 *Cahier* using surrealist imagery that asserts the power of the irrational. Césaire denounces the monstrous absurdity of colonial reason with a wilful affirmation of creative madness, clearly highly influenced by surrealist aesthetics. Addressing figures of colonial and racist authority, the poet retorts: 'nous vous haïssons, vous et votre raison, nous nous réclamons de la démence précoce, de la folie flambante, du cannibalisme tenace' ['we hate you, you and your reason, we claim for ourselves precocious madness, flaming folly, tenacious cannibalism'].[29] In memory of the slave ship, for example, the poet proposes a series of images of destruction and revolt, drawing on imagery of the Middle Passage but expressed through incongruous and shocking metaphors of environmental sickness and madness. The poem forms an important part of Césaire's development of the aesthetics of the *Cahier*, where negritude is associated with the expression of the revolt of the unconscious, with its internalisation of colonial history, and the recovery of African civilisation in terms far more rich and more explosive than those of mere identity politics.

If Césaire and his colleagues at *Tropiques* on the one hand sought to champion the Martinicans' connection with African civilisation and its belief in the integration between humanity and landscape, however, it may seem surprising that at the same time this aesthetic was combined with that of a European poetic tradition such as surrealism. The blurring of the influences of Frobenius and European surrealism also has problematic conceptual implications. It is implied, for example, that Caribbeans can get closer to their African roots via the unconscious, as if Africans represent a more 'primitive'

72 WARTIME MARTINIQUE

mode of being, in ways that reinforce problematic oppositions between the civilised and the primitive.[30] At times it seems as if closer proximity to the unconscious and the irrational is somehow a particularly African or Caribbean mode of being, a suggestion that would fuel the critique of forms of negritude poetry that end up reinforcing essentialised notions of black identity. Yet Césaire was on the whole less interested in distinguishing different types of civilisation than in using these various cultural influences to experiment with imagery that promoted energetic forms of liberation. He did not simply absorb Breton's influence, but rather developed and transformed surrealism, imbuing it at once with imagery of Martinique, of Africa and of the history of slavery to create an incendiary poetics of personal, cultural and political freedom. 'En guise de manifeste littéraire', moreover, is prefaced with a dedication to Breton, and yet, as Kora Véron also notes, it announces the rebirth of the poetic self, as the poet insists: 'c'est moi, rien que moi / qui prends langue avec la dernière angoisse' ['it is me, only me / who takes on language with the last anguish'].[31] Césaire may at times seem to suggest that it is by reconnecting with the unconscious that the Caribbean subject can find his past in Africa, but for the most part his poetic elaboration of this process of recovery foregrounds reinvention rather than return.

The affiliation between Césaire and Breton in the early 1940s was at the same time intense but not all-encompassing, and was ultimately fleeting, as Césaire became more overtly politicised. Breton published a eulogy to Césaire, 'Un grand poète noir', in *Tropiques* in May 1944, a text that would later serve as a preface to the 1947 editions of the *Cahier*, in which he praised the effervescent energy of Césaire's language, but also rather troublingly implied that it was particularly impressive that a black man should write in this way. Breton's *Martinique, charmeuse de serpents*, written together with André Masson and published first in the journal *Hémisphères* and as a book in 1948, presented Martinican culture and landscape through the lens of a painting by Henri Rousseau and unashamedly perpetuated exoticist myths of the Caribbean in ways that would no doubt have made Césaire uncomfortable. Césaire's engagement with surrealism inaugurated some of his most experimental poetry, as we shall see in the reading of *Les Armes miraculeuses*, but his use of surrealist aesthetics was also highly idiosyncratic as well as innovative, and it was combined in the later issues of *Tropiques* with a more overtly political stance.

Early issues of *Tropiques* expressed Césaire's and his colleagues' discontent with the political situation in contemporary Martinique, but as we have seen they conveyed this allusively rather than through direct critique. This did not prevent the journal from being censored between February and October 1943, as the Lieutenant de Vaisseau Bayle denounces the team's call for freedom as, 'freedom to poison minds, to sew hate, to destroy morale'.[32] It is in their response to that letter that the editorial team proudly claim their role as 'empoisonneurs d'âmes', as well as 'révolutionnaires', and even 'racistes' in the sense of the great antiracist thinkers such as Toussaint Louverture, Claude MacKay and Langston Hughes, and against extreme right figures such as Drumont and Hitler.

In the later volumes, however, and after Admiral Robert had fled, Césaire's political stance was expressed more clearly. In issue eleven, published in May 1944, Césaire wrote a long letter to Monsignor Varin de la Brunelière, Bishop of St-Pierre and Fort-de-France, denouncing the church's hypocrisy and complicity with regimes of enslavement, though some of this was once again censored. In issue twelve, published in January 1945, he offers a eulogy to Georges-Louis Ponton, governor of Martinique who took his own life, and here Césaire does not hold back from detailing the misery of the island both in the past and in the present, again using imagery of stifling: 'the horizon is low, the ceiling low, and the air thin'.[33] Finally, in issue 13–14, published in 1945, Césaire wrote his first homage to Schoelcher, figuring him as we saw in the Introduction as a symbol of freedom and equality, and emphasising his relevance for the contemporary period and the claim for freedom from the Vichy regime. The demand for liberation that was enacted by abolition is also here seen necessarily to come with a demand for economic equality, the lack of which is again represented with a metaphor of physical crushing: 'where there is no economic security, the foundations of freedom are nullified, and without freedom security is shaky, it cracks and vacillates, in the grip of its own fall, crushed by its own weight'.[34] Freedom remains the fundamental principle of both Schoelcher and *Tropiques*. Abolitionist thought is brought into the present through this connection between enslavement and the current regime of poverty and exploitation, where oppression is still experienced as a corporeal attack.

This increase in the militancy of Césaire's writings in the mid-1940s is accompanied by an expansion in his horizons and influence and by increasing connections with writers and thinkers beyond France and Martinique, as if to represent the growing resistance to the isolation and stultification noted at the beginning of this chapter. From 1943, *Tropiques* was no longer the main forum for the publication of Césaire's poems, since he started sending many of his poems to New York surrealist journals *VVV* and *Hémisphères*.[35] A version of the *Cahier* was scheduled for publication in *Hémisphères* in 1944, though there were tensions in the editorial team around the translation, and the editors were having difficulty sourcing paper for printing.[36] This version was subsequently published in New York by Brentano's in 1947. A Spanish version of the 1939 *Cahier* (translated by Lydia Cabrera) was published in Cuba in 1943, together with illustrations by the Cuban artist Wifredo Lam, whom Césaire met in Martinique in 1941 and with whom he formed a close friendship.

In addition, Césaire spent seven months in Haiti in 1944 on a mission of cultural diplomacy aimed at expanding the influence of French culture. There he gave lectures on major French writers including Baudelaire, Rimbaud, Mallarmé and Giraudoux, as well as presenting 'Poésie et connaissance' at the Congrès de Philosophie in Port-au-Prince in September 1944. The speech would have surprised its audience for its vehement championing of poetry and the arts over science and rationality, as Césaire celebrates the triumph of Dionysus over Apollo. The essay forms an important stage in his conception of negritude as the overturning of existing scientific concepts of race, as poetry is instead associated with the creation and liberated expression of a collective unconscious, conceived in the speech as 'the ancient, original, ancestral foundation beyond race' (though the reference to race here was cut from the *Tropiques* version).[37] More broadly, this period in Haiti was by all accounts pivotal for Césaire in developing his sense of Caribbean culture and history and crystallising notions of black consciousness and resistance. 'Poésie et connaissance' serves as the conceptual foundation for the poems collected in *Les Armes miraculeuses*, published by Gallimard in 1946. And, as we saw in the *Cahier*, Haiti for Césaire represented the land where, 'négritude se mit debout pour la première fois' ['where negritude rose for the first time'], and his stay there preceded his move into politics, where he too would stand up for the rights of Martinicans.[38] Ngal describes the trip to Haiti as the end of Césaire's youth, whilst biographers Toumson and Henry-Valmore note, 'he would come back shaken, his consciousness matured and expanded'.[39]

Les Armes miraculeuses

The poetry collection *Les Armes miraculeuses* can be seen as the synthesis of Césaire's creative work during the *Tropiques* years. Combining and extending the preoccupations and influences that shaped the journal, *Les Armes* contains some of his most ambitious and most challenging poetic work. The poems' anarchic forms perform the upheaval referenced in the Leiner interview cited earlier, and a visionary, surrealist aesthetic is used expansively in the assertion of cultural, psychological and, more obliquely, political freedom. Allusions to enslavement and assertions of revolt associated with negritude are juxtaposed with surrealist imagery, conjuring dynamic movement in the environment and the cosmos, and combining eclectic and powerful metaphors of stagnation and liberation. Césaire worked on the creation of the volume between 1943 and 1945, and the final version of the collection was preceded by earlier, more limited attempts to bring his poems together to form an anthology. Seven poems were published by Ivan Goll in *Hémisphères* in spring 1944 under the title 'Colombes et menfenil', and Césaire later sent this same collection to Breton in August 1945, along with another series entitled 'Tombeau du soleil'. Both series were experimental and incomplete, and Césaire continued to rework the poems contained within them, but they nevertheless form an important stage in the creation of *Les Armes miraculeuses*, which was eventually contracted to Gallimard in December 1945. The collection would include not only twenty-six of Césaire's poems of the early 1940s, but also the tragedy *Et les chiens se taisaient*. Many of the poems were substantially revised several times, suggesting that they were very much ongoing experiments, and even the final versions defiantly resist interpretive closure. This resistance is a crucial part of the challenge they offer against the oppressive rationality behind European systems of domination.

The volume's title offers a clue to Césaire's vision for poetry at this stage. The poems are 'miraculous' or marvellous visionary offerings, but they also have the power of weapons, as resistance is expressed here not yet through political activism but through explosive and incendiary poetic images and forms. They dramatise myths of origins and rebirth, drawing on Nietzsche to trace a trajectory from stagnation to revolt and revolution. In this way, they develop and extend the journey enacted by the *Cahier*, as indeed Césaire suggested that if the earlier work was '*the poem of a coming to consciousness* and the delimitation of a domain', then *Les Armes* was 'the in-depth *exploration* of that domain'.[40] Yet whilst the *Cahier*'s experimentalism nevertheless quite clearly articulated its underlying critique of the history of enslavement and exploitation, *Les Armes* refrains from communicating a clear message, rather achieving its effects through extraordinary juxtapositions of images, obscure symbols and eclectic, disorientating and dynamic verse forms. Freedom is once again the guiding principle of the collection; as Ngal argues, it could be dubbed Césaire's 'epic of freedom'.[41] But this goal is expressed not with reference to overt political revolt but through the allusive symbolism of the sun, as well as the air, stars, sky and ecological diversity, contrasted with the stultifying stagnation of marshes and swamps. Once again, the quest for freedom is carried out through the mining of the unconscious as well as through the renewed connection with Africa and embrace of the 'plant-human'. At the same time, the liberation of the poet's subjective consciousness is combined with a broader exploration of the history and experience of race that far exceeds the restrictive boundaries of identity politics.

The first poem in *Les Armes miraculeuses*, aptly entitled 'Avis de tirs', sketches the poet's vision of the explosive weapon of poetry and inaugurates the surrealist reinvention of negritude to be pursued throughout the volume. Although 'Avis de tirs' opens the Gallimard edition of *Les Armes*, it was written in 1943, later than major compositions such as 'Les pur-sang' and 'Le Grand midi', and was first printed in issue 8–9 of *Tropiques*. Placed at the beginning of the collection, the movement towards uprising that the poem records can be seen to comprise, according to René Hénane, 'the very definition of *Les Armes miraculeuses*' as well as 'a threat levied against the oppressor'.[42] Yet the revolt staged here does not explicitly dramatise the history of the slave trade, as does the depiction of the enslaved people's reclaiming of the slave ship in the *Cahier*. Rather, an atmosphere of oppression and stagnation is gradually replaced by imagery of explosion and fulguration, as the poet denounces the old order and ultimately celebrates the 'feu de brousse de la fraternité' ['the brush fire of brotherhood'].[43] The poem starts by evoking the poet's heavy eyelids, as if to suggest lethargy and stultification. Imagery of the slave ship, and the poet's 'haine de cargaison coulée' ['sunken cargo'], is juxtaposed with references to ecology and culture in other parts of the world, 'mes 6 arbres géants de Tasmanie' ['my six giant Tasmanian trees'] and 'mon château de têtes en Papousie' ['my castle of Papuan heads'], as the poem moves towards its explosive rejection of oppression. Noting on the one hand 'les jours sans viande sans yeux sans méfiance sans lacs' ['the days without meat without eyes without suspicion without lakes'] and on the other 'les feux de position des jours tout court et des avalanches / le pavillon de phimosis à dents blanches du Vomito-Negro' ['the navigation lights of days – period – and of avalanches / the white-toothed phimosis flag of the Vomito-Negro'], the poet juxtaposes suffering and deprivation with the call for dramatic change. The 'Vomito-Negro' refers to yellow fever, a disease that came from Africa and was transported to the Americas on the slave ships, but it is also conjured here as a figure for the expulsion of the master.

'Avis de tirs' is followed in the Gallimard collection by 'Les pur-sang', which was first published as 'Fragments pour un poème' in *Tropiques* 1. Translated as 'The Thoroughbreds', 'Les pur-sang' refers to Caribbean people using vocabulary associated with horse-breeding, and the term works as a statement of defiance towards European conceptions of race, subversively deploying the image of racial purity in order to denounce the colonial discourse that, as Hénane puts it, 'in three centuries of alienation and oppression has bastardised the race'.[44] These victims of racial discourse are also 'les cent pur-sang hennissant du soleil / parmi la stagnation' ['the hundred whinnying thoroughbreds of the sun / amidst the stagnation'], and here the French 'cent pur-sang' plays on 'cent pour cent' [a hundred per cent] to intensify the image of racial purity, whilst the appeal to the sun represents a call for freedom from the stultification of contemporary Martinique.[45] The horses are also associated with movement and agitation in protest against stagnation. The poem traces the movement of the speaker from this early imagery of suffering and oppression towards a heroic affirmation of liberation, a movement that is accompanied by a shift towards increasingly disordered syntax, as if to mirror the process of creative liberation. The line 'le ciel baîlle d'absence noire' ['the heavens yawn from black absence'], associates cosmic emptiness with the marginalisation of blackness, and then unleashes a sequence of images of cosmic disorder indicating the sickness of a world structured by racial oppression. The diagnosis of this human and cosmic pathology is succeeded in the poem by imagery of descent, of a plunging into the depths of the self and the earth akin to that enacted by the *Cahier*, though figured here more abstractly and allusively: 'd'un dodelinement de vague, je saute / ancestral aux branches de ma / végétation' ['with a wavelike doddling, I leap / ancestral into the branches of my / vegetation'].[46] In the final section, however, the heroic speaker joins with the cosmos in demanding freedom and renewal, and, like the 'homme-plante', is able to grow and ascend, after the descent into suffering and stagnation, to achieve a form of spiritual rebirth in harmony with the land: 'je pousse / comme une plante / sans remords et sans gauchissement / vers les heures dénouées du jour / pur et sûr comme une plante / sans crucifiement / vers les heures dénouées du soir' ['I grow, like a plant / remorseless and unwarped / towards the unknotted hours of day / pure and confident as a plant / uncrucified / towards the unknotted hours of evening'].[47] This movement of descent and ascent, again like that of the *Cahier*, reflects the embrace followed by the transcendence of the suffering of the black race in tandem with the earth, at the same time as the poet's introspection and recreation of the self.

'Le Grand Midi' was originally composed as the continuation of 'Les pur-sang' and printed in the second issue of *Tropiques*. Its imagery will therefore be briefly noted here even though it was printed nearer the end of the collection in 1946. The revolutionary cry articulated in the poem develops the movement towards uprising performed in 'Les pur-sang', though its nightmarish visions and its syntax are from the start more frenzied, more aggressive and more disordered. Sequences of images connoting flashes, outbursts and explosions, whilst lacking main verbs, record the poet's anger: 'essaim dur. Guerriers ivres ô mandibules caïnites / éblouissements rampants, paradisiaques thaumalées / jets, croisements, brûlements et dépouillements' ['harsh swarm. Drunken warriors oh cainite mandibles / rampant bedazzlements, paradisiac golden pheasants, / spurts, crossings, burnings and strippings'].[48] Again, imagery of the slave trade, of the Atlantic crossing, mixes with African tradition, as 'tam-tams de sang' ['tom-toms of blood'] serve to capture the striking but irregular rhythm that governs the poem. This frenzied imagery accompanies at the same time the poet's references to the search for self-expression, as he laments, for example, 'je bourlingue / gorge tendue à travers les mystérieux rouissements, les atolls enroulés' ['I toss about / throat stretched amidst mysterious rettings, rolled-up atolls'].[49] As the poem reaches its climax, however, the poet resolves to leave, perhaps making a break with the history of violence against which the poem revolts, to enter the rebirth symbolised by the noon of the title. In the final lines, he evokes the devastation of the cosmos with the image of stars rotting in their swamps, conjuring again the imagery of stagnation characteristic of the opening of the *Cahier* and the 'terre muette et stérile' of the inaugural essay of *Tropiques*. At this powerful climax, and in the face of this devastation, he evokes dynamic and liberated movement, again in harmony with ecological growth: 'ô vol courbe de mes pas! / posez-vous dans la forêt ardente' ['oh curved flight of my steps! / alight on the ardent forest'].[50]

This evocation of rich ecological diversity and celebration of the energy of the elements as part of the poet's revolt and self-affirmation continues in 'Conquête de l'aube', originally published in *VVV* in 1942 and printed in the middle of the Gallimard volume *Les Armes miraculeuses*. Again, negritude is not referenced explicitly, but the poet allusively portrays a history of violence against humanity and landscape before conjuring revolt through outbursts of incongruous imagery connoting upheaval in both poet and environment. The first four sections of the poem begin with the line 'nous mourons' ['we die'], the fourth specifying 'nous mourons d'une mort blanche fleurissant de mosquées son poitrail d'absence splendide où l'araignée de perles salve son ardente mélancolie de monère convulsive' ['we die a white death decking out its breast of resplendent absence with mosques where the spider-of-pearls salivates its ardent melancholy of convulsive moneron'].[51] The image of white death echoes that of the death of Toussaint Louverture in the *Cahier*, again associating obliteration with whiteness, whilst the mosque implies the presence of cultural difference, here reduced to the soulless convulsions of the moneron, an organism that reproduces through asexual fission. Successive images of death then give way to an equally surreal and incongruous series of visions connoting more dynamic movement, introduced by the single-word line 'jaillir' ['to spring forth'].[52] Metallic imagery suggestive of violence and oppression ('les genoux de fer de la nuit' ['the iron knees of the night']) is replaced by evocations of sexual energy, summoned by the poet and activated in the landscape.[53] Syntax becomes increasingly chaotic here, as threads of 'métaphores filées' or extended metaphors of sexual energy, of hermaphroditism, as well as of sleeping, waking and excretion weave themselves through references to the reinvented landscape. The poet stands in the middle of it all, 'je dressais mon sein mon gueuloir d'Antille verte' ['I raised against its breast my Antilles-green mugpiece'] and 'moi debout dans les champs du sang' ['I standing in the fields of blood'], giving himself a position of power and dominance whilst contemplating this visceral transformation of the land in terms that foreground corporeal experience and agency. The earth like a human body bears witness to, but also convulses in defiance of, a history of violence.

The surrealism and unstructured syntax found in 'Conquête de l'aube' are intensified later with the poem 'Les Armes miraculeuses', whose title indicates its significance in the volume. Unlike most of the other poems, it was not previously published elsewhere. In addition to denouncing the slave trade and its legacies, 'Les Armes miraculeuses' makes explicit the surrealist ambition to overturn the Western systems of rationality responsible for colonial and racial violence. At the same time, its form juxtaposing four longer passages of unpunctuated prose with sequences of rhythmical verses, some of which are structured by anaphora, amply performs this rejection of familiar frameworks of reason, verse and syntax. Reason is coloured red like blood, betraying its complicity with violence, and relentlessly crushes not just Caribbean people but humanity across the world, as the poet evokes 'le nouveau sang la raison rouge tous les mots de toutes les langues qui signifient mourir de soif' ['the new blood the red reason all words in all tongues that mean to die of thirst'].[54] Throughout the poem, sexual, zoological, chemical and religious images are piled on top of one another in this furious creative outburst. 'La plus belle arche' ['the finest arch'] figures a spurt of blood suggestive of brutality as well as of menstruation, and describes also a ring around the eye, an image that Hénane associates with the after-effects of an amorous encounter, only to be juxtaposed with the cross and 'la beauté eucharistique et qui flambe de ton sexe au nom duquel je saluais le barrage de mes lèvres violentes' ['the eucharistic beauty and which blazes from your sex in the name of which I hailed the barrage with my violent lips'].[55] Sexual energy fuses with Christian imagery in this rebellious expression of contestation, whilst the image of the arch references, according to Hénane, the Creation myth in Dogon cosmogony, and this mixing of religions works to celebrate human diversity in defiance of racial hierarchy. Recurrent references to the centipede invoke animal agency, while imagery of the sea unfurling and the force of the wind is interspersed with fragmented allusions to the Middle Passage. Lines and images cannot be separated into statements of either lamentation or resistance, but surreal and incongruous sequences mingle past and future, destruction and rebirth, in a dizzying, effervescent outpouring. African tradition is preserved in 'la berceuse congolaise que les soudards m'ont désapprise mais que la mer très pieuse des boîtes craniennes conserve sur ses feuillets rituels' ['the Congolese cradle-song that the old troopers untaught me but that the very pious sea of cranial boxes preserves in its ritual leaves'].[56] But tradition is also commemorated here alongside imagery of the sea crossing of enslaved peoples, of cranial measurements determining racial identity, as the leaves and the waves seem to contain and record this history of violence. This mingling of images and tones defiantly resists interpretation but conveys to the reader a vertiginous medley of connotations to imply revolt not only in the name of black identity but also on at once visceral and cosmic levels.

If negritude at its origin in *L'Etudiant noir* progressed through identifiable stages, from seizing to planting within the black subject 'le nègre immédiat', in *Les Armes miraculeuses* the focus of the revolt far transcends this account of lived experience. It is still a reclaiming of racial history, but it is also an abrupt rejection not only of established verse forms but also of reason and syntax, and it demands at once corporeal and environmental upheaval. The re-establishment of a connection with Africa is referenced in many of the poems, as we have seen above, and is accomplished most fully in poems such as 'Batéké' and 'Batouque'. They are, however, less sources of ancestral culture than sites where sexuality and vitality are celebrated as imbricated in ecology and the elements. Africa is conjured as a source of energy, the origins of the 'homme-plante', and its imagery fuels invention and renewal rather than return. If these references help to situate *Les Armes miraculeuses* under the banner of negritude, they also further prevent the reification of that concept and enact its evolution as an assertion of aesthetic liberation, the scope of which is continually expanding. 'Batéké' is the name of an area of plains and hills in the Congo, north of Brazzaville, but the rest of the poem gives the reader little sense of this region and its culture, and instead conjures multiple images of the female body whose power and eroticism is evoked through analogies with flora and fauna ('ton sexe à crocus', 'ton sexe à serpents nocturnes' ['your crocus sex', 'your nocturnal serpent sex'].[57] 'Batouque' refers to a Brazilian dance of African origin associated, according to the Africanist critic Aliko Songolo, with rebellion, and again humanity as well as the animals and plants in the

84 WARTIME MARTINIQUE

landscape join in the rebellious dance.[58] References to African places and cultures are interspersed with traces of enslavement as well as parts of Martinique, but also with broader forms of environmental destruction and rebirth. Sexual activity again plays a dominant part in this energetic and expressive movement. Yet whilst in 'Batéké' the poet conjured fantasies of female sexual energy, here and for the most part in *Les Armes* sexuality takes multiple forms blending humanity and ecology, and the masculine perspective intermittently evident in the *Cahier* is less clearly identifiable. At the end of the poem, the poet seems to acquit the enemy of his crimes of murder and rape in order rather to declare liberation, sexual connection and reawakening: 'liberté mon seul pirate, eau de l'an neuf ma seule soif / amour mon seul sampan / nous coulerons nos doigts de rire et de gourde / entre les dents glacées de la Belle-au-bois-dormant' ['liberty my only pirate, water of the new year my only thirst / love my only sampan / we shall slip our fingers of laughter and calabash between the icy teeth of the Sleeping Beauty'].[59] The calabash fruit of Martinique suggests life and nutrition, in contrast with the deathly connotations of European tradition, referenced here with the Sleeping Beauty.

Although many of the poems of *Les Armes miraculeuses* trace a form of movement from stagnation and oppression to revolt, some of Césaire's most surrealist experiments deny the reader the satisfaction of this teleology. Poems such as 'La Forêt vierge' and 'L'Irrémédiable' are among Césaire's most anarchic, they resist interpretation and consist rather in an explosion of sounds and images that deliberately defy logic and disorient the reader. 'La Forêt vierge' obliquely references enslavement by seemingly following the confused wandering of a maroon woman or runaway slave, apparently lost in a hostile and alienating urban environment. Authoritarian figures still seem to pursue her, whilst hints at a Martinican landscape are juxtaposed with that of the city, and in both environments the woman is pursued by death. The poem takes the form of one long prose sentence, with no punctuation, no verse or paragraph breaks, and reads almost as a piece of automatic writing, juxtaposing imagery of violence and loss in both wild and domesticated settings. The poem is less a narrative of the quest for freedom than an explosive expression of creative liberation, a throwing off of all literary constraints in a seemingly uncontrolled jumble of sounds and images. Moreover, 'L'Irrémédiable', a highly opaque sequence of fourteen prose sections printed in the 1946 Gallimard volume but excluded from those published in 1970 and 1976, does not even have a unifying figure such as that of the maroon woman in 'La Forêt vierge'. Rather, the refrain 'c'en est fait' ['it's all over'] introduces some of the sections to call for a definitive end to a past order, an upheaval captured also in both language and landscape: 'les mots se dépassent c'est bien vers un ciel et une terre que le haut et le bas permettent de distraire' ['words surpass themselves that's fine towards a heaven and an earth that high and low do not permit diversion'].[60] The title echoes 'L'Irrémédiable' by Baudelaire, where the poet charts, in a tightly structured verse form, the triumph of evil. In Césaire's version, there is no attempt to provide a reassuring aesthetic shape such as that deployed by Baudelaire, and instead of depicting evil in abstract form, imagery of enslavement and racial oppression again bursts forth in chaotic and disordered syntax.

If liberation is the underlying drive that propels the creative energy of *Les Armes miraculeuses*, this force is in no way shaped into a programmatic quest, but rather opens and disseminates the already dynamic energy of negritude revolt. The volume can be read as the direct successor to the *Cahier* in its clear vilification of enslavement and its legacy of racial inequality. However, the poet is no longer seeking a notion of black identity but is rather dramatising the very gesture of revolt through explosive imagery and fractured, disorientating poetic form. Africa is present not so much as a source of heritage but as a vast and powerful landscape, where humanity is conceived as embedded in the earth and the cosmos and where this integration between man and environment provides critical and creative energy. Revolt is depicted not so much as a process of human uprising but as an upheaval powered by both man and the cosmos, as the landscape too pronounces its refusal of historic systems of oppression. Césaire's rejection of constraint is at the same time enacted in his shattering not only of verse form but also of syntax itself, and in his effervescent and discordant imagery. This dramatisation of revolt through poetic language is then accomplished most fully in *Et les chiens se taisaient*, a hybrid text that shifted between tragedy, drama and oratorio, on which Césaire worked obsessively during the early 1940s and which was first published in the same volume with *Les Armes miraculeuses* in 1946.

Et les chiens se taisaient

Césaire's interest in theatre began during his years in Paris, where his friend Petar Guberina introduced him to the works of playwrights such as Giraudoux. Giraudoux's *La Guerre de Troie n'aura pas lieu* and *Electre* both use a Greek setting to portray the futility and destructiveness of war, and may have influenced Césaire, as he too deploys techniques inherited from ancient Greece. Césaire worked restlessly on *Et les chiens se taisaient* over several years in the early 1940s back in Martinique. Locally, there was little theatrical tradition, and his turn to theatre in that setting was therefore highly innovative. The form of the text preoccupied and troubled Césaire, who repeatedly returned to it, adapted it and rewrote it before publishing a first version (with the subtitle 'tragédie') in *Les Armes miraculeuses* in 1946. The text would change again when it was published as a drama in three acts by Présence Africaine in 1956, when the new edition helped to establish his aesthetic as a playwright ahead of the production of three more tragedies of decolonisation. The version included in *Les Armes* was already the culmination of a long period of experimentation. The earliest draft was more of a historical drama, initially intended to represent the Haitian Revolution led by Toussaint Louverture. James Arnold's discussion of the 1943 typescript

WARTIME MARTINIQUE

of *Et les chiens* tracks the specific historical references, including the naming of Toussaint and Dessalines. Arnold compares, for example, the setting of the Rebelle's death in the Jura to that of Toussaint, which is also evoked in the *Cahier*.[61] Césaire became unhappy with the historical drama during his stay in Haiti, perhaps because Toussaint's biography did not in the end fully adhere to his vision for negritude revolt. He ended up removing all the historical references in order to lift the play onto the universal and abstract level of myth.[62] The drama was recreated as a poetic 'tragédie' for publication in 1946, to be rewritten in a form slightly more adapted to the stage in 1956, and was later removed from the edition of *Les Armes miraculueses* published after 1970. This continued revision and reinvention of the work, like that of the *Cahier*, dramatises Césaire's restless and evolving aesthetic at the same time as the multiple and necessarily dynamic reincarnations of negritude revolt.

Et les chiens se taisaient nevertheless occupies a crucial place in Césaire's corpus in its staging of the act of revolt. Many critics have noted Césaire's insistence that it was the source of his inspiration for his later plays, as he claims it is 'the nebula from which all the successive worlds of my other plays emerged'.[63] If Césaire himself conceives it as an inauguration for his tragic universe, this is because of its tightly focused but universally resonant mapping of revolt as an assertion of destruction and liberation in both action and language. The play dramatises negritude by tracing the trajectory from struggle, through action, to the tragic denouement and call for rebirth. Whilst the poems of *Les Armes miraculeuses* use multiple forms of imagery to evoke the liberation of mind, body and cultural expression, *Et les chiens se taisaient* performs liberation through the nameless, universalised figure of the Rebelle, who murders the slave master to presage, after his death, the advent of a new world. The setting of the play is that of the hellish suffering of oppressed people, as the stage directions indicate: '*dans la barathre des épouvantements, vaste prison collective, peuplée de nègres candidats à la folie et à la mort; jour trentième de la famine, de la torture et du délire'* ['*in the barathrum of terror, a vast collective prison populated by black candidates for madness and death; the thirtieth day of famine, torture and delirium'*].[64] The Rebelle is present throughout, and the text is shaped by his consciousness as he is addressed by various figures, including a Narrator and Narratress, a chorus, several figures of authority, two madwomen, and the Beloved and the Mother, against whose compromises he articulates his ambition for complete renewal through the sacrificial act. The assassination of the master is figured as a symbolic act of refusal; it follows the Rebelle's murder of his own 6-month-old son after the master caressed the child, as if this sacrifice testifies to the horror of the regime of enslavement and its necessary destruction. The Rebelle is blinded as a punishment, before he himself is killed. The act is a clear demand for rebirth, an explosive claim for liberation that can be seen as the apotheosis of Césaire's revolutionary thinking during the early 1940s. This demand here takes the form of a myth, expressed at the same time through violence carried out on language. The political difficulties associated with revolution and revolt would be addressed explicitly only later in the 1950s, with the tragedies of decolonisation.

Et les chiens se taisaient is a performance of revolt, an aesthetic experiment that predates Césaire's political endeavours but that voices revolution through language and through myth. Influenced by Nietzsche's *The Birth of Tragedy*, Césaire's text enacts a Dionysian revolt, an uprising against the colonial order that takes the place of the gods in the structure he also analysed in 'Poésie et connaissance'. As Gregson Davis notes, the Rebelle is also akin to Aeschylus's Prometheus, 'a rebellious, titanic protagonist who is imprisoned by an omnipotent oppressor', though the Rebelle is visited by human characters and voices, albeit impersonal ones, rather than Aeschylus's abstract forces.[65] *Et les chiens* also respects the Greek unities, in that the drama is entirely formed by the single issue of Rebelle's murderous act and its tragic consequences, and it takes place across a day and a night in the vast prison setting.

Yet the highly innovative form of Césaire's dramatic text stems from its simultaneous deployment of European and African influences. Césaire draws on Egyptian mythology, as imagery of resurrection recalls that of Osiris. Césaire was clearly influenced in this by James Frazer's study of mythology in *The Golden Bough*, to which references can be found in the author's notes. The dogs of the title reference the dog-headed god Anubis, who bears the souls of the dead to the underworld, though at the same time the dogs allude to Caribbean history by recalling the hounds used to hunt down runaway slaves. Yet in blending Greek and Egyptian mythology, Césaire conceived these not as opposed but as closely related, as he insists in an interview with Rodney Harris: tragedy was 'a complete, total art for the Greeks' and this form was 'very close to Africa'.[66] Alongside Greek and Egyptian mythology, moreover, Césaire notes his debt to Shakespeare and Brecht. Arnold details in addition his use of Claudel's *Livre de Christophe Colomb*, evident in the play's explicit references to the history of enslavement starting with Columbus.[67]

The use of mythology, however, does not prevent the play from reflecting Césaire's personal struggles during the early 1940s. The anguished rewriting suggests Césaire was searching for a form and struggling to bring together his commitment to Caribbean history with his ambitious, universalising vision for freedom. He confessed to Breton that *Et les chiens* was a personal preoccupation and can be read as 'the uncertain and unsteady step of a man taking possession of himself, of his destiny, still frightened by his prophesies and being subjected to voices, of which the alternating and contradictory choruses never stop and seem to surround him completely'.[68] The Rebelle's assailment by different voices, his quest for leadership and troubled relationship with the world as it is incarnated by the Mother and the Beloved, on some level reflect Césaire's parallel search for a position. Arnold, moreover, reads the Rebelle as a sort of alter ego, the grounding of the 'je' of *Les Armes miraculeuses* in a unified but complex character, who dramatises the process of revolt as a lived experience carried out through action.[69] Fonkoua goes so far as to describe Césaire himself as the Rebelle, tracing links between the 1956 version of the play, the voices of the *Cahier*, and that of the poet himself in his endeavours to secure the autonomy of the Martinican people, whilst in his study of Césaire's theatre, Rodney Harris sees parallels between the isolation of the Rebelle and that of Martinique during the war.[70] If, as we shall see, the ending of the play retains some ambiguity in refusing to make it clear how a new, more liberated order can arrive, this ambiguity can be seen to reflect Césaire's self-questioning, as he too interrogates the process of revolt – not like the Rebelle through violence, but through language and aesthetic invention.

Throughout *Et les chiens* the Rebelle nevertheless makes it clear that he speaks for generations of enslaved people, so that this personal perspective is given a universal significance. The Rebelle can be seen to voice the poet's ambition in the *Cahier*, whereby '"ma bouche sera la bouche des malheurs qui n'ont point de bouche"' ['"my mouth shall be the mouth of those calamities that have no mouth"']. Whilst the quotation marks surrounding that statement in the *Cahier* indicated the poet's unease with that position, the Rebelle is for the most part more assertive in his role as spokesman.[71] In his exchange with the Beloved at the start of the play, the Rebelle greets her appeal to embrace life with references to starving black children, as if he is unable to share her optimism because of his responsibility to these innocent victims. Addressing the madwomen a little later, the Rebelle conjures imagery not just of his own revolt but of black revolution, 'la nuit bruissante de souffles d'esclaves dilatant sous les pas du christophore la grande mer de misère, la grande mer de sang noir, la grande houle de cannes à sucre et de dividendes, le grand océan d'horreur et de désolation' ['the night rustling with the breathing of slaves dilating beneath their Christophoric steps the great sea of destitution, the great sea of black blood, the great swell of sugarcane and profits, the great ocean of horror and desolation'].[72] Here, the imagery of breath recalls that of suffocation

WARTIME MARTINIQUE   91

explored earlier in *Tropiques*, as the Rebelle conjures the bare traces of life that endure the horrors of enslavement. The Rebelle's own uprising in this way follows this evocation of stifled resistance, and his status as leader is reflected by the chorus's repetition of 'ô roi debout' ['arise o king'].[73]

Césaire further enhances the broader resonance of the Rebelle's uprising by echoing the term 'debout' with the imagery of the rebellion on the slave ship, as well as of the Haitian Revolution in the *Cahier*. Later, in justifying his actions to the Mother, the Rebelle again insists on his universal representativity: 'il n'y a pas dans le monde un pauvre type lynché, un pauvre homme torturé, en qui je ne sois assassiné et humilié' ['there is in the world no poor bastard lynched, no poor bastard tortured, in whom I am not assassinated and humiliated'].[74] Nevertheless, in standing for the oppressed people, the Rebelle also cuts himself off from those around him. As the chorus chant 'ô roi debout' ['arise o king'], the Rebelle admits: 'et maintenant / seul / tout est seul / j'ai beau aiguiser ma voix / tout déserte tout / ma voix peine / ma voix tangue dans le cornet des brumes sans carrefour / et je n'ai pas de mère / et je n'ai pas de fils' ['and now / alone / everything is alone / however much I sharpen my voice / all deserts all / my voice labours / my voices pitches in the foghorn of mists without crossroad / and I have no mother / and I have no sons'].[75] As we shall see more extensively in the later plays, the rebellious leader figure occupies a difficult position, and the role of the mythical spokesman does not sit easily with personal human relationships. Césaire suggests that the Rebelle's solitude is part of his universality, yet this combination of isolation and representativity at the same time indicates that the spokesman resonates with other humans in an uneasy and partial way.[76]

The universal and mythic significance of the Rebelle is intensified by the temporality of his vision, which is lifted outside of ordinary chronological time in its prophesy of a wholly new order. The play opens with the Echo's comment that, 'bien sur qu'il va mourir le Rebelle' ['surely he is going to die the Rebel'], so that the present moment already augurs its inevitably tragic consequences.[77] Past and present contain an ominous future, a prophetic vision that disrupts linear time. Yet this prophesy also announces a new temporal structure that indicates that the play works not as a linear progression but as an aspiration towards a completely different world. This is associated not with political change but with cosmic renewal or reinvention. Césaire's subversion of temporality is analysed in structural terms in the recent critic Jackqueline Frost's reading of the text, in which she explores the invention of two alternative forms of temporality, that of Dionysian cyclical renewal and that of kairological 'right time', a time of justice at once on the horizon and yet unattained.[78] Although these structures are distinct, Césaire's use of imagery recalling both is suggestive of the chaotic upheaval that the revolt struggles to achieve while demanding a relinquishment of the existing order of progressive history. On the one hand, then, the rising up heralded by the chorus's repetition of 'ô roi debout' ['arise o king'] is suggestive of resurrection, and Frost notes that this is followed in the 1956 version by images of a new, purified landscape. On the other hand, imagery of rebirth is complemented with that suggesting an at once distant but imminent arrival. The Rebelle acts as a result of a long history, as he references 'l'épais crachat des siècles' ['the thick spit of centuries'] and the 306 years of enslavement in Martinique.[79]

Yet against this vast timescale is the possibility of a time of justice, a moment anticipated but not grasped, as the Rebelle earlier reflects: 'une minute trop lourde ou trop belle pèse sur moi depuis longtemps' ['a minute too heavy or too beautiful has weighed on me for a long time'].[80] This moment is formulated by the tempters as 'l'heure rouge, l'heure dénouée rouge' ['the red hour, the red unknotted hour'] and 'l'heure des nostalgies, l'heure des miracles' ['the hour of nostalgias, the hour of miracles'], as if it would contain both past and future in some cosmic turning point. The Rebelle's blindness is also significant here, it recalls that of Oedipus and also that of Tiresias, the blind prophet of Greek mythology, and suggests that the Rebelle sees beyond the immediately visible events of lived history and beyond, to more fundamental and far-reaching change. Whilst the Rebelle is on one level a lonely individual, the latest victim of the horrific regime of enslavement in the Caribbean, Césaire also portrays his revolt on this cosmic level that reorders the very form of human history.

The cosmic significance of the revolt enacted in *Et les chiens* is at the same time represented through imagery of meteorological upheaval and environmental change. On one level, the embedding of the Rebelle's experience and vision in the landscape again suggests a mode of existence associated with Frobenius's African civilisation, where humanity lives in dialogue with ecology without claiming mastery. On another level, the imagery of environmental sickness and the anticipation of elemental change enlarges the scale of the coloniser's wrongdoing and announces its overthrow as the advent of a new configuration of both time and space. Colonial destruction is recorded by flora, fauna and the elements, as alongside the imagery of starving black children the Rebelle observes: 'le parfum de la mandragore s'est séché; la colline chasse sur ses aussières; les grands remous des vallées font des vagues; les forêts démâtent, les oiseaux font des signaux de détresse où nos corps perdus bercent leurs épaves blanchies' ['the scent of mandrake has evaporated; the hill is dragging its hawsers; the great eddies of the valleys are making waves; forests are losing their masts, birds are making signs of distress in which our lost bodies are rocking their whitened wreckage'].[81] The anticipation of change, moreover, is conjured through the rising of the sun, a symbol for freedom here and throughout *Les Armes miraculeuses*, as the Narratress intones: 'il monte. Il monte. Le soleil est un lion qui se traîne fou brisé de pattes dans la cage qui tremble' ['it rises. It rises. The sun is a maddened lion that drags itself paws broken in the shuddering cage'].[82] The Rebelle then indicates that this rising of the sun in the hope of freedom is accompanied by movement in the waters: 'le flot noir monte' ['the dark flood rises'], as rivers and seas bearing witness to violence participate in the tempestuous revolt. Environmental change works as a metaphor for the Rebelle's eruptive language, as his words 'par la grâce des terres jeunes et du bassin sismique' ['by the grace of young lands and the seismic basin'] ask the landscape for renewal before he bursts out with 'ma parole puissance de feu' ['my word power of fire'].[83]

If the imagery throughout *Et les chiens se taisaient* suggests that the environment conspires in this all-encompassing rebellion in pursuit of cosmic change, however, the Rebelle remains an embattled figure. He may be portrayed as a Promethean hero representing a universalised act of revolt, but he does not voice a unified perspective, and the play at the same time signals the difficulties of this mythic pursuit. As Carrie Noland has argued, whilst the Rebelle may on one level function as a universal spokesman, leader and role model, his various interlocutors can be read as internal voices, as if the text tracks his inner consciousness responding to the world around him as well as to his own doubts.[84] Figures such as the Bishop and the Jailer spout colonial discourse, denigrating the Rebelle and the enslaved population and catalysing his assertion of resistance. The Narrator and Narratress both recite and summon the action, fuelling the Rebelle's quest, though they also taunt him, as the narrator comments, for example, 'voici le nautonier noir de l'orage noir, le guetteur / du temps noir et du hasard pluvieux / muré dans la passion noire du voyage noir' ['behold the black boatman of the black storm, the watchman of black weather of rainy luck / walled up in the black passion of the black voyage'].[85] The Narrator repeats the term 'noir' as if to mock negritude revolt and reduces the Rebelle to 'un vieillard têtu, fragile noire interrogation du destin dans le cycle / perdu des courants sommaires' ['a stubborn old man, frail black interrogation of fate in the lost / cycle of summary currents'].[86] More disturbingly, the Tempters voice his uncertainty, pointing out the emptiness of his words and mocking his status as king, whilst the Chorus first summon him as king and then later also belittle him.[87] Most pressingly, the Beloved reminds him of the beauty of life, to prevent him from sacrificing himself, whilst the Mother preaches fidelity to humanity before abstract principles. From the point of view of the Rebelle, the Mother represents feeble compromise, as she fears the prophetic vision he conjures from the murder: 'j'ai peur de la balle de tes mots' since 'ce ne sont pas des mots humains' ['I fear the bullet of your words' since 'they are not human words'].[88] Yet if the Mother calls for compromise in the name of human love, the Rebelle ranks freedom over love, and the demand for freedom structures his entire ethos. In this sense the play offers, as we saw earlier, a fitting culmination to Césaire's work with *Tropiques* against asphyxiation and stultification, and yet the presence of these other characters makes evident the challenges of pursuing freedom as an overriding and abstract principle.

Et les chiens se taisaient is no doubt one of the most assertive performances of revolt to be found across Césaire's corpus. The Rebelle personifies the act of seizing freedom and demands a rupture from the past. His call for a transformed future is articulated both through his revolutionary act and through the text's vibrant, fulgurating language. Yet at the end it remains unclear whether this better future will come into being. After the death of the Rebelle, the Narrator and Narratress continue to conjure imagery of destruction, though there are hints of rebirth, expressed, for example, in the renewed growth of angry vegetation: 'plantes parasites, plantes vénéneuses, plantes brûlantes, plantes cannibales, plantes incendiaires, vraies plantes, filez vos courbes imprévues à grosses goutes' ['parasitic plants, venomous plants, burning plants, cannibal plants, incendiary plants, true plants, weave your unforeseen curves in great droplets'].[89] The closing lines of the play announce the fusion of the Narrator and Narratress with the islands, in an embrace again reminiscent of Suzanne Césaire's 'homme-plante', as if this reintegration with the earth might bring an end to the history of colonial mismanagement. The final stage directions also conjure a bright vision of the Caribbean environment, as we are left with a '*vision de la Caraibe bleue semée d'îles d'or et d'argent dans la scintillation de l'aube*' ['*vision of the blue Caribbean sown with gold and silver stars in the scintillation of dawn*'].[90] Césaire himself encourages this optimistic reading in affirming his allegiance to Nietzsche and conceiving tragedy as a stimulation or a commitment to change: '*because, beyond the failures, beyond death, it is nevertheless in the end an adherence to life*'.[91]

Yet there is no doubt that the world of the play is throughout steeped in violence, and there is no indication of how a new order could be instated. Femi Ojo-Ade's reading of the play in his study of Césaire's theatre stresses the Rebelle's isolation, the individuality of his revolt, and suggests that if he were somehow to return after his death, this would only allow the repetition of the act of violence. According to Ojo-Ade, the Rebelle does not succeed in bringing about change, and the play leaves us with a sense of ambivalence about the future: 'Césaire's imagery never ceases to be deliberately two-faced, positive and negative, with death and life jostling for position, and rebellion finding it difficult to conquer reaction'.[92] Although the imagery in the play's final speeches occasionally hints at rebirth, this promise is by no means free from connotations of destruction. Césaire insists on the demand for liberation, but it seems he too perceives the future as uncertain. *Et les chiens se taisaient* is his most ambitious dramatisation of the claim for freedom, but the history of violence and enslavement still bears its weight on the present. In his later plays, Césaire would use a more historically grounded form to explore both revolution and its consequences, and in so doing would explore the ambiguous aftermath of revolt that remained unexplored in the early dramatic experiment of *Et les chiens se taisaient*.

The early 1940s bear witness to an intensification in Césaire's antiracist critique, expressed now as an urgent, aesthetically explosive call for freedom both from the stultification of contemporary Martinique and from the longer history of slavery.

He expresses this contestation in increasingly challenging ways, experimenting with myth and surrealism, both to universalise the act of revolt and to perform its disruptive force through language, in *Tropiques* and *Les Armes miraculeuses*. His most famous work, the *Cahier d'un retour au pays natal*, moreover, continued to evolve during this period, as the poet kept revising and making additions in part as a result of his dialogue with André Breton and surrealism.

A further edition of the *Cahier* was published (together with an English translation by Lionel Abel and Ivan Goll, a preface by Breton and three illustrations by Wifredo Lam) several years later in 1947 by Brentano's in New York, but the work for this edition was done during the early 1940s. This version remains notably different from the 1947 edition published in Paris by Bordas, to be discussed in the next chapter. The Brentano's edition reflects Césaire's preoccupations, as they are borne out in the works discussed here, in a form briefly worth noting. Five new strophes are inserted at the end of the first section, as the poet breaks off the depiction of the rotting city of Fort-de-France. He recasts the poet as 'un homme-juif / un homme-cafre / un homme-hindou-de-Calcutta / un homme-de-Harlem qui ne vote pas' ['a Jew-man / a kaffir-man / a Hindu-from Calcutta-man / a man-from-Harlem-who-does-not-vote'] as well as 'un homme-pogrom, un chiot, un mendigot' ['a pogrom-man / a puppy / a beggar'], as if to amplify his claim to speak universally for oppressed peoples.[93] Like the Rebelle, the poet here represents not just black people in Martinique but all those who are downtrodden, repeating the term 'homme' at the same time to restore their human dignity. Most notably, the lines here are briefer and more staccato than in much of the 1939 edition, and this passage is succeeded by one figuring the landscape with imagery of sexual prowess, as if to fuse elemental and ecological revolt now with the surrealist release of unconscious desire. A further fifty-six strophes are added at strophe 63, before the famous passage evoking the dynamic activity of negritude, containing references to Africa: 'à force de penser au Congo / je suis devenu un Congo bruissant de forêts et de fleuves où le fouet claque comme un grand étendard' ['I have thought and thought of the Congo and so, I have become a Congo rustling with forests and rivers'].[94] This imagery enhances the connection with Frobenius, evoking the re-establishment of an African heritage and the 'homme-plante' whilst also making a clear reference to the enslaved past. This long added section is at the same time striking for its disordered structure and syntax and for its explicit affirmation of irrationality ('que 2 et 2 font 5 / que la forêt miaule' ['that 2 and 2 make 5 / that the forest mews']).[95] The poet's aesthetic rebellion is now captured in chaotic sequences of defiant imagery composed in a highly jolting form, lurching from curt assertions of dissent to convoluted and surreal visions of upheaval.

Read alongside *Tropiques* and *Les Armes miraculeuses*, this revised *Cahier* announces Césaire's ambitious aesthetic revolt. Explosive juxtapositions of imagery conjure the poet's anger and reframe negritude as an incendiary refusal of all forms of oppression, associated here not only with political regimes but also with Western rationalism. The Rebelle's murderous act is articulated in this *Cahier*, and in 'En guise de manifeste littéraire', with the stark and uncompromising assertion: 'ASSEZ DE CE SCANDALE' ['ENOUGH OF THIS OUTRAGE'].[96] The authoritarianism of Robert's regime as well as of past regimes is addressed directly with a riposte to the 'flics et flicaillons' ['cops and rozzers'] whose brutal reason is rejected in the poet's furious celebration of madness.[97] If, as we saw at the beginning of this chapter, Césaire's imagery of suffocation ominously anticipated the slogan of the contemporary Black Lives Matter movement 'I can't breathe', this denunciation of police brutality once again indicates that even this surrealist aesthetic can be connected with more recent activist responses to injustice. The call for revolt in *Tropiques*, together with its performance and dramatisation in *Les Armes, Et les chiens*, and the Brentano's edition of the *Cahier*, is crystallised here as a vilification of the violence committed by policemen as well as by slave owners in the past. Césaire was not yet politically active, but it was only a matter of time before the call for liberation from the shackles of authority would come to inform his political endeavours after 1945.

3

Departmentalisation, *Soleil cou coupé* and *Corps perdu*
'I shall command the islands to exist'

In 1945, Césaire's career took a decisive change of direction. Although his discontent towards the political situation of Martinique was quite clear in the essays and poetry published in *Tropiques*, it was in that year that he moved from the role of commentator to that of political actor. Standing in the municipal and legislative elections in May and October, Césaire was elected *conseiller municipal* and Mayor of Fort-de-France, and *conseiller général* for Martinique. In November, he was elected Deputy at the Assemblée Nationale representing the Communist Party, where he began a long and energetic career fighting for the rights of Martinicans.

Although, as Kora Véron notes, Césaire himself was modest about his political ambitions at the time and agreed to stand because his colleagues asked him to and because as a result he saw it as his 'moral duty', this turn to politics clearly evolves out of his earlier interests.[1] Whereas in the early 1940s it was above all through the oblique critique offered by *Tropiques* that he expressed his political dissent, from 1945 onwards he was determined to act. He chose to join the Communist Party in this endeavour, moreover, because, as he himself declared in 1946:

> In a world that has not healed from racism and where the ferocious exploitation of colonial populations persists, the

Communist Party incarnates the will to work effectively for the advent of the only social and political order that we can accept, because it would be founded on the right to dignity of all men without distinction in origin, religion, or colour.[2]

At the same time, whilst the poetry volumes *Soleil cou coupé* and *Corps perdu* (published in 1948 and 1950 respectively) continue to experiment with surrealism, the latter in particular expresses the ambitions of negritude in more direct and affirmative terms by comparison with *Les Armes miraculeuses*. The closing line of the poem 'Corps perdu', 'je commanderai aux îles d'exister' ['I shall command the islands to exist'], at once asserts the island's status and the claim for the rights of its people, and represents the poet's demiurgic stance, whereby poetry itself brings a new geography into being.[3]

On 26 February 1946, Césaire presented the proposal, devised together with the Martinican politician Léopold Bissol, that Martinique and Guadeloupe should be classified as French départements. The law was then voted through unanimously on 19 March. Gaston Monnerville fought for the establishment of the same law in Guiana, and Léon de Lepervenche and Raymond Vergès secured departmentalisation for Réunion. The move may seem surprising given Césaire's anticolonial rhetoric throughout *Tropiques*, but, as Nick Nesbitt suggests, it was a 'politics of principle' and a paradigm shift in its aim 'to transform colonial subjects into full citizens of the Fourth Republic subject to its rights and laws without discrimination'.[4] It was conceived as a bold and practical means to improve the living conditions of the people of Martinique and Guadeloupe, and although there were a few dissenters (particularly in Guadeloupe), Césaire had the support of the vast majority of Martinicans.[5] The Communist Federation of Martinique insisted in its journal that they wanted 'a complete assimilation', not a cultural assimilation but a democracy that would allow Martinicans to benefit from the same advantages as those living in metropolitan France.[6]

102   DEPARTMENTALISATION

Césaire's presentation of the bill at the Assemblée Nationale on 12 March reflects the urgency behind this call for equality. He began notably with a homage to France and argued that if Martinique and Guadeloupe had been French since 1635, then this new integration would be 'the normal endpoint of a historical process and the logical conclusion of a doctrine'.[7] Yet rather than proceeding to this end point, he insisted that the process of integration had stalled, but that departmentalisation would be a fitting continuation of Republican principles. His strategy at this point was to claim the rights of Martinicans by praising French Republican ideology, challenging the status quo from within to take a practical step forward in improving the lives of his people. Insisting on parity between Martinicans and French, he then virulently denounced the unequal treatment of his compatriots:

> A French citizen like those who live in Paris or Bordeaux, the Martinican for example now finds himself as little protected from social risks as the inhabitant of the forest or the desert. In a country where salaries are abnormally low and where the cost of living is perceptibly very close to the cost of living in France, the worker is at the mercy of illness, disability, and age with no security.
>
> No benefits for women giving birth.
> No benefits for the sick.
> No benefits for the elderly.
> No benefits for the unemployed.[8]

The speech reaches a crescendo with Césaire beseeching the French administration to remain true to the ideals of Schoelcher, and to make a decisive break with the legacy of slavery that still affects relations between the colony and the metropole. His arguments privilege ethics over economics, conjuring images of a France capable of unifying diverse cultures with its fidelity to principles of equality and fraternity, and entreating the assembly to remain true

DEPARTMENTALISATION

to itself rather than to pander to metropolitan economic self-interest.

The Assemblée Nationale agreed to the departmentalisation of Martinique, Guadeloupe, Guiana and Réunion; however, it did not agree to the automatic application of metropolitan laws or benefits to these territories. Césaire would therefore continue to use his oratorical powers to demand freedom and equality in Martinique. Speaking on 11 April 1946 on the project of the new constitution, he championed the 'Union française' as a salutary alternative to the historic French Empire, envisaging a freely chosen, non-hierarchical union, where citizens themselves would be able to choose greater or lesser degrees of autonomy. He conjured a new era, suggesting that the Fourth Republic would put an end to the colonial myth and would establish a real and lasting democracy for all French territories. Yet, as we see across his work, his rhetoric veers between visionary idealism, deployed to drum up support, and a more pragmatic realism, as he notes that the new constitution by no means spells the end of colonialism but that it is a progressive step. The new constitution was rejected, moreover, and on 14 September 1946 Césaire defended the citizenship of the people of the new French territories, though again his pragmatism is juxtaposed with incendiary indictments of the history of the French colonial enterprise and is capped by a rousing vision of emancipation: 'a great hope has arisen in colonised countries: the hope that out of their suffering and sacrifice they will witness the birth of a more just world, where their duties will be equally balanced with their rights'.[9] The new constitution was approved in October 1946, and Césaire was safely re-elected in November, to return to Martinique full of hope for concrete rewards, such as the establishment of a proper benefits system. If it was initially expected that the assimilation law would be implemented in January 1947, however, this was then delayed, and although préfets were named in 1947, the application of the new law did not occur until January 1948. It was already becoming evident that the promises of departmentalisation would not be met in the ways that Césaire had hoped.

During the course of 1947, Césaire quickly became disillusioned with departmentalisation. In April 1947, de Gaulle's *Rassemblement du peuple français* (RPF) was highly successful in the municipal elections, leading to the expulsion of Communist ministers, and a period of social unrest began, with large-scale strikes across multiple sectors. These strikes would affect Martinique in 1948, with an outbreak of violence in February. The RPF organised a protest in Martinique, and a peaceful counterprotest was then held. In a way that perhaps anticipates the intensive police presence at recent Black Lives Matter protests in the US, the counterprotesters were met with violence, whilst the RPF protest was not. Georges Gratiant, Deputy Mayor, was arrested on the orders of the Prefect Pierre Trouillé, and the police turned violent towards the protesters. A few days later, on 1 March, three workers on strike in a dispute over pay were killed, further fuelling tensions between the people and police authorities.

Outraged, Césaire spoke out for justice, calling in February and March at the Assemblée Nationale for the government to be held to account and evoking the 'atmosphere of terror' that as a result reigned on the island. In May, Césaire condemned the government for its silence on the events and directly incriminated Trouillé for his brutality. Césaire's activism at this point is not just that of a political negotiator, then, but directly challenges the indiscriminate use of violence against black people asserting their rights. Césaire himself did not take to the streets, but spoke up in the name of the protestors in the halls of power, using his rhetorical skill to shame the savage brutality that gave the lie to Republican principles. These incidents also marked a turning point for Césaire, whose moderate vision for departmentalisation was now badly damaged. His focus would become a more explicit denunciation of colonial violence and injustice.

In the months following these violent incidents, Césaire's political interventions became increasingly embittered. In an article published in the Communist journal *Justice* in July 1948, he demanded the removal of Trouillé and evoked the sorry state of Martinique under his power: 'Martinique presents the spectacle of a department that an administration unable to control it is gradually leading to ruin, poverty, and revolt'.[10] Trouillé is portrayed as a stunted tyrant, governing without collaboration and ordering police aggression at will. Also in July 1948, Césaire participated in a tense and hostile debate at the Assemblée Nationale concerning social security in the overseas departments, citing the high cost of living and the risk that local dissatisfaction would be stirred up into revolt. The discussion was punctuated with protests and exclamations, testifying to the anger now directed against metropolitan hypocrisy. This anger was also expressed outside the political arena: shortly after the incidents, in April 1948 Césaire delivered an address at the Sorbonne at the commemoration of the centenary of the abolition of slavery in praise of Schoelcher, but took the opportunity to point out that nothing of Schoelcher's ideals could be found in contemporary Martinique. Detailing the abolitionist's emancipatory ideals, he nevertheless insisted that the same grievances plague Martinicans as those that mobilised Schoelcher and that, 'looking at certain recent events, who could say that the administration has completely unlearned the methods that Schoelcher denounced a century ago'.[11] Césaire's intervention is astonishing in its implication that the legacy of enslavement still lingers into the current regime; indeed, as Véron notes, it was reported in *L'Époque* as a scandal.[12] His more detailed account of Schoelcher's work in his introduction to *Esclavage et colonisation* also ends with the intimation that the abolitionist's work is not yet complete.

It was in May 1948 that Césaire published a first draft of what was to become his most famous and most incendiary essay, *Discours sur le colonialisme*. The 1948 essay was just a few pages long, entitled 'L'impossible contact', and was composed in response to an invitation from the right-wing journal *Les Chemins du monde*. The editors clearly expected a moderate appraisal of departmentalisation and would no doubt have been discomfited by Césaire's incendiary anticolonial statements. The crux of the argument was the failure of the colonial project to bring about any 'contact' or collaboration between peoples because of its brazen, unmediated self-interest. The essay opens with an excoriating definition of colonisation not as a beneficent enterprise but as 'the decisive gesture of the adventurer and the pirate', supported by a civilisation in pursuit of 'its antagonistic economics'.[13] Césaire's incandescent rhetoric is on display here in full force, as he lists the hypocrisies and crimes of the colonial system in colourful and hyperbolic vocabulary. Whilst it was claimed that colonialism would be the harbinger of civilisation, Césaire insists on the contrary that its brutality dehumanises the coloniser. Europe has been forced to confront its own dehumanising practices, moreover, with the 'boomerang effect' of Nazism, when finally the barbarity of Western civilisation played out on its own territory. If the bourgeoisie of Europe could not tolerate Hitler's humiliation of the white man, Césaire reminds his reader that this humiliation had been imposed by Europe on its colonies for centuries. He goes on to vilify European humanists (such as Ernest Renan) for their racist thinking, which he connects directly with that of Hitler, to argue that the barbarism of Nazi ideology can be found at the very heart of European thought. Colonial beneficence is nothing but a sham: 'no human respect, but relationships of domination and submission which transform the coloniser into a pawn, an army sergeant, a despot, a slavedriver, and the indigenous man into an instrument of production. It is my turn to propose an equation: *colonisation = thingification*'.[14]

As we shall see in later chapters, the fury expressed in 'L'impossible contact' and later in *Discours sur le colonialisme* unleashed what Césaire was unable to say explicitly in the political debates at the Assemblée Nationale. Read alongside those speeches, however, the essay showcases the revolutionary vision that Césaire was forced to moderate while seeking practical solutions to the unequal provision for Martinicans despite the promises of departmentalisation. Through 1949 and 1950, these speeches testify to his increasing exasperation, as he evoked the lamentable living conditions in the overseas departments and pointed out the failings of the regime to address ongoing inequality. In July 1949, he made a detailed call for further investment and documented the miserable state of the cities in Réunion Island, of Pointe-à-Pitre in Guadeloupe and Fort-de-France in Martinique. He denounced the absence of a proper sewerage system, the stench of the rubbish collecting in the streets, the dilapidated state of the schools and hospitals, and the omnipresence of poverty. Repairs and development works promised in 1947 (and again in 1948) never took place, and Trouillé is again condemned, this time for his inefficacy in putting plans into operation and for spending funds to which he had no right. Césaire's language is precise and measured here, and yet his incrimination of Trouillé was met with criticism, to which he in turn objected in frustration: 'so, ladies and gentlemen, it is as a result of such faults that have accumulated and remained unpunished, faults which have been treated with indifference, that age-old friendships are becoming undone and fidelities are weakened'.[15]

On 15 March 1950, the tension at the Assemblée Nationale reached new heights. Césaire vilified the persistent lack of attention to overseas departments other than when it was a question of repressive laws, or, in the case of the debate on that occasion, of a military pact between France and the US. The speech became an impassioned denunciation of the failures of departmentalisation, as he offered a torrent of detail indicating the poor living conditions and the terrible state of hospitals and healthcare in Martinique. This diatribe led Césaire to contrast the Union française with the more egalitarian values of the Soviet Union, and to describe the Union française as nothing other than 'a prison of the people'. In response, he was told he was insulting the fatherland and he was ungrateful.[16] Even Léon-Gontran Damas, representing Guiana and who had been associated with Césaire and the negritude movement in Paris during the 1930s, commented that Césaire's arguments detracted from the debate at hand.

108 DEPARTMENTALISATION

After this debacle, Césaire made a few further brief interventions at the Assemblée Nationale over the summer of 1950, notably on the payment of *fonctionnaires* in Martinique and in favour of an improvement in the provision for schools, before returning to Martinique in October. He did not return to the Assemblée until 1952 and would from then on intervene with less frequency than he did during those first years. This period between 1945 and 1950, however, was one of highly intense activity, as he shifted from the visionary hopes of departmentalisation to profound disillusionment and to a bitter condemnation of the persistence of the racism and inequality that structured the colonial history of the Antilles. The 'incandescent speech' evoked by René Hénane in his introduction to the volume of Césaire's speeches at the Assemblée Nationale is amply in evidence during this period, moreover, and indeed this rhetorical flourishing can be seen to unfold in parallel with a period of fervent cultural development and dialogue.[17]

Cultural Connections and Poetic Reinventions

Césaire's cultural and poetic vision flourished and matured during the late 1940s. The final issue of *Tropiques* came out in September 1945, but the end of this cultural enterprise gave way to a richly productive period leading to the publication of a further version of the *Cahier* in 1947, and to the remarkable poetry volumes *Soleil cou coupé* in 1948 and *Corps perdu* in 1950. Césaire continued to explore surrealism during this fertile period, recrafting surrealist influences to forge his own unique aesthetics of invention and revolt in the Caribbean. His relationships with other writers and artists also evolved and expanded in highly productive ways. He worked in dialogue less intensively with Breton and the New York avant-garde, (which were major interlocutors of his in the early 1940s) while forging links with Parisian writers, as well as international artists Wifredo Lam and Pablo Picasso.

Césaire's contact with Breton became less frequent after the War, though Aimé and Suzanne Césaire were warmly welcomed by surrealists in New York when they passed through in November 1945 on the way to Paris. In December 1945, Pierre Loeb hosted an exhibition of Lam's work at his Galerie de la rue des Beaux-Arts in Paris, and Véron surmises that it was here that Césaire also met Michel Leiris, who connected him with other surrealist writers such as Tristan Tzara.[18] Leiris would then visit the Caribbean as ethnographer in 1948, a project that further fuelled the intellectual connections between the two writers. As testimony to Césaire's ongoing links with surrealism, his poem 'Couteaux midi', a highly surrealist vision of revolution figured through the uprooting and projection into the air of the trees on the Champ de Mars in front of the palace in Port-au-Prince (or also at the site of the École militaire in Paris), was displayed at the *Exposition internationale du surréalisme* organised by Breton at the Galerie Maeght in Paris in 1947, before its publication in *Soleil cou coupé*. Moreover, the volume's title testifies to Césaire's ongoing engagement with and reworking of surrealism by referencing the last line of Guillaume Apollinaire's 'Zone', from the anthology *Alcools* published in 1913. Apollinaire's poem evokes the jarring emergence of urban modernity using highly incongruous and surrealist imagery, mixing religion and mythology with technological progress. The final image suggests at once sunrise, a new dawn, and fear of the destruction it might bring. For Césaire, the sun – a highly polysemic figure that recurs throughout his work and is associated by turns with the poet and his revolt, liberation and rebirth as well as destructive force – here in part represents freedom, but its decapitation connotes the French revolution and its brutal repression.[19] At the same time, in an apt example of the polysemy of Césaire's imagery, René Hénane suggests that the 'cou coupé' is also a large-beaked bird, so this title associates bird and fire as if in a reference to the phoenix and its rebirth.[20]

Césaire's writing so far bears the mark of his immersion in French poetry and prose (from Baudelaire and Rimbaud to

110 DEPARTMENTALISATION

Apollinaire and Breton), whilst creatively mixing references to such figures with allusions to African mythology and Voodoo spirituality. In addition, his evolving relationship with artists Lam and Picasso became increasingly important during this period. Césaire met Lam along with Breton in Martinique back in 1941, and Lam illustrated the Cuban edition of the *Cahier d'un retour au pays natal* in 1943. Lam also illustrated the short collection 'Colombes et menfenil', which contained some of the poems later printed in *Les Armes mirculeuses* and which was published in *Hémisphères* in 1944. Pierre Mabille wrote a long essay on Lam and his famous painting 'La Jungle' for *Tropiques* in January 1945, further demonstrating his significance for the reinvention of Caribbean art and culture during this period. One of Lam's illustrations was then included with the 1947 Bordas edition of the *Cahier*. Césaire had already dedicated a copy of the *Volontés* edition of the *Cahier* to Lam, moreover, and 'Simouns' (in 'Colombes et menfenil') as well as 'À l'Afrique' (in *Soleil cou coupé*) are also dedicated to the Cuban artist. Much later, in 1982, Césaire would compose a series of poems for Lam for his volume *moi, laminaire. . .*

Césaire's dialogue with Lam is significant for its role in developing his thinking on the relationship between anticolonial thought and ecology, as Lam's art blurs human, plant and animal to envision a more integrated symbiosis between living things. Indeed, in 1946, Césaire praised Lam's energised reinvigoration of Caribbean art in an article first printed in *Cahiers d'art*:

> Painting is one of the rare weapons we have left against the sordidness of history. Wifredo attests to this. And this is one of the meanings of Wifredo Lam's painting, which is richer than all others: it stops the epic of the conquistador; it represents the failure of the bloody epoch of the bastardisation with its insolent affirmation that something is happening in the Antilles. . . .
>
> And it is free, free from all aesthetic scruples, free from realism, free from any attempt at documentary, that Wifredo

Lam, magnificent, holds the great and terrible meeting: with the forest, the swamp, the monster, the night, the flying seeds, the rain, the liana tree, epiphyte, the snake, fear, the leap, life.[21]

This description of Lam's work captures Césaire's own aesthetic as it developed in the 1940s, where anticolonial contestation is combined with affirmation of the dynamic, interconnected life of human, landscape and cosmos.

Lam was already closely affiliated with Picasso, having met him in Paris in 1938. Lam, Picasso and Césaire shared their commitment to the denunciation of authoritarianism, their reinvention of the human through the plant world and their reinvigoration of African cultures. Picasso was a source of inspiration for the Cuban painter, who saw his work as an 'inciter of freedom'.[22] Whilst Lam and Césaire both sought to reconnect with Africa as if to rediscover their roots, Picasso was interested in detaching himself from his origins to denounce colonial barbarism and to access an alternative vision of the world to that represented by Western modernity. Césaire met Picasso in Wroclaw in Poland in August 1948 at the *Congrès mondial pour la paix*, where delegates discussed the aftermath of the Second World War and the emergence of the Cold War. Césaire's speech included passages from 'L'impossible contact', advocating freedom across the globe using the rhetoric of universal humanism. After the conference, several delegates (including Césaire) spent ten more days in Poland, visiting Warsaw, Krakow and Auschwitz-Birkenau. Césaire wrote the poem 'Varsovie' as testimony to this harrowing experience and sent a copy to Picasso. It was in the months after this visit that Césaire and Picasso devised the idea that the latter would illustrate Césaire's poems. Whilst it seems that originally Césaire had thought of reprinting for this project some of the poems from *Les Armes miraculeuses*, ultimately 'Corps perdu' consists of ten new poems written in a fresh new style, less hermetic than the previous two volumes. Picasso worked on his illustrations in March 1949, adding the opening image 'Tête de nègre' later that year, experimenting with anthropomorphic forms blending humans and plants as well as erotic imagery in a way that beautifully complements Césaire's deployment of landscape imagery in his poems. Véron evokes in Picasso's works their 'nature vigoureuse, souvent anthropomorphique: femme-plante, fleur-sexe, homme-tige' ['vigorous often anthropomorphic nature: woman-plant, flower-sex, man-stem'], an aesthetic that the painter developed in his portrait of Françoise Gilot in 1946 but which also clearly resonates powerfully with the imagery of Césaire's poems.[23]

Césaire's work during this period testifies to the expansion of his cultural dialogue with other writers and artists. His collaboration with Picasso implicitly references the engagement they both had with Lam, and both were also clearly thinking of Apollinaire: Picasso's 'Tête de nègre' is like a mirror image of a portrait he painted at that time of Apollinaire, and references to the latter's poems recur in *Corps perdu*. Césaire's relationship with Breton became increasingly distanced, however, as he embraced Communism, a move that does not fit comfortably with surrealist aesthetics. His great poetic volumes of the period retain their extraordinary, visionary form, though at the same time it is possible to see how his political engagement starts to leave a mark on his poetry. He published two poems in the journal *L'Humanité*, organ of the French Communist Party, in 1949 and 1950, the form of which was much less inspired and original than those of *Soleil cou coupé* and *Corps perdu*. These poems demonstrate the uses of poetry in political activism but fail to display the extraordinary energy and creativity found in Césaire's best-known works. Reading his poetry alongside his political work during this period, however, testifies to the diversification of his interests, and his political activity is strikingly juxtaposed with an evolving aesthetics that reveals both his poetic inventiveness and his awareness of the urgency of political change at that time.

The Bordas edition of the *Cahier*, published in Paris in 1947, provides revealing insight into Césaire's changing aesthetic vision. Despite being published in the same year as the

DEPARTMENTALISATION 113

Brentano's edition, this version underwent significant changes and is clearly the product of Césaire's thinking during the latter part of the 1940s. As Arnold notes, if the Brentano's edition testifies to Césaire's collaboration with Breton, the Bordas edition is the work of the new mayor of Fort-de-France and can be read against the background of the tumultuous political changes to which he was bearing witness.[24] It is this edition that crystallises Césaire's stance as an anticolonial militant, and it would have been this edition that revolutionary thinkers Frantz Fanon and Jean-Paul Sartre read and interpreted as a poetic expression of political revolt. Césaire notably added two new sections, one at the very start and one at the end, before the final strophe leading to the poem's triumphant conclusion. The effect of both is to clarify and intensify the political message of the poem, a change conceived by Arnold as a clear shift away from the spiritual resonances of the *Volontés* and Brentano's editions, though the references to the brutal history of slavery and oppression in those early versions already served to voice Césaire's anticolonial critique.

In the Bordas edition, the poem opens with a furious riposte to figures of authority, addressed using aggressively pejorative slang words: 'va-t-en, lui disais-je, gueule de flic, gueule de vache, va-t-en je déteste les larbins de l'ordre et les hannetons de l'espérance' ['get lost I said you cop face, you pig face, get lost, I hate the flunkies of order and the cockchafers of hope'].[25] The poem bursts into life with this new assertion of revolt, which in turn leads to an unleashing of poetic fury ('je délaçais les monstres' ['I unlaced monsters']) onto the putrefying city languishing under 'un sacré soleil vénérien' ['a blessed venereal sun']. With this addition Césaire introduces the 'je' at a much earlier stage than previously, reinforcing the assertiveness of the poetic voice. He also takes an active stance that contrasts markedly with the passivity in the evocation of the city that follows and that constituted the opening of the *Volontés* and Brentano's versions. At the end of the poem, moreover, Arnold identifies in the added lines clear references to the Cold War ('épervier qui tiens les clefs de l'occident' ['listen you sparrowhawk who hold the keys to the Orient'], 'squale qui veille sur l'occident' ['shark who watches over the West'], 'chien blanc du nord' ['white dog of the north']).[26] Césaire's interest in Communism and in the Soviet Union as offering an alternative political model to that of Western modernity is evident in these lines. The poet also speaks back directly to the slave owner, forcing him to confront the brutal system of transportation of slaves and goods known as the Atlantic triangle: 'et pour ce, Seigneur aux dents blanches, les hommes au cou frêle / reçois et perçois fatal calme triangulaire' ['and for this, Lord, fragile-necked men receive and perceive fatal triangular calm'].[27]

The other significant change is the movement of the section added to Brentano's, which opens with the strophes that make up 'En guise de manifeste littéraire', to a much earlier point in the poem. Césaire now inserts the passage evoking the poet's association with the forests and rivers of the Congo, so that it follows on directly from the passage on Toussaint Louverture and his death in the snow of the Jura. The passage brings in the connection with Africa earlier in the poem, as well as the poet's ensuing address to the 'flics et flicaillons', which uses imagery of madness and irrationality to denounce the barbarity of colonial reason. This inclusion of imagery of resistance earlier in the poem clearly gives it a more focused mission and distracts attention away from the poet's introspective quest and towards the insistence on contestation. The displaced section at the same time includes new lines, notably those repeating the sound 'vroum rooh oh' and which conjure the animals and the elements to join in the revolt: 'à charmer les serpents à conjurer les morts' and 'à contraindre la pluie à contrarier les raz de marée' ['to charm the snakes to conjure up the dead' and 'to force the rain to counteract the tidal waves'].[28] The imagery here seeks to resist death and stagnation, with the repeated sound suggesting a visceral, rhythmic insistence. The opening rebuttal to the police and to the colonial master is extended here, as if the poet draws the landscape in to contribute to this expression of refusal, and cosmic change is framed by this explicit political challenge. The following added strophe juxtaposes an image of the poet as a child with that of a man with a rope around his neck, then that of a man in a circus wearing a crown of thorns. These lines thereby establish the connection between the speaking voice, the history of enslavement, and a biblical scene of torture as if to dramatise the expanded resonance of the poem.

These changes betray Césaire's political preoccupations at the time whilst the text preserves the surrealist experimentation he started with the earlier version and with *Les Armes miraculeuses*. Read alongside his political writings and speeches and alongside *Soleil cou coupé* and *Corps perdu*, the revised poem reveals the at times complementary and at times conflictual layers of Césaire's evolving aesthetic. This period was undoubtedly a turning point, as the explosive, incongruous and at times baffling creations of *Les Armes miraculeuses* give way to a slightly more grounded aesthetic in *Soleil cou coupé*, despite the volume's still defiant embrace of surrealist imagery. *Corps perdu* can be seen as the greatest expression of Césaire's revolt expressed on a cosmic scale, where his creative energy is transcribed most directly and where landscape and the elements play a clear role in the anticolonial rebellion. The Bordas edition of the *Cahier* captures this transition to a more immediate expression of revolt, whilst the poetic quest of the original version and the surrealist experiments of the second remain present. In this way it bridges the anger and disillusionment of 'L'impossible contact' and the inventive power of *Soleil cou coupé*.

Soleil cou coupé

Soleil cou coupé was published in 1948 – just two years after *Les Armes miraculeuses* – by the surrealist publishing house 'K' and was illustrated with engravings on the front and back covers by the abstract artist Hans Hartung. Although a few poems were previously published in Parisian journals, most were freshly written for the anthology, with the result that they were clearly composed very quickly during a period of intense activity on both a creative and a political level. Arnold argues that *Soleil cou coupé* uses more surrealist imagery than any other volume of Césaire's, though as Toumson and Valmore point out, the poems are less abstract than those of *Les Armes miraculeuses* and more often contain references to black history.[29] In this they clearly continue the work of the negritude movement and ally poetic form with the affirmation of anticolonial revolt, while couching this revolt in magical and mythical form rather than as a political ambition.

Furiously visceral, erotic and sensory imagery is combined with both Christian and African spirituality in an astonishingly eclectic expression of rebellion against the history of enslavement. Yet although the poems are startling in their use of incongruous juxtapositions, they are also carefully structured, and the whole volume is neatly unified by the title and the recurrent references to the sun, associated by turns with liberation, revolt and violence. The collection also announces a movement towards lucidity and justice. It opens with 'Magique', where the island is figured with a horrifying image of a death ('vous bêtes qui sifflez sur le visage de cette morte' ['you beasts hissing into the face of this dead woman']) before the magician-poet calls the stars to redress the balance, so that they resurrect the oppressed people and 'réajustent un dieu noir mal né de son tonnerre' ['reinstate a black god ill born of his thunder'].[30] The collection ends, however, with 'Jugement de lumière', which centres on 'un jet d'eau de victorieux soleil / par lequel / justice sera faite' ['a water jet of victorious sun / through which / justice shall be done'], as if the sun's illumination overcomes the darkness against which the stars of 'Magique' had struggled.[31]

Soleil cou coupé is Césaire's largest collection of poetry, and there will be space here to offer a glimpse of just a few of its highlights. The two formally very different 'Lynch' poems provide insight into Césaire's explosive combination of protest

DEPARTMENTALISATION 117

against violence and injustice with poetic experimentation. The first is an outpouring in prose that seems reminiscent of the surrealist method of automatic writing in its piling up of shifting associations around the central term 'lynch'. Yet the poem follows a structure in moving from an ironic rejection of spring as a symbol of awakening to a sequence reimagining lynching and moving towards the poet's apparent self-sacrifice in the hope of the rebirth of a better order. There are no references to concrete acts of lynching and the poem is not a political response to a particular crime. The imagery of the first part evidently connotes violence at once materially and aesthetically: 'le lynch c'est six heures du soir dans la boue des bayous c'est le mouchoir noir agité au haut du mât d'un bateau pirate c'est le point de strangulation de l'ongle au carmin d'une interjection' ['lynch it's 6 p.m. in the mud of the bayou it's a black handkerchief fluttering atop a pirate ship mast it's the strangulation point of a fingernail in the carmine of an interjection'].[32] Yet this is succeeded by an oneiric frenzy of images, some of which are erotic or suggestive of castration, as if the speaker is mutilated or disempowered until the intimation of rebirth at the end, a moment that is also captured through sexualised imagery of surging and spilling. The prose shifts from brutality to wild, delirious and at times blasphemous imagery (lynch is 'le sourire bleu d'un dragon ennemi des anges' ['the blue smile of a dragon enemy of angels']) to erotic protest (lynch is an 'aimable compagnon bel oeil giclé large bouche muette' ['loveable companion beautiful squirted eye huge mouth mute']), in order to finish 'dans la meurtrière sommaire de mon ouïe assassinée' ['in the succinct murderess-hole of my assassinated hearing'].[33] Far more than a reflection on race crime, then, this profusive prose poem recasts protest as this surrealist refusal of expectations and as an irreverent affirmation of sexuality and rebirth. Intriguingly, 'Lynch II', printed much later in the collection, is a much more succinct explosion, taking the form of nine lines of verse conjuring the shaking of fists against a broken sky before protesting against a history of silencing: 'un perfide chant vivant / dans les ruines indestructibles de son silence' ['a perfidious chant alive / in the indestructible ruins of his silence'].[34]

'Le coup de couteau du soleil dans le dos des villes surprises' directly references the title of the collection, though here the sun is not the victim but the aggressor acting in the name of change. Césaire again dramatises a movement from oppression to renewal, couched throughout in terms that imagine the human in relation to animals and elements calling for transformation. The poem has two parts, the first consisting of three visions of monstrous, hybridised creatures bearing marks of suffering, followed by a prophesy in the second part. James Arnold shows how the poem closely references passages from the Book of Revelations and indeed uncovers very clear parallels in the imagery which conspire to intensify Césaire's 'prophetic and apocalyptic design'.[35] The animals of the first part are surrealist creations that combine attributes of multiple creatures at once to suggest a form of monstrosity and to evoke connections between species, hinting at the transmission of human suffering as a result of oppression into the animal world. The first animal has 'un corps de crocodile des pattes d'équidé une tête de chien' ['a crocodile body equine feet a dog's head'], but on closer look bears scars, the signs of 'un corps longtemps soumis à d'obscures épreuves' ['a body long subjected to obscure ordeals'].[36] The second creature is a hairless dog lost in cities that have not been rebuilt after destruction by a volcano, and Césaire clearly refers here to the eruption of Mount Pelée and the destruction of St Pierre in Martinique in 1902. The third is an earthworm that continues to grow, as if to counter the preceding images of destruction with one of defiant rebirth. The next section seems to reclaim the agency of the poet's voice, noting first the apathy of the landscape 'dans une clairière de paupières sommaires, velours' ['in a glade of pithy, velvet eyelids'] but moving towards an increasing expression of refusal: 'le bariolage sauta livré par les veines d'une géante nocture' ['the medley of colours exploded surrendered by the veins of a nocturnal giantess'].[37] Césaire also combines the biblical intertext with a reference to the

Voodoo 'vever' or mandala, a sign sprinkled on the ground using cornmeal, here used as if to herald the change foretold in the final line of the poem: 'nous fondîmes sur demain avec dans nos poches le coup de couteau très violent du soleil dans le dos des villes surprises' ['we built on tomorrow having pocketed the sun's very violent knife-stab in the back of the surprised cities'].[38] Césaire's mixed spiritual traditions contribute to the powerful vision for destruction, directed here against cities, perhaps associated with modernity, subjected to the explosive defiance of the elements.

The figure of the sun returns in 'Défaire et refaire le soleil', a much more rhythmic, incantatory poem in which the denunciation of past violence and the poet's demand for change are expressed more directly. The first part is a sequence of lines introduced with the term 'demeure' ['dwelling'] used in an anaphora that forges a powerful rhythmic force and portrays images connoting oppression in quick succession, sometimes directly and sometimes indirectly. With its staccato repetition, the form contrasts with the seemingly uncontrolled prose of 'Lynch', though the overall structure again moves from the suggestion of past violence to defiance. At the end, the poet shifts away from this staccato rhythm and adopts a liberated prose form that perhaps mimics the action of breaking free. He addresses the jailer in a tone reminiscent of the Rebelle of *Et les chiens se taisaient*, and heralds a new environment in which to dwell, one of freedom and fertility, agency and rebirth: 'demeure faite de votre impuissance de la puissance de mes gestes simples de la liberté de mes spermatozoïdes demeure matrice noire tendue de courtine rouge le seul reposoir que je bénisse d'où je peux regarder le monde éclater au choix de mon silence' ['dwelling made of your impotence of the power of my simple acts of freedom of my spermatozoa dwelling black womb hung with a red curtain sole altar I may bless while watching the world explode as my silence chooses'].[39]

The anaphora of 'demeure' is also used in 'Demeure I', which speaks back to 'Défaire et refaire le soleil' with its riposte to the jailer, and where the imagery of chains and yokes more directly connotes the enslaved past. The remaking envisaged at the end of this poem again references the volcano and its self-destructive reconnection with the sea in a cleansing gesture. The recrafting of dwelling is conjured a further time in 'Demeure antipode', another surrealist creation again using apocalyptic biblical imagery and in which the elements reshape the world and work with the demiurgic power to drive transformation: 'luciole et eau je me construirai moi-même en petites gouttes d'eau de feu trop belles pour un autre architecte' ['firefly and water I shall assemble myself in little drops of water of fire too beautiful for any other architect'].[40] The poem ends with revolver shots suggestive of the poet's self-sacrifice, and again the sun – here 'le méridien sans ombre' ['the shadowless meridian'] – seems to watch over the scene. The extended web of metaphors of the sun, the volcano, the apocalypse, self-sacrifice and rebirth, weaves itself through these poems as if to re-enact the transformative drama of negritude.

This network of metaphors is expanded further with 'Couteaux midi', the title of which resonates with 'Le coup de couteau du soleil dans le dos des villes surprises'. The inclusion of this poem in the exhibition at the Galérie Maeght is indicative of its significance as a prime example of Césaire's use of surrealist aesthetics in the revolutionary demand for freedom. The opening image of black revolution uprooting trees on the Champ de Mars turns habitual symbolism on its head by figuring the white coloniser as a tree to be displaced. The French 'ils tirent à blanc' is translated by Arnold and Eshleman as 'they fire blanks', but it is important that the French could also suggest that white people are the target.[41] It is the midday sun that crystallises the rebellion, however, as the poet invokes, 'Midi? Oui, Midi qui disperse dans le ciel la ouate trop complaisante qui capitonne mes paroles et où mes cris se prennent' ['Noon? Yes, Noon dispersing in the sky the too complacent cotton wool that muffles my words and traps my screams'].[42] The noon or sun listens and

DEPARTMENTALISATION 121

bears witness to the poet's cursing before unleashing movement, conjured here as trains running along hands, as if bodies had been hindered and are now being reinvested with dynamism.

After two dense paragraphs of surrealist prose, the poem breaks into verse, as storm and wind are invoked to join in the fury. The poet's screams of riposte are also punctuated with calls to the African filao tree, known for growing in cemeteries, so thought to connect with the world of the dead. The anaphora of 'filao' contributes to the sense of the poet's spitting in the face of the coloniser and the slave owner. This furious invective then shifts in the next part of the poem to anaphora around the word 'doux', as if the poet moves from anger to sweet triumph, captured in particular by the line 'doux comme le parfum de l'étoffe rouge sur la respiration bruyante d'une peau noire' ['sweet as the perfume of red fabric on the heavy breathing of a black skin'].[43] Red here connotes life, and the line is rich in erotic imagery celebrating sexual energy, though the colour red is also suggestive of blood, as if black skin is given new life after the brutality to which it has been subjected. This metaphor is extended through the poet's affirmation, once again, of his upright stance, 'debout dans mes blessures où mon sang bat contre les fûts du naufrage' ['upright in my wounds where my blood beats against the shafts of shipwreck']. He also re-enacts here his role as spokesman, speaking for the people's feet, hands, breath and faces, honouring the bodies of the oppressed without rancour, shame and distrust. At the end of the poem, simple anaphoric lines detailing this stance are succeeded by a more extended prose sentence evoking black people searching in the dust for gems and 'l'ardoise lamelleuse dont les sorciers font l'intime férocité des étoiles' ['the fissile slate out of which sorcerers make the intimate ferocity of stars']. Out of the destruction of the past, out of the dust, there emerge magical flashes of light in a further image of fulgurating renewal.

Alongside these surrealist visions of revolution and freedom, *Soleil cou coupé* contains poems more clearly directed towards

122 DEPARTMENTALISATION

Africa, among which the most notable is perhaps 'A l'Afrique', dedicated to Wifredo Lam. A revised version of a poem first published in *Poésie* in 1946, 'A l'Afrique' in *Soleil cou coupé* is distinctive in introducing a concrete geographical reference to Africa of the sort that, as Pierre Laforgue notes, was absent from the poems of *Les Armes miraculeuses*.[44] The poem opens with the image of a peasant striking the soil ('paysan frappe le sol de ta daba' ['peasant strike the soil with your pickhoe']), the 'daba' referring to a tool used in West Africa, only for this act to unleash a mythic past.[45] The poem then evokes a sequence of signifiers of a dying civilisation, referencing, as Arnold suggests, the seven plagues of the Book of Revelation.[46] These images project the poem into the realm of the mythological, as Africa is referenced only through the title and through the reference to the 'daba', and the poem otherwise tells a broader tale of destruction and rebirth. The sequence detailing stages of extinction is punctuated by the incantatory repetition of the image of the peasant striking the soil, giving way to erotic imagery suggestive of new life and again linking human with landscape:

> Attente passementaire de lamproies j'attends d'une attente
> vulnéraire une
> campagne qui naîtra aux oreilles de ma compagne et verdira
> à son sexe
> le ventre de ma compagne c'est le coup de tonnerre du
> beau temps
> les cuisses de ma compagne jouent les arbres tombés le
> long de sa démarche

> [passemented lamprey expectation I await with vulnerary
> expectations a
> countryside to be born in my mistress's ears and to turn
> verdant in her sex
> the belly of my mistress is a thunderbolt of fine weather
> the thighs of my mistress play at being trees fallen along
> her stride][47]

DEPARTMENTALISATION   123

Here the poet anticipates healing created by the wedding of his mistress with the land, as if sexual energy also brings about activity in the elements. The merging of the poet and the woman also seems to return both to the land, as they are compared in a chaotic sequence to guavas, seaweed, seed, a bubble, recollection and a precatory tree. This reincarnation then brings the poet back to the Caribbean, as the wave in which the lovers are swallowed serves to 'parfaire une île rebelle à naître' ['perfect an island rebelling against birth'].[48] The recrafting of the island landscape is coupled with a rejection of Christianity, moreover, and an invocation of the Babylonian Mother-Goddess Ishtar, associated with storms and rain but also with fertility. The end of the poem returns to the peasant tilling the soil, this time evoking the poet himself as his son, and suggesting awakening through imagery of the 'iguanes inassoupis' ['undozing iguanas'] and of a woman who promises a future of friendship.[49] The poem testifies to Césaire's interest in Lam in its interweaving of human, plants and elements in the process of renewal, while at the same time suggesting through the image of the peasant a rebellion against a history of submission.

The poems discussed so far explore extended webs of metaphor, weaving together apocalypse and rebirth, destruction and renewal, and human and landscape. Passages of irregular verse are interspersed with sections written in a form closer to prose, where images are connected without punctuation and without being divided into neat syntactic units. The form across the volume expresses extraordinary creative freedom and energy, even as the reworking of images and tropes across poems establishes a sense of unity. The proliferating style of the poems referenced above, however, is offset by shorter, sometimes more rhythmical pieces, one example of which is 'Barbare', which serves as a fitting prelude to 'Corps perdu'. Anticipating 'Mot', the opening poem in 'Corps perdu' in which Césaire seizes and reinvents the word 'nègre', 'Barbare' too reappropriates this derogatory term and makes of it a signifier of resistance: 'Barbare / du langage sommaire / et nos

124   DEPARTMENTALISATION

faces belles comme le vrai pouvoir opératoire / de la néga-
tion' ['Barbarity / of rudimentary language / and our faces
beautiful as the true operative power / of negation'].[50] Once
again Césaire uses anaphora to track the evolution and transformation of meaning, and here the structure is staccato and
succinct as if to convey an acerbic message of rebellion. The
poems of 'Corps perdu' are all longer than 'Barbare' but use
fragmented and staccato forms to articulate this most direct
expression of negritude revolt.

Corps perdu

The ten at once explosive and highly readable poems of *Corps
perdu*, juxtaposed with the illustrations by Picasso, make this
volume one of Césaire's most powerful poetic works. Written
over a relatively short period, the collection is more unified
in style than both *Les Armes miraculeuses* and *Soleil cou coupé*.
The poems are roughly similar in length to one another
(with the exception of the slightly longer concluding poem,
'Dit d'errance'), and consist of brief punchy lines arranged
in rhythmical forms with none of the proliferating prose of
the earlier volumes. They are also organised in a tight structure tracking a clear movement, as the opening poem 'Mot',
performing the rebirth of the word 'nègre', progresses to
utterance in 'Dit d'errance'. As James Arnold notes, the poems
testify to Césaire's abandonment of the quest for spiritual
transcendence in their simpler and more explicit assertions of
resistance to oppression and injustice.[51]

   There is, however, perhaps some irony in the presentation of this assertion of revolt and uprising in the form of
an expensive volume of artworks. The first publication of
'Corps perdu' with Picasso's illustrations consisted of just
219 luxury volumes and would have been inaccessible to most
Martinicans, in whose name the poet was seeking to speak.
The artworks nevertheless weave intriguingly through the
volume, not so much serving as precise illustrations of particu-

lar poems but rather showcasing both the poet and the artist's preoccupations with the suffering and self-affirmation of the body, tinged with erotic references and shaped by the connection between humans and plants. The volume opens with Picasso's stunning 'Tête de nègre', the disembodied head of a man wearing a crown of thorns, aptly anticipating the conjuring of black punishment as well as self-affirmation in 'Mot' and throughout. The image also references the volume's title, which suggests both decapitation and self-loss, though 'à corps perdu' can also be translated as 'at breakneck speed', as if to herald the energetic and dynamic movement of resistance out of past acts of violence. 'Tête de nègre' would be displayed at the *Premier congrès des écrivains et artistes noirs* in Paris in 1956, further linking it with black cultural activism.

The volume opens with the poem simply entitled 'Mot', referencing the brutality and dynamic reclaiming of that contested word 'nègre'. The poem is prefaced by an aquatint etching by Picasso resembling a mask, with 'mot' inscribed in the centre, and set alongside two etchings conjuring the sexual reproduction of a plant, again not directly indexing the poem but drawing out Césaire's aesthetics combining erotic energy with a vision of the reinvention of the human through its integration with the organic growth of plants. 'Mot' is less steeped in ecology than many of Césaire's poems, but can rather be read as the very poetic performance of Lamine Senghor's reclaiming of the word 'nègre' as 'a watchword' and 'a rallying cry', as the poet moves from a position of disablement and oppression to recraft the word as a living signifier. The poem starts from the poetic self, but references a history of silencing and self-loss against which the poet himself and his people more broadly continue to struggle:

le rare hoquet d'un ultime spasme délirant
ma face perdue ta face éperdue
ensemble fondu intimes confondues
toute chose miroitante toute chose clapotante
entre nos corps balançés par naufrage

126 DEPARTMENTALISATION

[the rare hiccup of an ultimate raving spasm
my face lost your face distraught
fused together intimate confused
every glistening thing every lapping thing
between our bodies rocked by shipwreck][52]

Before the word itself is uttered, the poet unleashes a non-verbal gasp in the name of the lost bodies of slaves as they were destroyed during the Middle Passage. Out of this history of violence and suffering, however, emerges the dynamic movement of the word, 'vibre mot' ['keep vibrating word'], a sonorous, lived vibration fighting against the imagery of containment. The word itself is not used until the second page, but is recorded first for its dynamic vibration, heralding its capacity for change, until it explodes on the second page: 'le mot nègre / sorti tout armé du hurlement / d'une fleur vénéneuse' ['the word nègre / emerged fully armed from the howling / of a venomous flower'].[53] The poet then unleashes the word by repeating it, each time succeeded by imagery suggestive of the brutal treatment of slaves: 'le mot nègre / tout pouacre de parasites / le mot nègre / tout plein de brigands qui rodent / de mères qui crient / d'enfants qui pleurent' ['the word nègre / all filthy with parasite / the word nègre / loaded with roaming bandits / with screaming mothers / with crying children'].[54] Again Césaire uses anaphora not just for emphasis but to track the movement and recreation of meaning. Here, the ghastly history of the term 'nègre' is laid bare as increasingly disturbing images emerge under its banner, as if to tear it open to reveal the layers of horror that are covered by this single word. At the end of the poem, however, the poet reminds us that words themselves can be made into forces for counter-attack: 'et comme le mot soleil est un claquement de balles / et comme le mot nuit un taffetas qu'on déchire' ['and as the word sun is a banging of bullets / and as the word night is a ripping of taffeta'].[55] The sun is here a signifier of freedom and revolt, and its illumination of the history of violence fires a bullet at the slave owner, whilst the darkness of the night is ripped open. Finally, out of this imagery of destruction there emerges a new meaning:

> le mot nègre
> > dru savez-vous
> du tonnerre d'un été
> > que s'arrogent
> > > des libertés incrédules

> [the word nègre
> > dense, right?
> from the thunder of a summer
> > appropriated by
> > > incredulous liberties][56]

Thick with the connotations of enslavement, the word here seems to galvanise that thickness and energy as if in a thunderstorm that unleashes anger to clear the sky for cleansing. Having voiced this brutal word and laid bare the horrors it contains, the poet heralds its new provision of 'libertés incrédules' – incredulousness suggesting an unanticipated release or a freedom not yet imagined.

If 'Mot' opens *Corps perdu* with this vibrant dramatisation of the rebirth of the term 'nègre', 'Corps perdu' can be found at the centre of the volume and displays Césaire's most powerful and dramatic self-assertion as the lyric voice of negritude. Indeed, Clayton Eshleman describes the poem as 'the most jarring rollercoaster ride of the negritudinal self, turning and being turned by inner and exterior self and social forces'.[57] If 'Mot' records the explosive reclaiming of the word, 'Corps perdu' combines this aesthetics of eruption with a vision of the recreation of the self, staged through the summoning of and fusion with the land and the elements. The Picasso etching that prefaces the poem is a simple pared-down image of a body with a curious triangular shape, whilst two further abstract etchings are set alongside the poem, one suggestive of a human face printed onto a leaf. The poem opens with the poet's identification of his voice with those of the volcano Krakatoa, the monsoon and speedy dog Laelaps (whose name means 'storm wind'), to infiltrate his poetic stance with this elemental energy. These opening lines are an explosive juxtaposition of sounds, where nouns function as verbs to foreground the aesthetics of dynamic action:[58]

> Moi qui Krakatoa
> moi qui tout mieux que mousson
> moi qui poitrine ouverte
> moi qui laïlape
> moi qui bêle mieux que cloaque
> moi qui hors de gamme

> [I who Krakatoa
> I who everything better than monsoon
> I who open chest
> I who lailaps
> I who bleat better than cloaca
> I who outside the musical scale][59]

The poem then proceeds through three stages, starting with the poet's self-dissolution and blending with the earth, 'jusqu'à me perdre tomber / dans la vivante semoule d'une terre bien ouverte' ['to the point of losing myself falling / into the living semolina of a well-opened earth']. Here, after the demiurgic power of the opening lines, the poet's voice is humble and expresses a sense of exile and self-loss in a disordered ecological environment, though the poet at the same time attempts to grasp the connectedness between the elements within that environment in a vision of 'RENCONTRE BIEN TOTALE' [SPLENDID TOTAL ENCOUNTER]. Next, from this state of disorientation and dispossession in the land, the poet gradually awakens, noting the loss of a connection with the past (suggestive of Africa) and searching for roots but mimicking the posture of the slave at once labouring and railing against his position:

Ma terrible crête de racines ancreuses
qui cherchent où se prendre
choses je sonde je sonde
moi le porte-faix je suis porte-racines
et je pèse et je force et j'arcane

[my terrible crest of anchor-like roots
looking for a place to take hold
things I probe I probe
I the street-porter I am a roots-porter
and I bear down and I force and I arcane][60]

The poet insists 'j'omphale j'omphale' ['I omphale I omphale'] in a polysemic reference conjuring both the Greek term for the navel of the universe, as if the poet reaches into the very depths of the earth, and the Lydian queen who enslaved Hercules, connoting an inversion of the relationship between master and slave. Embracing the wind in this endeavour to bond with the earth, however, the poet then once again hears the murmuring of that brutal word brought by the wind: 'nègre nègre nègre depuis le fond du ciel immémorial' ['nègre nègre nègre from the depths of the timeless sky'].[61] The word is followed with imagery of horses and dogs, like those that chase the runaway slaves, yet the poet again turns this history of violence into a cry for freedom, as he voices the revolt of the slave whilst demanding an upheaval that will be so far-reaching as to be recorded in the cosmos. Once again, the aesthetic is explosive, disruptive, shattering: 'je me lèverai un cri et si violent / que tout entier j'éclabousserai le ciel' ['I shall raise so violent a cry / that I shall splatter the entire sky'].[62] But it also blurs human and nonhuman in calling for the transformation of the land at the same time as the rebellion of the people, in a vision of complete renewal that the poet himself engenders: 'je commanderai aux îles d'exister' ['I shall command the islands to exist']. This line is an extraordinary assertion of poetic power and can be seen as the apotheosis of Césaire's vision for negritude in its reinvention of the Caribbean islands and their people ravaged by colonial history. Here, Césaire moves away from the vibrant mythical and spiritual synergy found in earlier volumes to a more immediate transformation, an urgent demand for change in the here and now.

'Mot' and 'Corps perdu' move from histories of violence, slavery and self-loss to confident expressions of poetic reinvention, and plumb the depths of the suffering of the poet and his people to voice their rebirth. The final poem in *Corps perdu*, 'Dit d'errance', is an equally powerful expression of resistance, and at the same time it hints at the incipient doubts of the poet towards the seemingly demiurgic power he claims elsewhere in the volume. The poem is prefaced by an aquatint etching by Picasso of stick figures seeming to float aimlessly, and then printed alongside abstract images suggestive of vegetation and insect life. The figures in the aquatint etching seem lost, however, referencing the wandering referred to in the poem's title, and if the imagery of vegetation often connotes in Césaire's aesthetic a rediscovery of selfhood through landscape and ecology, here the abstract images convey less confidence about the integration of the human. The 'dit' referred to in the poem's title, moreover, references a medieval form of spoken poem, which would tend to use the first person and include observation and reflection. Césaire's use of the form betrays an attachment to European poetic form even as he deploys it to record the colonial ravaging of Caribbean islands. The poem opens with imagery of mutilation, expressed here in much less chaotic form than in poems such as 'Lynch I' in *Soleil cou coupé*, initially using lines of six, nine and twelve syllables as if to approximate to an ordered verse form, though this sense of order dissolves after the first few lines:

> Tout ce qui jamais fut déchiré
> en moi s'est déchiré
> tout ce qui jamais fut mutilé
> en moi s'est mutilé
> au milieu de l'assiette de son souffle dénudé
> le fruit coupé de la lune toujours en allée

[Everything that ever was torn
in me has been torn apart
everything that ever was mutilated
in me has been mutilated
in the middle of the plate stripped of its breath
the cut fruit of the moon forever on its way][63]

If many of the other poems in the volume express anger and revolt, the tone here is rather one of disillusionment. It is the moon – and not the sun – whose throat is cut here, and the upshot of the violence is less an assertion of revolt than a sense of disorientation. Later, Césaire again conjures imagery of the brutal treatment of slaves and of the very cosmos ('ciel éclaté courbe écorchée / de dos d'esclaves fustigés / et des yeux grands des exilés' ['exploded sky flayed curve / of flogged slaves' backs / and wide-open eyes of exiles']).[64] But the poet seems less to reclaim black history than to doubt his ability to access this brutal past ('grimoire fermé mots oubliés / j'interroge mon passé muet' ['grimoire closed words forgotten / I question my mute past']).[65] There follows an anaphora redefining the word 'île' ['island'], conjuring its destruction and tentatively linking it with Africa through references to Benin and to Ife, a sacred place according to Yoruba mythology, yet the evocation of the island as a widow suggests separation from these putative origins. There is a hint of self-ironisation in the lines 'j'ai inventé un culte secret / mon soleil est celui que toujours on attend' ['I invented a secret cult / my sun is the one always awaited'], suggesting both that his poetic vision has not been shared and that the symbol of freedom never arrived. If rebirth is suggested through references to Isis and Osiris and through the figure of the phoenix, the trajectory from descent to recreation is evidently less assured here. The poet also wonders 'serais-je le jouet de la nigromance' ['might I be the sport of nigromancy'], a possible reference to negritude as black magic, a cult form in which the poet himself ended up the victim. The more ordered, though not neatly structured, form of 'Dit d'errance' coupled with its imagery of self-loss and self-doubt indicates a shift in this last utterance of *Corps perdu* and signals the start of the poet's movement away from his vision for demiurgic poetic power.

James Arnold reads 'Dit d'errance' as an abandonment of the belief in poetry as revolution. The closing assertion 'j'abats les arbres du Paradis' ['I fell the trees of Paradise'] can be seen to affirm the destruction of the image of a promised land, yet in the penultimate line the poet still crafts himself as a regal figure: 'je suis sultan de Babiloine' ['I am sultan of Babiloine']. 'Babiloine' is the medieval spelling of Babylon, affiliating the poet with a pre-Christian era and perhaps suggesting the Tower of Babel and the vision for a unified humanity that was halted with the multiplication of languages. The combination of imagery of rebirth and disillusionment, of self-doubt and self-assertion, makes 'Dit d'errance' a complex, highly eclectic, transitional poem. It reorients the poetic power envisioned through *Corps perdu* to anticipate its recrafting in subsequent volumes, where Césaire's aesthetics are less explosive, less visionary, less experimental. If the late 1940s saw Césaire's entry into politics and the profound dissatisfaction with the political arena that followed, his poetry at that time testifies to this highly energised but highly shifting period. It was perhaps during these years that Césaire was the most prolific, speaking regularly at the Assemblée Nationale whilst producing some of his richest poetry. Although much of the poetry of this period testifies to this extraordinary energy, the closing lines of 'Dit d'errance' suggest that this energy would soon change in character and be redirected.

4

The Political Upheavals of the 1950s
'History I tell of the awakening of Africa'

The 1950s was a period of dramatic change for France and its colonies. This was the decade when France's colonial ambitions crumbled, when French colonies in Africa claimed their independence, and when the status of the French Antilles became a question of heightened tension. This was also a period of intense activity and change for Césaire, who found his previous ideals shattered and whose aspirations for Martinique were forced to change tack along with his aesthetics and his vision for cultural practice. Roger Toumson and Simonne Henry-Valmore comment on how in 1950 Césaire's career was flourishing: his authority in Martinique was uncontested and he was brimming with creative energy, well-connected with both the Communist intelligentsia and with major avant-garde writers and artists. And yet throughout the decade, 'tout semble basculer' ['everything seems to be overturned']. Césaire's beliefs and practices were tested on multiple levels, and these challenges meant that, 'Orphée se change en Prométhée' ['Orphée transforms into Prometheus'], the poet became a political actor.[1] Toumson and Henry-Valmore first cite as central to this sense of crisis Césaire's divorce from his wife Suzanne in 1963, and yet during the 1950s Césaire's other connections were also tested and he essentially had to recraft himself and his political and cultural

134 THE POLITICAL UPHEAVALS OF THE 1950S

role. Having fought during the late 1940s for better provision for Martinicans after departmentalisation, he became thoroughly disillusioned, and inspired by African independence movements, sought greater autonomy from France. At the same time, he became increasingly dissatisfied with the French Communist Party and ultimately severed his ties with them in 1956. This was the same year that Césaire published a new edition of *Cahier d'un retour au pays natal*, in which the poem's African and anticolonial resonances are foregrounded. This shift gave way to a new, more direct politically contestatory aesthetic in the poetic volume *Ferrements*, published in 1960.

The explosion in Césaire's anticolonial rhetoric and stance began with the publication in 1950 of one of his best-known and most cited works, *Discours sur le colonialisme*, at the foundation of which was the 1948 essay 'L'Impossible contact', now considerably extended and developed. The 1950 edition was published by Réclame, who were associated with the Communist Party, and Césaire added a further thirty-eight pages to the eleven that had been printed in *Chemins du monde* in 1948. This version did not merely stick to generalities but attacked key parliamentary figures and denounced the violent repression of anticolonial revolts in Madagascar and Indochina. Its militant style also contributed to what Romuald Fonkoua sees as a veritable popularisation of Césaire's work, as the wide circulation of the text in the Caribbean was supported by the Communist Party in Martinique, who printed extracts in their journal *Justice*.[2] A further edition was published by Présence Africaine in 1955, including another fifteen pages with some more detailed references to the horrors of colonial history, a critique of the French thinker Roger Caillois and a homage to the Senegalese anthropologist Cheikh Anta Diop's *Nations nègres et culture*. The emphasis in this final edition shifted slightly away from Communism and towards increased attention to Africa, in line with editor Alioune Diop's vision for the press.

In the 1950 version and again in 1955, Césaire clearly vented his fury towards the hypocrisy of the French bour-

THE POLITICAL UPHEAVALS OF THE 1950S   135

geoisie and French humanist thought. If the *Chemins du monde* article sketched out his anticolonial critique, the 1950 edition was, in James Arnold's terms, a 'rhetorical firework', whilst the 1955 version sharpened its political actuality.[3] The work in all its incarnations was inflammatory and foreshadowed both Césaire's abandonment of his belief in departmentalisation and his evolution of a more militant poetic practice. Whilst at the Assemblée Nationale he had been arguing for specific improvements in living conditions for Martinicans, in the *Discours* he voiced a damning critique that went to the core of French culture, as he later recounted: 'I put everything into it and expressed all my resentment. It was like a pamphlet and a bit like a provocation. It was to some extent for me the opportunity to say everything I did not manage to say on the platform of the Assemblée Nationale'.[4]

The text opens with a vilification of the idea of 'civilisation', the hypocritical belief that France's 'mission civilisatrice' bestows its beneficent principles on the colonies. Added in 1950, the opening lines have a carefully crafted tripartite structure laying bare the failings of this myth and setting the tone for the essay's acerbic denunciation of French ideology in sweeping terms:

> A civilization that proves incapable of solving the problems it creates is a decadent civilization.
> A civilization that chooses to close its eyes to its most crucial problems is a stricken civilization.
> A civilization that uses its principles for trickery and deceit is a dying civilization.[5]

Césaire goes on to condemn outright the violence of European colonialism, asserting that *'Europe is indefensible'*, as is testified by the brutality with which anticolonial protests in Indochina, Madagascar, Africa and the Antilles were met. The coloniser is himself dehumanised by these acts of violence despite his ostensible pursuit of civilisation: 'without his being aware of it, he has a Hitler inside him'.[6] He is a

136   THE POLITICAL UPHEAVALS OF THE 1950S

hypocrite who can tolerate violence against other peoples but is only horrified when it turns against the white man. Césaire quotes as an example of this hypocrisy Ernest Renan, a thinker associated with nationalism and humanism, but who he shows clearly advocates domination rather than equality and upholds a belief in racial hierarchy. There follows a sequence of quotations from French thinkers, such as Albert Sarraut, R. P. Barde and R. P. Muller, all insisting on white supremacy and drawing distinctions between civilised and supposedly barbarous peoples. Césaire adds to this critique a series of references to particular colonial atrocities, such as those undertaken during the conquest of Algeria: 'these heads of men, these collections of ears, these burned houses, these Gothic invasions, this steaming blood, these cities that evaporate at the edge of the sword'.[7] The upshot is that, in treating the colonised like a beast, the coloniser is himself transformed into a beast.

Colonialism also, according to Césaire, destroys local cultures. As we saw in 'L'Impossible contact', colonialism reifies colonised cultures, and capitalism replaces their communitarian, democratic and fraternal structures. Césaire takes the risk of idealising precolonial cultures here, celebrating their naturalness and harmoniousness, but makes the point in order deliberately to undermine the idea of progress on which the colonial mission was built. His intermittent eulogies of precolonial culture could equally be read, as Michael Rothberg suggests, to anticipate the stereotypes of colonial discourse, as if to disorient the reader and to force us to question our assumptions about both progress and regression.[8] Césaire then accuses various parliamentarians for the brutal suppression of the insurrection in Madagascar in 1947, listing ministers by name to make his political point crystal clear, before condemning the connection between these atrocities and French humanist thought. An extraordinary passage vilifies in an explosive list the mean-spirited proponents of European knowledge, with journalists, academics, ethnographers and theologians caricatured in monstrous terms alongside governors and politicians. A hyperbolic panoply of

THE POLITICAL UPHEAVALS OF THE 1950S 137

grotesque colonial sympathisers exemplifies Césaire's impassioned rhetoric at its height, and he concludes by dismissing them all for their charlatanism: 'sweep out all the obscurers, all the inventors of subterfuges, the charlatans and tricksters, the dealers in gobbledygook'.[9] The Belgian ethnographer Placide Tempels, who set out to understand Bantu philosophy, is then denounced for maintaining the hierarchy between Bantu and European culture, and the French psychoanalyst Octave Mannoni is condemned as racist for his theory of the complicity of the Malagasy in their own servility. Writers such as Balzac, Baudelaire and Lautréamont are cited for their depictions of the rotting at the heart of French society, before Césaire launches in the 1955 edition into his critique of Roger Caillois' defence of the notion of Western rationalism. This explosive tirade concludes with the warning that Europe will be destroyed if it does not jettison this supremacist ideology. Césaire calls not for a revolution in European methods but for *Revolution*, meaning the definitive substitution of the proletariat for the bourgeoisie. If in 1955, the more precise references to Africa and comments on Diop diluted some of the Communist rhetoric of the 1950 *Discours*, its conclusion retains this clearly Marxist influence.

Césaire's *Discours sur le colonialisme* is a rhetorical *tour de force*. There may be little consideration of particular experiences of colonialism, and the form of the new society he demands in the wake of colonialism remains unsubstantiated. But the text is a powerfully ambitious and broad-brush excoriation of colonialism, capitalism and bourgeois thought, fuelled by its author's witnessing of anticolonial revolts in Africa and Asia. Whilst the 1950 edition had a relatively modest impact, the 1955 version of the essay created shock waves in France whilst inspiring anticolonialists across the world. In the immediate aftermath of its publication, Yves Florenne and Roger Caillois responded furiously to Césaire's critique of their work with an article published in *Le Monde* on 25 April 1955 in which they denounced Césaire himself as racist.[10] Conversely, in a testimony to the text's inspirational force, Frantz Fanon opened

138   THE POLITICAL UPHEAVALS OF THE 1950S

the introduction of his 1952 denunciation of French racism, *Peau noire, masques blancs*, with a citation from the *Discours*. He referenced in addition Césaire's insistence on the presence of Nazism in European thought and developed his critique of Octave Mannoni's concept of the dependency complex of the colonised in his chapter 'Du prétendu complexe de dépendence du colonisé' later in the same work. Fanon also repeatedly evoked the reification and paralysis of colonised culture in his 1961 volume *Les Damnés de la terre* in terms that clearly recall Césaire's 'thingification' in the *Discours*. More recently, the power of Césaire's vision and rhetoric is exemplified in Nelson Mandela's observation after his liberation that the text helped to shape his struggle against Apartheid in South Africa.[11] The controversy of the *Discours* lives on, moreover, as it was proposed as a set text for the French baccalauréat in 1994, but it had to be withdrawn because of the tension this caused at the Assemblée Nationale. On 23 February 2005, the French passed a law that required teachers to emphasise the positive benefits of colonialism and of the French presence abroad when teaching colonial history. In response to the law, Césaire refused to meet Nicolas Sarkozy during a planned visit to Martinique in 2005, and the visit was cancelled whilst thousands demonstrated in the streets of Fort-de-France.

The militancy of *Discours sur le colonialisme* was accompanied during the early 1950s by a turbulent series of political interventions by Césaire, where the sweeping rhetoric of the *Discours* is complemented by more focused and yet increasingly frustrated demands for global justice as well as for equality in Martinique. After his return to Martinique in 1950, Césaire did not speak at the Assemblée Nationale until 1952, but he was actively involved in city politics in Fort-de-France and with the Communist Federation of Martinique. He wrote frequently for *Justice*, notably voicing his critique of Harry Truman's support for the use of the atomic bomb in the Korean conflict if necessary and defending the pursuit of peace. In December 1950 he gave a speech for the bicentenary of the birth of Abbé Grégoire, who had campaigned for the

THE POLITICAL UPHEAVALS OF THE 1950S   139

abolition of slavery at the time of the 1789 revolution and after its reinstatement in 1802. Césaire's speech praised the lucidity and lyricism of Grégoire's defence of black people in *De la littérature des nègres*, published in 1808, and insisted that it continues to speak to all colonists, all racists and all those who attack and oppress others. He continued to write in support of Martinicans' demands for equality, moreover, supporting the strikes in March 1951 and condemning the repression of workers protesting for reasonable pay. In the legislative elections of June 1951, he again campaigned for economic justice for Martinicans, demanding specific measures to address the difference in provision between Martinique and France, and denouncing the systemic inequality of French colonialism. He was comfortably re-elected as Deputy, though would return to the Assemblée Nationale only in November 1952, when he spoke up about the need for the reconstruction of housing in Martinique and for proper urban planning and development. Re-elected again in April 1953, he returned in June 1953 to articulate a broader attack at the Assemblée Nationale against departmentalisation and against France's failure to deliver on its promises, deploying his incendiary rhetoric in all its force:

> The successive governments that have ruled France since 1947 have hurried to do nothing more than to empty the law of 19th March 1946 of its content, to denature and mutilate it, and it is in this way that the old colonies of Martinique, Guadeloupe, Réunion and Guiana have become caricatures of French departments; yes, caricatures of French departments, because against a background of terrible poverty, economic stagnation and unemployment, we have seen the reappearance, rejuvenated and fortified, of the ghost of the old colonialism with its procession of inequalities, prejudices, and oppression.[12]

Césaire's language suggests he no longer sees departmentalisation as a structure within which to militate for equal rights.

140 THE POLITICAL UPHEAVALS OF THE 1950S

Rather, as it currently operates it merely perpetuates inegalitarian colonial structures under a new name.

Césaire's argument here about the resurgence of the ghost of colonialism is fleshed out in a more detailed discussion entitled 'Le colonialisme n'est pas mort', published in *La Nouvelle critique* in January 1954. The article clearly complements the discussion in *Discours sur le colonialisme* and insists from the outset that colonialism is by definition violent – a point that will be reiterated by Fanon in stark terms at the opening of *Les Damnés de la terre* in 1961. Citing Albert Sarraut's *Grandeur et servitude coloniales* (published in 1931), as well as Vigne d'Octon's *À la gloire du sabre* (published in 1900), Césaire again punctures the myth of colonialism as civilisation and insists that the logical end of the colonial project is the destruction of indigenous peoples. If the thinkers he cites were critical of the excesses of colonialism whilst supportive of its vision, moreover, Césaire's response indicates that for him this underlying violence necessitates the imminent collapse of that entire system. At the same time, the essay reveals his increasing interest in colonial injustices in Africa. He vilifies the expropriation of land in Algeria, Madagascar and sub-Saharan Africa, and records the numbers of deaths at the suppressed protests in Algeria in 1945 and Madagascar in 1947. He also denounces the racism that underpins the colonial system, evoking poverty across the colonised world and the lack of both healthcare and schooling. The essay ends by summoning the forces of contestation and warning of the impending collapse of this destructive imperialist project.

Césaire's interest in colonialism in Africa in 'Le colonialisme n'est pas mort' can be read alongside an intervention at the Assemblée Nationale in March 1954, where he details the poor state of education systems in Africa. The speech shows Césaire attentive as ever to detailed examples of colonial injustice, which support his generalising anticolonial rhetoric, and the dissent with which his assertions were met testifies to the inflammatory power of his political arguments as well as his philosophical vision. Césaire's support for decolonisation in

THE POLITICAL UPHEAVALS OF THE 1950S 141

Africa was concretised later, in his address entitled 'La mort aux colonies' at the *Comité d'action des intellectuels contre la poursuite de la guerre en Afrique du Nord* in the Salle Wagram in Paris, January 1956. The speech was published in *Les Temps modernes* in March to April of that year, and in it Césaire notes the significance of the Bandung Conference in 1955, where representatives of twenty-nine Asian and African states agreed to cooperate to contest colonialism in all its forms, and he goes on to call for an end to the war in Algeria. In expressing his support for Algeria he again condemns the subjugation of colonised peoples, though at this stage he maintains a belief in the possibility of a free Algerian state but which would remain 'united with France by laws of friendship and solidarity, and no longer by ties of subjection and domination'.[13]

It was in the mid-1950s, however, that Césaire himself experienced conflicts that profoundly reshaped his cultural and political thinking. Indeed, 1955–6 was a pivotal moment, one where the poet and politician found himself in battle against significant figures with whom he had previously been closely affiliated and where he finished by profoundly revising his views on Caribbean poetics, on Communism and on the future status of Martinique. The first of these conflicts was a dispute with the Haitian writer René Depestre, in conjunction with the formerly surrealist, Communist poet Louis Aragon, over the form of politically engaged poetry. The dispute contributed to Césaire's unease towards the Communist Party and probably fuelled his decision in 1956 to break with it and to develop an anticolonial vision in new terms. Césaire had previously written appreciatively about Depestre's writing, producing a preface for the latter's *Végétations de clarté* in 1951. Césaire compared Depestre's art with that of the great Haitian writer Jacques Roumain in *Gouverneurs de la rosée* published in 1944, and praised Depestre's integration of actuality into his use of poetic form and his capturing of the sensory richness of local experience: 'he is the poet of freshness, of rising sap, of the blossoming of life, of the river of hope that irrigates the fertile ground of the present and of man's work'.[14]

142 THE POLITICAL UPHEAVALS OF THE 1950S

However, a shift in Aragon's vision for poetic form that profoundly influenced Depestre and triggered him to criticise Césaire's aesthetics led in 1955 to an embittered change of heart. In December 1953, Aragon had published in *Les Lettres françaises* (a journal of which he was chief editor) an article entitled 'Sur la poésie nationale', later gathering a series of related articles in *Journal d'une poésie nationale* at the end of 1954. Aragon argued for a national poetry, which should be regular in its rhythm and adhere to traditional rules of French poetry, to be approachable to ordinary people. Poetic form was essentially regulated and tamed to promote the expression of a political message. Depestre expressed his support for Aragon and his pursuit of realism in poetry in a letter to one of the editors of *Les Lettres françaises*, Charles Dobzynski, in June 1955; Dobzynski published extracts from the letter in the same month. Depestre's allegiance with Aragon here was coupled at the same time with direct criticism of negritude, which he dubbed 'a petit-bourgeois metaphysics blind to the historical realities of class struggle'.[15]

Césaire's response to Depestre made his disagreement and disappointment clear. In the April–July 1955 issue of *Présence Africaine*, he published the poem 'Réponse à Depestre poète haitien (Éléments d'art poétique)', which evokes the Haitian Revolution as a reminder to Depestre of his nation's claiming of its freedom and which calls upon the poet too to liberate his art from the constraints to which he has subjected it by affiliating himself with Aragon. Dutty Boukman and Jean-Jacques Dessalines, the leaders of slave revolts in Haiti, are commemorated in a reminder to Depestre to remain faithful to the principle of freedom, and the poet too is cast as a runaway slave. Linking Aragon's insistence on traditional form with the colonial regime, moreover, Césaire calls for a poetry of 'marronnage':

Ouiche! Depestre le poème n'est pas un moulin à
passer de la canne à sucre ça non
et si les rimes sont mouches sur les mares

sans rimes

toute une saison

loin des mares

moi te faisant raison

rions buvons marronnons.

[Ouch! Depestre a poem is not a mill for
crushing sugar cane stalks not at all
and if rhymes are flies on ponds

without rhymes

all season long

I justifying to you

let's laugh drink and maroon.][16]

Césaire's own disregard for regular verse and rhyme, the dynamic movement of the words on the page, and the festive association of freedom with laughter and drink gives his poem a vibrant, energised, sensory quality that enacts his disregard for Aragon's far more restrictive poetics. The use of poetic form itself for the expression of this critique performs Césaire's liberatory disregard for generic conventions and classifications. In the following issue of *Présence Africaine* published in October–November 1955, moreover, Césaire's article 'Sur la poésie nationale' clarifies his critique of Depestre for subjugating his poetry to traditional French prosodic form. The result is that 'Depestre, under the pretext of aligning himself with Aragon's position, falls into a detestable assimilationism'.[17] At the same time, he criticises Depestre's idea of African poetic form, conceiving this as a concept mired in exoticism, so that in his view Depestre finishes by constraining poetry between these two falsely static frameworks of French and African tradition. Finally, he objects to the category of 'national poetry', championing instead the poem as a signifier of life with its own creative autonomy.

Depestre produced a response to Césaire's poem in the same issue of *Présence Africaine* as the latter's essay, however, which appeared to soften his opposition as well as to defend

144   THE POLITICAL UPHEAVALS OF THE 1950S

the vibrancy of his own poetic practice. He explains that his invocations of French and African poetic form were in no way intended to imply that these were static categories; rather he wanted to celebrate their evolution and synthesis.[18] He elaborates on a specifically Haitian poetic art and argues that poetry is created out of shared histories and idioms, whilst continuing to regard the idea of a shared black culture as excessively generalising. Haitian art, he insists, should be anchored in the people's experiences and can convincingly be expressed in French because of the proximity of French and Creole and because of the profound embeddedness of the French language in Haitian cultural life. Poets need to make themselves understood, moreover, by anchoring their work in forms with which their addressees would be familiar. The last part of Depestre's essay picks up on certain lines in Césaire's poem and acerbically criticises the latter's 'marronnage' of poets such as Aragon. Whilst celebrating the use of traditional poetic forms alongside their evolution in new contexts, moreover, he condemns poetry whose form can be seen as individualist. Despite the vibrancy of Depestre's poetic vision in this defence, however, Césaire's long-standing collaborators Senghor and Gratiant expressed their support for Césaire's position in the subsequent issue of *Présence Africaine*. Senghor argued that black writers need to reach beyond the restrictive framework of realism to create a more authentic black art, whilst Gratiant challenged the idea of 'national' poetry and emphasised the importance of the poet's attachment to a broader black culture. Both, like Césaire, perceived Depestre's affirmation of realism as a sign of his assimilation by Western thought. Later, however, in an article in *Les Lettres Nouvelles* printed in January 1957, Depestre seemed to concede defeat and align himself more closely with Césaire.[19]

If the aesthetic questions raised in this dispute with Depestre ultimately turned out not to divide the poets as decisively as they had thought, however, the political tensions of the debate fuelled Césaire's uncertainties about the uses of Communist thought in the anticolonial context and

THE POLITICAL UPHEAVALS OF THE 1950S   145

left deeper scars. Césaire's relationship with the Communist Party had always been tinged with ambivalence. He had been unsure about the Marxist agenda of *Légitime Défense* back in Paris in the 1930s and remained sceptical about the capacity of Marxist thought properly to address the question of colonialism. Toumson and Henry-Valmore note the slight uneasiness surrounding Césaire's affiliation with the Parti Communiste Français (PCF) in the 1940s, recounting the anecdote that the Martinican poet missed his first meeting with Maurice Thorez, the leader of the party, causing Thorez to respond with irritation.[20] However, Césaire did meet Thorez in Moscow in 1953 and at that time commented enthusiastically on Thorez's interest in Martinique.[21]

The dispute with Aragon and Depestre two years later nevertheless fuelled other reservations that had been brewing in Césaire. On 24 October 1956, he wrote his famous 'Lettre à Maurice Thorez' announcing his departure from the Communist Party, sending a copy of the letter to *France-Observateur*, who published key extracts the following day. The support of *France-Observateur* was significant, in that the newspaper was widely read, and it helped to link Césaire's position with that of other non-Communist left-wing thinkers. Romuald Fonkoua details the internal tensions leading up to Césaire's dramatic gesture, the upshot of which was that he continued to feel that the Party was unable to provide a concrete response to the difficulties caused by the colonial situation in Martinique.[22] The insurrections against the Stalinist regimes in Poland in June and in Hungary in October also no doubt galvanised Césaire. In cutting his links with the Communist Party Césaire joined Breton (who back in the 1930s had criticised those intellectuals who idealised Soviet politics) as well as the American writer Richard Wright (who had experimented with working with the Communist Party in the US and had become disillusioned in the mid-1940s).

Césaire's letter can be read as one of his most divisive political statements, and his denunciation of Communism was uncompromising. He starts by unveiling the violence of

146   THE POLITICAL UPHEAVALS OF THE 1950S

Stalin's methods, as they were exposed by Khrushchev earlier in 1956, by vilifying the exploitation of workers by state power, and by arguing that the bureaucracy of numerous socialist regimes in Europe transformed the socialist dream into a nightmare. The French Communist Party, he continues, has failed to dissociate itself from Stalinism and to judge its crimes. Whilst the PCF could have taken the opportunity to revise its position on Stalinism at its Congress in Le Havre in July 1956, Césaire accuses its representatives of stubbornly clinging to lies. Most importantly for Césaire, however, is the separation between the concerns of the Party and his own preoccupation with racial inequality. The PCF's support for Guy Mollet's government's continued power in North Africa in turn reinforces his realisation that anticolonial struggle is distinct from the struggle of French workers against capitalism and cannot be understood to be a part of it. Césaire as a result accuses members of the Party for 'their inveterate assimilationism; their unconscious chauvinism; what could reasonably be seen as their basic conviction, that they share with all bourgeois Europeans, of the superiority of the West', and he vilifies in a characteristically profuse diatribe their belief in myths of Civilisation and Progress.[23] His target, he insists, is not Marxism itself, but the uses it has been put to, and Marxist thinking continued to inform Césaire's work throughout his career.[24] Here, however, he argues that it is time that Communism work in the service of black people, not the other way round. The regeneration of Martinique will come, he suggests, from its contact with Africa, not with Europe. The letter concludes with a forceful summary of Césaire's priorities:

> To build organisations capable of honestly and effectively helping black peoples in their struggle for the present and the future: the struggle for justice; the struggle for culture; the struggle for dignity and freedom; in a word, organisations capable of preparing them in all areas autonomously to take on the heavy responsibilities that history currently weighs on their shoulders.[25]

THE POLITICAL UPHEAVALS OF THE 1950S   147

Césaire makes his points with his customary hard-hitting rhetoric. The repercussions of this dramatic statement had an immediate impact and plunged Césaire into a dispute that would catalyse his evolution of a new politics. Thorez responded with an article in the journal *L'Humanité* on 28 October, in which he expressed his surprise towards Césaire's sudden volte-face and his disappointment in the face of this publicly aggressive gesture while also suggesting that the latter was betraying the workers' cause. On 29 October, the same journal printed a letter by Rosan Girard, Deputy for Guadeloupe, criticising Césaire's betrayal and affirming the Antillean people's ongoing support for the PCF. On 1 November, Césaire's former friend the philosopher Roger Garaudy also published a letter in *L'Humanité* (reprinted later that month in *Justice*) in which he too denigrated Césaire's action and accused him of being too bourgeois. Although Garaudy recognised the errors of Stalinism, he defended Communist principles and argued that it stood for all those enslaved by capitalism. The Communist Federations of both Martinique and Guadeloupe went on to exclude Césaire from their ranks, and several of Césaire's former allies (including René Ménil, Léopold Bissol and Georges Gratiant) also broke their ties with him. Nevertheless, only days later, on 4 November Soviet forces entered Hungary, crushing the insurrection and causing thousands of casualties, a development that would have vindicated Césaire in his decision.[26] Césaire was also of course not alone as an intellectual in distancing himself from Communism at that time, as many French writers and thinkers broke their ties with it in the wake of the Soviet intervention in Hungary.

In order to address the controversy head-on, after his return to Martinique Césaire gave a long speech to a large crowd at the Maison du Sport on 22 November, in which he further justified his decision. Clearly wounded by accusations of betrayal and by his exclusion from the Communist Federation of Martinique, in his speech he nevertheless stands firm in his belief that he acts for Martinicans in good faith. He adds to his 'Lettre à Maurice Thorez' a more specific

148   THE POLITICAL UPHEAVALS OF THE 1950S

critique of the Federation and does not hold back from condemning its blind commitment to Stalinism: 'the Federation continues to see Stalinism as the normal, completed form of socialism, whereas I see it as a deformation, a vicious, monstrous, tyrannical form'.[27] He also defends his position by reminding his audience that distinguished intellectuals such as Jean-Paul Sartre have disaffiliated themselves with the leaders of the PCF, and cites a letter from Leiris informing him that Picasso too had denounced the Party's silence. He refers again to the Khrushchev report to evoke the horrific crimes committed under the aegis of Communism, noting nevertheless that the leaders of the PCF have failed to take on board these crimes. He goes on to argue that one of the consequences of this preoccupation for the Federation was that it made them incapable of properly addressing the needs of Martinicans. He argues that the PCF did not always support measures he had been fighting for on behalf of Martinique, such as the establishment of the island as a critical zone for the development of new industries and for the employment of workers. As a result, Césaire proposes the creation of a 'Front martiniquais' to establish a unified approach to the various social and economic difficulties on the island. He also defends his insistence on promoting connections between the Caribbean and Africa by emphasising the importance of Africa in contemporary global politics, an argument for which he had been accused of racism. Finally, he concludes that he is not seeking the independence of Martinique and that, 'I consider our belonging in the French Union to be permanent and definitive'.[28] For Césaire, departmentalisation was never akin to assimilation, and yet a new model is needed to allow for the increased participation of Martinicans in the management of their own affairs.

Césaire's political vision for Martinique would continue to develop in more concrete ways in the late 1950s. Césaire already sketched the beginnings of this vision in an article entitled 'Décolonisation pour les Antilles' published in *Présence Africaine* in April/May 1956 and reprinted as the Introduction

THE POLITICAL UPHEAVALS OF THE 1950S   149

to Daniel Guérin's *Les Antilles décolonisées*. He notes that Guérin's study outlines the shared experiences of the French Antilles and suggests that a new independent federation could pave the way for a new democracy. Whereas Guérin identifies a growing racial and social consciousness, Césaire explores the development of national consciousness over the previous ten years, since the disappointments of departmentalisation became entrenched. Departmentalisation, he suggests, turns out to be nothing more than a 'ruse of history', based on the pursuit of abstract equality of a form that would never be achieved in practice.[29] The growth of national sentiment testifies for Césaire to the failings of that vision, and at this point he undermines Guérin's pursuit of the grouping together of French Caribbean islands, arguing that it is the idea of the Antillean nation that needs to be nourished and developed. Césaire nevertheless notes that Guérin's study certainly contributes to this process of construction of 'Caribbean nations in their infancy and uncertain in their being', and the essay ends with this tentative vision for the early stages of political change.

As Gary Wilder notes, Césaire comes unusually close to promoting nationalism here, though the argument serves mainly as a critique of departmentalisation, and certainly nationalism in the sense of state sovereignty was not something he pursued.[30] Instead, after separating from the Communist Federation of Martinique, Césaire sought to imagine a form of autonomy for Martinique that would avoid the problems associated with both assimilation and nationalism or independence. Whilst in 1957 the Communist Federation of Martinique recreated itself, in the absence of Césaire, as the new Martinican Communist Party, Césaire set about inaugurating his own party. In March 1958, he founded with Pierre Aliker the Parti Progressiste Martiniquais (PPM), which would seek autonomy for Martinique within a federal union with France. The creation of the new party also came after the establishment of the European Economic Commission in 1957, with which Césaire expressed his dissent at the Assemblée Nationale because he

150   THE POLITICAL UPHEAVALS OF THE 1950S

saw that within it the French overseas departments would not have their own representation.[31] Césaire's proposed federation, including Martinique, Guadeloupe and Guiana within a French federal republic, turned out not to be dissimilar to Guérin's federation envisaged in *Les Antilles décolonisées*. Its form would be detailed in a report presented for the constitution of the PPM as a third way between assimilation and autonomy, and would consist in the creation of 'regions' akin to those included in the Italian Constitution of 1948.[32] This federation of regions is clearly presented by Césaire as the way out of the current impasse, as he argues that in making this transformation, 'we will have succeeded in bringing together our dual concern to remain linked with France and to be good Martinicans, and without falling into a separatism that would be fatal to us, we will have triumphed over another separation which can also in the long term turn out to be fatal, the separation of man from himself'.[33]

The Parti Progressiste Martiniquais gained support and publicity through its journal *Le Progressiste*, which launched in April 1958 and which Césaire filled with numerous articles explaining the party's politics and commenting on the impending vote for the new French Constitution of 1958. On 12 April he clearly set out the priorities of the party as part of his campaign for the district elections, which he won with a comfortable majority on 20 April. He argued that the party shared the Martinican people's concern for social and economic progress, the promotion of Martinicans within the French Union, and the triumph of morality in public affairs.[34] Once again, the creation of a federal Republic was held up as the solution to current inequities. Césaire also during this period offered his provisional support for de Gaulle and for the new constitution. He had repeatedly expressed his dissatisfaction at the lack of attention to the status of the overseas departments in the new constitution, and until early September was instructing Martinicans to vote no. After meeting with de Gaulle, his Chief of Staff Georges Pompidou and Minister of State André Malraux in Paris, however, and after hosting a visit from Malraux on 20 September in Fort-de-France, he was persuaded to vote yes to the constitution on 28 September. The promise that the difficulties of Martinique would subsequently be addressed was enough for the time being, and Césaire called on Martinicans to vote with him, since, 'a great contract has been proposed by the great country of France and little Martinique, a contract of fraternity, help, and mutual comprehension'.[35] Ninety-three per cent of Martinicans voted with Césaire, and most of France's African overseas territories voted yes too, with the exception of Guinea, where Sékou Touré voted no, and independence was granted on 4 October. Césaire would soon once again become disillusioned by the failed promises of the French government, and subsequently expressed his admiration for Sékou Touré's vision and decisiveness, producing an adulatory article on him in *Présence Africaine* in December 1959–January 1960, before Sékou Touré's regime became tyrannical.

Anticolonial Culture at the Time of African Decolonisation

This period of change in Césaire's political outlook testifies to his embattled position, constantly seeking to reconcile visionary ideals with practical strategy. During the 1950s, Césaire's political ambition was at its height, as can be detected in the incendiary critique presented in *Discours sur le colonialisme* as well as in his fidelity to the principle of racial equality in 'Lettre à Maurice Thorez' and in his, perhaps utopian, pursuit of the idea of a federal republic. His fundamental commitment to equality, freedom and justice by turns inflated his rhetoric with hopeful ideals and furious denunciations. At the same time, he continued doggedly to provide details of particular injustices, citing unequal salaries and benefits and evoking vivid scenes of poverty. He skilfully interwove idealism and practicality, long-term ambition and short-term strategy, in a range of forums.

It was also during this period, however, that Césaire's cultural vision was expressed with the most urgency and

152   THE POLITICAL UPHEAVALS OF THE 1950S

immediacy, as the visionary force of cultural activity was celebrated in ambitious terms while his cultural output became more grounded and focused. Writing and art are conjured in utopian language as powerful tools for creating change, but the extraordinary aesthetic experimentation of the 1940s is slightly tempered now as Césaire seeks to ally poetry more closely with history and politics. For James Arnold, this increased politicisation results in a deflation in his poetic artistry and obfuscation of his spiritual quest.[36] Yet although the 1950s no doubt marks a change in the style of Césaire's poetics, this decade also shows his art achieving a more direct force by shifting deftly between the visionary and the immediate, between utopia and focused critique in ways that reflect his parallel political journey. The avant-garde experimentalism is not lost during this period; rather it is coupled with a political urgency that can be read as a powerful supplement to, but not a betrayal of, the earlier work.

Césaire's participation in two major conferences for black writers and artists (in Paris in 1956 and in Rome in 1959) serves to crystallise his vision for anticolonial culture and position him as an inspirational figure for black revolutionary thinkers, notably in Africa. The first conference at the Sorbonne in September 1956 was organised by the Senegalese writer and editor of *Présence Africaine*, Alioune Diop, in the wake of the Bandung conference in 1955, to bring together black writers and artists in the hope of amplifying the role of African culture in the anticolonial project articulated at Bandung. Césaire's significance was underlined by Picasso's presentation of his 'Tête de nègre', from *Corps perdu*, for display at the conference, with a dedication referencing writers and artists returning to a shared native land that reinforced the connection with Césaire.[37]

One of the aims of the conference, and of Césaire's own intervention, would be to elucidate the common goals and visions of black cultures in different parts of the world. In his speech 'Culture et colonisation', Césaire's anticolonial vision and his aspiration for a broader black cultural revolution are

THE POLITICAL UPHEAVALS OF THE 1950S   153

presented in rousing terms. He uses the term 'civilisation' as the umbrella under which national cultures come together in their common experience of colonialism and with their shared history in Africa. Colonialism in all cases, for Césaire, destroys the culture of the colonised, who lose any sense of cultural synthesis as the imposed culture fractures and disperses their identity. Césaire's response is not to recommend the invention of a completely new culture but to emphasise the importance of connecting with traditional African cultures and to rebuild an authentic culture in the present out of that connection. His speech ends with an impassioned summons to his colleagues:

> At the moment we are in a cultural chaos. Our role is to say: liberate the demiurge that alone can organise this chaos into a new synthesis, a synthesis that will deserve to be called a culture, a synthesis and transcendence of the old and the new. We are here to say and to claim: let the people speak. Let black peoples enter onto the great stage of history.[38]

Césaire's rhetoric here is as ambitious and as galvanising as ever. He at once responds to the current moment and projects a far-reaching image of the regeneration of black cultural creativity. He moves away from his previous use of Frobenius, and the latter's conviction that culture is born out of man's emotion before the cosmos, to argue with Hegel for the crucial influence of politics on culture.

Yet Césaire's intervention, though helping to relaunch him as an African thinker, was controversial and provoked extensive debate among delegates.[39] American colleagues, including Mercer Cook and John Davis, objected to his emphasis on colonialism and called for a more inclusive vision of cultural activism that would account for the distinct nature of black Americans' experiences. Richard Wright noted the relevance of the debate launched by Césaire's intervention but demanded a more concrete vision of African culture and lamented the overuse of abstractions. Senghor spoke up to nuance Césaire's negative portrayal of métissage, arguing that all great civilisations are based on cultural mixing and that métissage is the necessary consequence of the contact between civilisations. Senghor agreed with Césaire's insistence that cultural mixing should be chosen rather than imposed, but insisted more positively that métissage can be productive. Despite this critique, we should note that Césaire's vilification of the imposition of colonial culture on colonised culture was never meant to deride all forms of métissage. Most cuttingly, however, Senghor objected to the vagueness of Césaire's political vision. Finally, Louis-Thomas Achille argued that Césaire's presentation did not apply to all black peoples and insisted at the same time on the impossibility of the notion of cultural purity that he perceived to persist in Césaire's vision.

Césaire was clearly aggrieved to have offended some of his colleagues and replied to the effect that he was committed to understanding the shared experiences of black people and that the situation of blacks in America was necessarily bound up with colonial history. He also reinforced his conviction that culture is a crucial part of civilisation but did not sharpen his political vision in response to Senghor's seemingly damning critique. When the Congress met again in Rome in March–April 1959, however, Césaire's address attested to his more authoritative position, addressing African intellectuals from the perspective of having established a new coherent vision for Martinique with the Parti Progressiste Martiniquais. His speech, entitled 'L'homme de culture et ses responsabilités', once again celebrates the role of intellectuals, writers and artists in establishing complete decolonisation. For both Fanon and Césaire, decolonisation involves the definitive destruction of colonial structures, and Césaire stresses the connections between African and Central or Latin American cultures, since the latter still struggle with the legacy of colonialism even after independence. The upshot is the incendiary insistence that *'true decolonisation will be revolutionary or it will not be'*.[40] In a shift from his earlier 'Culture et colonisation', however, Césaire affirms the importance of national culture,

THE POLITICAL UPHEAVALS OF THE 1950S 155

to which writers and artists give vision and form. It is here that he dubs the writer not, as Stalin did, an 'engineer of the soul', but an 'inventor of the soul' in a vocabulary that implicitly references Stalin but at the same time emphasises freedom and creativity rather than manipulation. The writer should contest the 'cultural anarchy' created by the imposition of colonial culture and should instead 'create order from the cultural chaos'.[41] If this process is now bound up with nationalism, moreover, by the end of his speech Césaire speaks of this invention of a culture of decolonisation as a universal symbol of human freedom. Relinquishing the vocabulary of negritude and pan-Africanism, he intones, 'it is finally for the whole world that we fight, to liberate it from tyranny, hatred, and fanaticism'.[42]

Césaire's speech in Rome positions him as an inspirational figurehead for anticolonial intellectuals while clearly championing his renewed, politically engaged vision for cultural practice. In *Tropiques*, the critical role of culture was expressed in veiled terms, and in the poetry volumes of the 1940s, the denunciation of colonial history was articulated through surrealist visions of cosmic upheaval; here, culture is to convey a much more direct and immediate political message. Césaire's interventions at the two Congresses in this way provide a revealing background to his reorientation of the *Cahier d'un retour au pays natal* in 1956 to a more explicitly anticolonial political agenda. As we have seen, 1956 was a pivotal moment for Césaire, following the publication of *Discours sur le colonialisme*, the dispute with Depestre and his separation from the PCF. James Arnold calls 1956 the 'year of reframing' of Césaire's work in the light of his affiliation with *Présence Africaine* in publishing a new edition of this inaugural work.[43] According to Arnold, the new text served in the campaign for the 1956 Congress in Paris. Both the poem and Césaire's speech inspired journalists and served to crystallise his recrafting as an African intellectual. As Arnold also notes, however, it was the framing and paratext that most altered the orientation of the *Cahier*. Various textual changes contributed to

156   THE POLITICAL UPHEAVALS OF THE 1950S

the concretisation of his anticolonial political message, even though most of the text remained the same as that published by Bordas in 1947. These changes, together with the reframing by Présence Africaine, however, show the *Cahier* evolving from the poet's soul-searching quest in 1939 to a more affirmative political critique in 1956, having passed through but also moved on from a period of intensified surrealist experimentation during the 1940s.[44]

The changes Césaire made to the *Cahier* in 1956 tend to streamline the text's political critique and temper some of its surrealist and erotic imagery. One of the passages that Césaire reworked follows the section evoking Toussaint Louverture's death in the snowy landscape of the Jura. Notably, the highly surrealist image of the 'terre mer almée retroussant tes aumusses mugissantes' ['land sea almah rolling up your howling fur sleeves'] is cut from the Présence Africaine edition and replaced with a return to the opening refrain and a more direct reference to the eradication of colonised culture: 'au bout du petit matin ces pays sans stèle, ces chemins sans mémoire, ces vents sans tablette' ['at the brink of dawn these countries with no stela, these road with no memory, these winds with no tablet'].[45] This imagery resonates with that of the arguments Césaire made in 'Culture et colonisation', where he denounced the coloniser's emptying out of the culture of the colonised and called for cultural reinvention. The change signals the closer alliance between the poet and the essayist, as well as his growing belief in the intervention of culture into political discourse.

Césaire also reordered much of this section and then cut some of the passages that had been taken from 'En guise de manifeste littéraire', including for example the riposte to the 'flics et flicaillons' ['cops and rozzers'].[46] The evocation of their 'impulsion satanique' ['satanic impulse'] with the colourful cosmic imagery of 'lunes rousses de feux verts de fièvres jaunes' ['red moons of green fires and yellow fevers'] is excised. The poet's rejection of colonial reason is therefore expressed in more direct terms. As Arnold points out, moreover, the lyric first person 'je' is replaced in this section in the Présence

Africaine edition with the collective 'nous': 'nous dirions. Chanterions. Hurlerions. / Voix pleine, voix large, tu serais notre bien, notre pointe en avant' ['we would speak. Sing. Scream. / Full voice, wide voice, you would be our right and our pointed spear'].[47] This change in tone to that of a political summons is then continued by further intermittent omissions of some of the most bizarrely sexual lines from the Bordas edition, such as, 'il y a les souris qui à les ouïr s'agitent dans le vagin de ma voisine' ['there are mice that can be heard agitating in my neighbour's vagina'], as well as the reference to Onan spilling his sperm to fertilise the land as the poet moves towards his revolt.[48]

The most significant addition to the poem comes close to the end, where in the middle of the section in which the poet insists on his acceptance of the horrors of the slave past, he evokes the work on the sugar plantations before commemorating those who have been forgotten by citing their names. He evokes the 'sol de boue. Horizon de boue. Ciel de boue' ['soil of mud. Horizon of mud. Sky of mud'], before summoning individual victims: 'ô noms à réchauffer dans la paume d'un souffle fièvreux' ['oh names to warm up in the palm of a feverish breath'].[49] Siméon Piquine, Grandvorka and Michel Deveine are named in a gesture of resistance to their effacement, and the poet pursues their revolt in order not to acquiesce to their horrific brutalisation: 'Présences je ne ferai pas avec le monde ma paix sur votre dos' ['Presences, I will not sign a peace treaty with the world on your backs'].[50] The imagery of the rest of this added section represents the violence against slaves as ongoing scars inflicted on the islands' landscapes, whilst the poet's words allow the landscape to speak. A further return to 'the brink of dawn' then brings together human and environmental destruction in a climactic fury, where the poet again voices his acceptance in a form that further unifies the poem and crystallises his all-encompassing revolt.

These textual changes are amplified, however, by the text's repackaging by Présence Africaine. Whilst Breton's preface to the 1940s versions emphasises the poem's surrealism, Petar

158   THE POLITICAL UPHEAVALS OF THE 1950S

Guberina's preface to the 1956 version situates the text in the context of movements in the developing world and of the Bandung conference of 1955.[51] Guberina also acknowledges the Sartrean reading of the poet's descent into hell but eclipses the mythical dimension and foregrounds the poet's call for revolution. At the same time, the back cover of this new edition emphasises the importance of the work for an African audience.[52] Although the blurb on the back cover is unattributed, it could well have been written by Mário Pinto de Andrade, an Angolan writer and thinker who was one of the editors at Présence Africaine during that period. Andrade would have been overseeing the changes to the text. He founded the Popular Movement for the Liberation of Angola and participated in the founding of the Communist Party in Angola, and his Marxist pursuit of African decolonisation would have shaped his vision for the press. The day after publication, the press organised a 'Journée du livre africain' in which Césaire participated and which helped present the poet and his text as African.

After the publication of the Présence Africaine edition of the *Cahier*, the previous versions were for a long time not widely available. In 2013, James Arnold printed all four versions of the *Cahier*, as well as 'En guise de manifeste littéraire', in *Poésie, Théâtre, Essais, et Discours* to allow readers to track the poem's evolution. Arnold laments that the 1956 version has tended to eclipse the other versions, with the result that the poem's complex journey and Césaire's personal, cultural and political evolution have been sidelined by readers keen to celebrate the expression of revolutionary politics through poetry. Analysis of the successive drafts of the *Cahier* in 2013 uncovers his trajectory. Césaire's incendiary revolt is certainly evident in the 1939 version, but his experimental aesthetics embellish this artistic process during the 1940s, before the poet's political motivations reshape it, together with Présence Africaine, in 1956. There is a clear continuity between the versions, but Césaire's rewritings reflect his changing ideas about aesthetics and about the role and form of culture in anticolonial politics

THE POLITICAL UPHEAVALS OF THE 1950S   159

at the same time as they perform his commitment to dynamic reinvention in their very plurality. The core text remains the same despite the revisions, yet the 1956 reworking and reframing aptly reflect the preoccupations of its author at one of the intense and transitional moments in his career.

This reframing occurred at the same time as Césaire was working on a revised version of *Et les chiens se taisaient* suitable for the theatre, a project that reflects Césaire's growing concern to make his work more accessible and address the public directly. This arrangement was set in motion by Césaire's German translator, Janheinz Jahn, who wanted to create a version for the radio to be broadcast to German listeners. Jahn's suggestions included highlighting the Rebel's political destiny; Césaire added a scene portraying a meeting between the Rebel and a new character, the Administrator, which contained a debate about colonialism that would have resonated with the current political situation.[53] Yet Césaire changed his mind about these additions and was reluctant to produce a dramatically different version of the play in French. Although Présence Africaine published a new edition in 1956 which divided the script into three acts and maintained the character of the Administrator who seeks to justify the colonial project, the revisions made to the text were in the end minimal. Nevertheless, it is once again revealing that Césaire chose to present his work under the aegis of Présence Africaine, even if there was now a slight tension between the blurb's characterisation of the Rebel as revolutionary and the text's mythical and spiritual quest. Jahn's German version maintained the more ambitious changes with which Césaire had experimented, thereby demonstrating further the malleability of his work as it was recreated and reframed in different contexts.

Ferrements

Ferrements, published in 1960, was Césaire's first new volume of poetry since *Corps perdu* published ten years previously,

160   THE POLITICAL UPHEAVALS OF THE 1950S

and it aptly showcases his new aesthetic as it shifted through the 1950s. The poems are markedly different in style from the surrealist heights of the 1940s; their language is more clearly referential, at times they name particular African states and evoke real workers and victims of racism in addition to conjuring the effects of slavery through the disturbance of landscape and cosmos. According to Gregson Davis, the poems of *Ferrements* are 'more lucid in texture' than those of earlier volumes, and manifest a 'drive towards concision and economy, and a radical pruning of luxuriant imagery'.[54] For another critic, Nick Nesbitt, along with the speeches at the two Congresses, they testify to Césaire's adherence to the model of the engaged intellectual, 'able to enlighten his readers and lead them to revolutionary consciousness'.[55] They display the poet's affiliation with the anticolonial cause, though in so doing refer more often to Africa than to the Caribbean, and are at times more historically grounded than his earlier collections. They also portray Césaire's growing global consciousness, reflecting on the politics of race and decolonisation in the Cold War system.[56] Nevertheless, their form remains varied and concrete historical references are set alongside imagery that is by turns visceral and cosmic to create a poetic volume that is more focused on decolonisation but no less original than his previous poetry.

The title *Ferrements* has a double meaning, which helps structure the volume and explain the poems. On the one hand it refers to the irons in which slaves were shackled, but on the other it suggests 'ferment', which Aliko Songolo reads as the 'maturation, the transcendence of the condition of degradation, an inevitable becoming'.[57] The title in this way crystallises the movement seen in many of Césaire's poems between imagery of enslavement and oppression, and visions of revolution and rebirth, reflecting shifts between past and future, between history and impending change. In James Arnold's reading, the collection comprises three voices which can be seen to foreground distinct temporalities across the poems. These are, in Arnold's words citing from Eshleman

THE POLITICAL UPHEAVALS OF THE 1950S   161

and Smith's earlier volume of translations: 'commitment to anticolonialist struggle; a "fantastic evocation of black bondage throughout history"; and an elegiac voice marked by an aesthetic "distance from the scene it evokes"'.[58] If this first voice is anchored in the demands of the present, the second connects the present movement with a longer history of colonial brutality, whilst the third takes the poet outside the structure of linear progress to offer a more timeless reflection.

These different voices and temporalities are at the same time accompanied by variable aesthetic forms. A section of prose poems in the middle of the collection contains wildly proliferating sequences of surrealist imagery, whilst some of the poems printed early in the volume are more elliptical and telegraphic, and some towards the end move closer to realism and are anchored by their address to other anticolonial figures or victims of colonialism. These varying forms have encouraged critics to read the volume in many different ways, as Christopher Bonner outlines, noting that *Ferrements* has been construed both as an expression of revolutionary anticolonialism (by Nesbitt, for example) and as conveying the poet's incipient disillusionment with radical politics (by René Ménil).[59] Bonner's discussion of the volume also tracks the different figures for movement and journeying, evocative by turns of dynamic change and of stagnation, as the poet negotiates the tension between despair and renewal.

The form of the first poems of *Ferrements* is most reminiscent of Césaire's aesthetic of the 1940s. The opening poem (itself entitled 'Ferrements') allusively evokes the slave trade, with the poet seeking to unite with its victims through imagery of a shared journey enveloped in a sense of obscuration. Yet if the imagery of the landscape reflecting the experience of enslaved peoples recalls that found, for example, in *Les Armes miraculeuses*, the message affirming unity between the poet and the oppressed people is now more directly and succinctly expressed. It is possible to read in the opening line, 'le périple ligote emporte tous les chemins' ['the periplus binds sweeps away all roads'], the repeated circular movement of the Middle

162 THE POLITICAL UPHEAVALS OF THE 1950S

Passage, figured through the unusual term 'périple' suggesting an ironic reworking of Ulysses' meandering voyage.[60] The poem is then broken in the middle by the interjection of the word 'esclaves' ['slaves'], establishing the victims of colonialism at its centre, surrounded by imagery of the slave ship, of suffering and protest. At the end of the poem, the speaker addresses the slaves using intimate vocabulary and confirms he accompanies them, also sickened but implying in his affiliation that his poem speaks in protest for them. His language is intermittently sexual, and the binding hints at intercourse, as if to link the surrealist eroticism often found in *Soleil cou coupé* with this militant affirmation of solidarity. The poem is not yet anchored in present struggles, but combines an indirect and evocative vision of enslavement with a firm insistence on the poet's present role. 'Ferrements' is later echoed by 'Ferment', moreover, whose title announces the poet's anticipation of a new order, and where entrapment is portrayed through reference to Prometheus, with renewal foreshadowed through the image of a 'soubresaut d'aube démêlé d'aigles' ['eagle-disentangled jolt of dawn'].[61]

Another poem printed early in the collection, 'Spirales', recalls the aesthetic of both *Les Armes miraculeuses* and *Corps perdu*, associating revolt with changes in plants and animals. Here the poet repeatedly conjures upwards movement in a form that echoes the final lines of the *Cahier*, but each line affirming ascent is followed by a line that blends the poet's movement with activity in the landscape, which in turn represents the people for whom he speaks, for example: 'nous montons / les balisiers se déchirent le cœur sur le moment précis / où le phénix renaît de la plus haute flamme qui le consume' ['we ascend / the balisiers tear open their hearts at the precise moment / when the phoenix is reborn from its highest consuming flame'].[62] The balisier flower was the emblem of the Parti Progressiste Martiniquais, and its red spikes are here associated with human hearts bursting open and bringing rebirth. As Davis also notes, the spiral form references Dante's circles of hell, as if to conjure again the horrors out of which

THE POLITICAL UPHEAVALS OF THE 1950S   163

uprising might occur.[63] Halfway through the poem, the movement switches, turns downwards and becomes enmeshed in tighter circles of entrapment, as Césaire conjures a hell where 'nous rampons nous flottons / nous enroulons de plus en plus serré les gouffres de la terre' ['we crawl we float / we coil tighter and tighter the chasms of the earth'].[64] The movement of descent is again comparable to that of the *Cahier*, this time mimicking the poem as a whole as it plunges into the poet's unconscious and the past suffering of black people, before he is able to commence the movement upwards. This time, the descent follows the ascent as if to express disillusionment, though the poet's project of resistance seems to be salvaged at the end by the image of the undertow, carrying those who are lost back 'dans un paquet de lianes / d'étoiles et de frissons' ['in a tangle of lianas / of stars and shudders']. The last three lines are indented to mark a separation from the movement of descent, and the liana here, as elsewhere in Césaire, is suggestive of growth in a coiling movement that weaves together the human and the ecological environment, leading both out into the cosmos in the staccato movement enacted by the poem.

In the early pages of *Ferrements*, however, Césaire already makes concrete reference to Africa in his eulogy to newly independent Guinea. Like 'Ferrements' and 'Spirales', 'Salut à la Guinée' represents change through movement in the landscape and the elements and with intonations of spiritual rebirth. Yet it can be read as a much more optimistic celebration of decolonisation, a reading that is bolstered in turn through comparison with Césaire's *Présence Africaine* article on Sékou Touré, even though he does not here make any specific reference to political change. It is also a more direct and succinct address to Guinea than that articulated in 'Ode à la Guinée' in *Soleil cou coupé*, where the poet's salute is surrounded by much more extensive, visceral imagery of suffering and oppression as well as of resistance. The poem opens with a list of names of rivers and cities in Guinea, with lines broken and spaced across the page in a highly musical arrangement:

164 THE POLITICAL UPHEAVALS OF THE 1950S

Dalaba Pita Labé Mali Timbé
  puissantes falaises
    Tinkisso Tinkisso

eaux belles
  et que le futur déjà y déploie toute la possible chevelure

[Dalaba Pita Labé Mali Timbé
  mighty cliffs
    Tinkisso Tinkisso

Beautiful waters
  and may the future already display there the fullest
  possible chevelure][65]

These lines celebrate in an idealised vocabulary the beauty and power of the landscape, anticipating a future of growth and fertility. The poet then again conjures the image of the volcano, though here the change and renewal it brings is represented in nurturing rather than destructive terms. The rock itself moves 'd'un maternel meandre' ['with a maternal meander'], and the 'liberté fragile' ['fragile liberty'] which caps the poem and which crowns its movement is gently rocked and protected by this nurturing mineral landscape.

Before moving on to a sequence of poems more securely anchored in history, *Ferrements* contains a series of experimental pieces showcasing the diversity of the volume's style, with the telegraphic, fragmented lines of 'Beau sang giclé' contrasting, for example, with the series in effusive prose that succeeds it. 'Beau sang giclé' consists of just eight lines, and moves from imagery of the mutilation of a bird to a call to justice. Césaire references the Creole story of Yé (about a peasant who kills an enchanted bird), which can be understood to represent violence against black people as well as survival and rebirth. The poem's dense and allusive lines evoke severed limbs, blood, lost warblings and scattered feathers, forming a startling retelling of the familiar Creole story to create a stark and arresting

THE POLITICAL UPHEAVALS OF THE 1950S   165

aesthetic that is not at all, unlike some of the poems in the volume, grounded in political reality. Rather, the economical style, pared down to key words without conjunctions, can be seen to be reminiscent of an African style evoked by Senghor in his study of black African poetry.[66] The brief, allusive lines of 'Beau sang giclé' contrast markedly with the prose form of poems such as 'Bucolique', whose title ironically suggests a subversion of conventional pastoral poetry. Here, revolt is suggested through the stirring of the earth, captured in two paragraphs each consisting of single sentences, gathering force as their imagery accumulates. The aesthetic here is again reminiscent of *Les Armes miraculeuses*, though the poem tracks a more distinct teleology than some of Césaire's earlier pieces. The poem evokes the earth growing a mane like a horse in an image that recalls 'Les pur-sang', though as it launches into motion it also carries away rocks, rivers, horses, horsemen and houses. As in 'Salut à la Guinée', the very earth shifts in pursuit of a new order, though whilst in the former the tone is more secure and celebratory, in 'Bucolique' this springing into life heralds a more destructive gesture, concluding with the image of a 'bon berger roux, qui d'un bambou phosphorescent pousse à la mer un haut troupeau de temples frissonants et de villes' ['good russet shepherd, which with a phosphorescent bamboo pushes into the sea a tall herd of shuddering temples and cities'].[67] Césaire conjures an apocalyptic movement of disruption here, a vision of nonhuman environmental upheaval that far transcends his more programmatic evocations of decolonisation and figures revolt on a cosmic level.

The later pages of *Ferrements* attach the poet's vision for revolt to a series of more specific historical moments. In 'Le Temps de la liberté', for example, Césaire alludes to the violent repression of protests in Côte d'Ivoire in 1950, describing 'petits fleuves au ventre gros de cadavres' ['little rivers their bellies swollen with corpses'] and then figuring the protest as the start of the call for independence: 'Histoire je conte l'Afrique qui s'éveille' ['History I tell of the awakening of Africa'].[68] The poem idealises the power of Africa, the bravery

166   THE POLITICAL UPHEAVALS OF THE 1950S

of its revolutionaries but also its simultaneous preservation of tradition and reinvention in the future, so that the 'time of freedom' referred to in the title is both the immediate present and Africa's larger containment of both past and future. The 'Mémorial de Louis Delgrès' tells a story of revolt in more detail, this time shifting to Guadeloupe and commemorating Delgrès' campaign for the liberation of slaves in 1802, playing the violin to calm his soldiers and then blowing up his camp rather than conceding defeat to the French General Richepanse. The poem is prefaced with two extracts introducing these two images of Delgrès: the first from the Larousse encyclopaedia noting his birth in Martinique and comparing him to Tyrtaeus (the poet of Sparta), and the second from Jean-Jacques Dessalines' proclamation to Haitians on 4 April 1804, celebrating Delgrès as a 'magnanimous warrior' and reminding readers that if Delgrès was defeated, Haiti went on to achieve independence two years after his death.

The poem sets the scene for Delgrès' defiant sacrifice at Matouba by evoking the 'tissu de bruits de ferrements et de chaînes sans clefs' ['texture of the noise of ferraments of chains without keys'], then building tension across the three days of Delgrès' and his men's entrapment, when 'tout trembla sauf Delgrès' ['everything trembled except Delgrès'].[69] The narrative of the encirclement and subsequent explosion is then followed by an affirmation of the poet's song, which recasts Delgrès' heroic gesture as a promise for future hope. The historical precision of the poem is combined with an elegiac tone, suggesting liberation and growth, notably, once again, with the image of the liana representing both evolution and connection:

Je veux entendre un chant où l'arc-en-ciel se brise
où se pose le courlis aux plages oubliées
je veux la liane qui croît sur le palmier
(c'est sur le tronc du présent notre avenir têtu)

[I call for a song in which the rainbow can break
in which the curlew may land on forgotten strands

THE POLITICAL UPHEAVALS OF THE 1950S   167

I call for the liana that grows on the palm tree
(on the trunk of the present it is our obstinate future)][70]

These lines form part of an irregular sonnet and are as a result much closer to a regular form than most of Césaire's work, and although the lines are of uneven length, their neater organisation portrays the action of resistance in a timeless, musical form. The evocation of Delgrès' music is in this way echoed here in Césaire's own musical poetic composition, just as past rebellion is connected with Césaire's call for a different future.[71] Delgrès' sacrifice is also reminiscent of that of the Rebelle in *Et les chiens se taisaient*, and the poem can be seen to provide a historical example to concretise the play's mythical, universalising vision whilst also remaining shaped by that vision.

There are also poems in *Ferrements* grounded in recent history, as if to express a more direct activism. 'À la mémoire d'un syndicaliste noir' commemorates Albert Cretinoir, a union leader from Basse-Pointe, Martinique; in doing so, the poem clearly shifts the focus much closer to home than those referring to Africa. Whilst the poem honours Cretinoir's brave resistance and describes him as a 'maître marronneur des clartés' ['master marooner of clarity'], however, its language is still often cosmic rather than historical, and the syntax of the opening lines is highly complex. Césaire has certainly moved away here from the language of his earlier surrealist experimentation, but history is still combined with lyric complexity, and the poem cannot be reduced to an activist statement. '... sur l'état de l'Union', however, is perhaps Césaire's most concrete activism in poetic form. The poem is addressed to the American Congress, with the Union referring to the meeting in the House of Representatives where the three branches of government, the executive, the legislative and the judiciary, gather once a year. The poem narrates the horrific murder in August 1955 of 14-year-old Emmett Till, who was tortured and killed by two white men who claimed he had been flirting with one of their wives. The assassins were acquitted for

168   THE POLITICAL UPHEAVALS OF THE 1950S

this brutal crime, which led to the printing of a photograph of Till's mutilated body on the front of the Afro-American magazine *Jet* in protest against this injustice and against the extent of racist violence at that time. Césaire names Till in capital letters in a statement of solidarity and recognition, but also uses his example to vilify the long history of violence against black people, as on his eyes, the poet notes, there weighed:

> plus que tous les gratte-ciel, cinq siècles de tortionnaires de
> brûleurs de sorcières,
> cinq siècles de mauvais gin de gros cigares
> de grasses bedaines remplies de bibles rancies
> cinq siècles de bouche amère de péchés de rombières
> ils avaient cinq siècles EMMETT TILL
> cinq siècles est l'âge du pieu de Caïn

> [more than all the skyscrapers, five centuries of torturers of
> witch burners
> five centuries of cheap gin of big cigars
> of fat bellies filled with slices of rancid bibles
> five centuries mouth bitter from the sins of biddies
> they were five centuries old EMMETT TILL
> five centuries is the ageless age of Cain's stake.][72]

Césaire in this way deftly links a direct critique of America's current racist society with the devastating history captured through his other poems. Till's name is repeated three times in capital letters in commemoration, while the poet also cites 'GARÇON DE CHICAGO' twice in a reference to the racist term 'boy' used during this period of segregation. The poem denounces capitalism in America, through references to its wealth and resources, as well as this murderous racist underside.

It is through references to Africa, however, that Césaire expresses his contemporary political preoccupations most clearly in *Ferrements*. We have already seen how, in 'Salut à la Guinée', Césaire articulated his affirmative support for

THE POLITICAL UPHEAVALS OF THE 1950S   169

decolonisation in celebratory, even idealistic terms. While 'Salut à la Guinée' celebrates independence, however, 'Afrique' is more of a summons, as the poet addresses Africa as a whole and affirms its power in entering combat. 'Afrique' can be compared with 'À l'Afrique' in *Soleil cou coupé*, but the earlier poem addressed to Lam is a much more visceral evocation of the peasant's toil leading to a surrealist vision of possible rebirth. 'Afrique' in *Ferrements* is by turns both a more direct summons and a more abstract, utopian 'song of combat', to use Arnold's term. Césaire's affirmation of solidarity with Africa during this period of decolonisation is capped by 'Pour saluer le tiers monde', in which the poet evokes a vision of a unified continent where the nations together affirm their independence. The poem was written soon after the second Congress in Rome and is dedicated to Senghor, and it testifies to the sense of solidarity produced at that meeting. It opens with the poet evoking the troubled state of his own native island before he celebrates Africa standing firm but also nurturing, with maternal imagery suggesting a romanticised longing for origin:

> Je vois l'Afrique multiple et une
> verticale dans la tumultueuse péripétie
> avec ses bourrelets, ses nodules
> un peu à part, mais à portée
> du siècle, comme un cœur de réserve
>
> [I see Africa multiple and one
> vertical in the tumultuous peripeteia
> with her folds of fat, her nodules,
> slightly to the side, but within reach
> of the century, like a heart in reserve.][73]

As in 'Afrique', Césaire emphasises the unity of Africa here. He may name the independent states of Guinea and Ghana, as well as Mali which achieved independence in 1960, unlike in 'Afrique', but he also conjures a single, ancient land capable of

170   THE POLITICAL UPHEAVALS OF THE 1950S

rebirth and potentially serving as an example to all oppressed peoples, its hand 'tendue, / brunes, jaunes, blanches, / à toutes mains, à toutes les mains blessées / du monde' ['extended / brown, yellow, white, / to all hands, to all wounded hands / in the world'].[74] This salute to Africa is also a universalised call for justice and equality regardless of colour, and this last line again suggests that the poet connects his interest in African decolonisation with his disillusionment in the face of continued inequality in Martinique.

Whilst the voice and tone of the poems of *Ferrements* vary across the work, the poet's stated support for decolonisation and impassioned evocation of particular instances of injustice and of liberation reflect the influence that independence movements in Africa were exerting on his thought. It is perhaps revealing that the orientation of the volume is now far removed from that of *Tropiques*, which was devoted to the reinvigoration of local culture, as if by the time of *Ferrements* Césaire was clear that departmentalisation ultimately betrayed that objective and the only option left for the poet was to look elsewhere. Africa is repeatedly portrayed as a place of hope and possibility, it is an ancient motherland with a vibrant culture and a figure for resistance and solidarity. Whilst Césaire here more than anywhere else in his poetry is attuned to current political events, he persists in conjuring Africa in utopian terms as an almost mythical site of solidarity and revolution. This most politically grounded volume of poetry is also for this reason at times curiously ungrounded, as the poet struggles to unite political commitment with mythology and with a fantasised dream of unity and solidarity.

Nevertheless, if this combination at times gives the poet's voice an excessive confidence, and if this engagement fails to match up to the aesthetic sophistication of his earlier volumes, the reader should remain attentive to the sense of uncertainty that arises from the collection's fluctuating tone. Whilst decolonisation in Africa is celebrated, the poet's critique of oppression in poems such as 'Mémorial à Louis Delgrès' and '. . . sur l'état de l'Union', for example, does not clearly lead

THE POLITICAL UPHEAVALS OF THE 1950S 171

to a vision of change. The poet's apparently secure position in those poems that salute African independence, moreover, contrasts with the expressions of doubt found in poems such as '. . . mais il y a ce mal'. Here the speaker acknowledges the capacity of his imagination to fly free like the 'menfenil' or sparrowhawk but laments the vulnerability of these visions and portrays the pain of self-doubt in imagery that again captures the history of destruction and oppression:

> et moi je le suis
> au bec du vent du doute de la suie
> de la nuit ô cendre plus épaisse vers le cœur
> et ce hoquet de clous que frappent les saisons

> [and I I am prey
> for the beak of the wind of doubt of soot
> of night oh cinder denser towards the heart
> and this hiccup of nails driven in by the seasons][75]

The language of the poem becomes increasingly syntactically complex whilst the imagery becomes more allusive and surreal, as he evokes his blood coursing ferociously, only to trip, before 'mon mensonge' ['my lie'], isolated in a line on its own, seems to be overtaken by 'l'original sanglot noir des ronces' ['the original black sobbing of brambles'].[76] The poet's fantasy, crafting his voice as the harbinger of freedom, is crushed here, as we saw in the *Cahier* in the scene of his crisis before the black man on the tramway, and the poem ends with an image of black suffering.

Ferrements clearly marks a particular moment in Césaire's poetic trajectory. He moves away from the intense surrealist imaginary of his earlier volumes and replaces the hermeticism of his most experimental poems with a more lucid style. The result is not, however, a homogeneously militant tone, and the form of the poems varies considerably, from the melancholic longing of 'Ferrements' to the assured political critique of 'sur l'état de l'union'. Allusive lamentations expressing

172 THE POLITICAL UPHEAVALS OF THE 1950S

disillusionment towards the state of Martinique contrast with celebratory eulogies to African decolonisation, though these also incongruously combine a political message with mythical and utopian vocabulary. The syntax, moreover, is pared down and explosive in poems such as 'Spirales' and 'Beau sang giclé', whilst it is proliferating and convoluted in prose poems such as 'Bucolique'. At the same time, moments of surrealism are juxtaposed with seemingly more direct statements of political commitment. The uncertain aesthetic that ultimately shapes the collection perhaps indicates Césaire's shifting principles, as he struggles to relate his impassioned support for African decolonisation with his dissatisfaction back home in Martinique. He is also evidently now disillusioned with his own pursuit of departmentalisation and is seeking other ways to work for Martinicans, both with the PPM and by addressing them with a different form of poetry. Although he went on to rework some of the poems of *Soleil cou coupé* and *Corps perdu* in *Cadastre* in 1961, Césaire took a break from poetry during the next decade and instead wrote for the theatre, hoping to find a medium in which to speak to the public more directly. Whilst *Ferrements* clearly testifies to his search for a more politicised aesthetic, it is in the plays published during the 1960s that he finds a more popular, more historicised and more activist literary voice.

5

The Theatre of Decolonisation
'One does not invent a tree, one plants it'

While the 1950s was a decade of significant political and personal change for Césaire, his repositioning in 1958 with the creation of the Parti Progressiste Martiniquais in no way led to the establishment of a more secure political situation for Martinique – or for Césaire himself. On the contrary, the 1960s and 70s brought further unrest to Martinique, and, in the light of ongoing tensions and inequalities, Césaire continued to militate for its increased autonomy even as he found his stance increasingly embattled. After publishing *Ferrements* in 1960, he produced *Cadastre* in 1961, which contained revised versions of poems from *Soleil cou coupé* and *Corps perdu*, but from then on Césaire found his time increasingly taken up with political activity. *Cadastre* excluded some thirty of the poems from the preceding volumes and tempered much of the more experimental, surrealist imagery, presumably to create a more direct and approachable work, consistent with his strengthening belief in the political role played by culture. *Cadastre* would be his last poetic volume for twenty years, however, as the poet shifted his attention to the immediate demands of Martinican politics while switching to theatre as his principal forum for cultural expression. Both Césaire's political interventions and his plays during this period were focused on the precarious position of the nation as it emerges from colonial rule.

174   THE THEATRE OF DECOLONISATION

Without calling for the outright independence of Martinique, his visions for autonomy came increasingly close to a form of nationalism, whilst two of his plays, *La Tragédie du roi Christophe* (1963) and *Une Saison au Congo* (1966), explore the new forms of tyranny seen in Haiti in the wake of independence in 1804 and in the Democratic Republic of the Congo after independence in 1960. In *La Tragédie*, the abolitionist William Wilberforce writes a letter to Christophe warning him that the nation, like a tree, is not simply invented but must be planted and nurtured: '*une nation n'est pas une création, mais un mûrissement, une lenteur, année par année, anneau par anneau*' ['*a nation is not a creation, but rather a gradual ripening, year by year, ring by ring*'].[1] During the 1960s and 1970s Césaire was evidently preoccupied with the difficulties hampering at once the creation of African nations in the wake of decolonisation and his own Martinique as it struggled to establish a workable form of autonomy alongside its connection with France.

The political situation in Martinique in the early 1960s was becoming increasingly tense. In March 1961, a strike by agricultural workers in the Lamentin district was brutally repressed: three people were killed, while sixteen protesters and six policemen were injured. A few days later Césaire published an article in *Le Monde* arguing that these events testified to a crisis at the heart of departmentalisation. He vehemently denounced the continuing colonial status of the Antilles at the time when African colonies were achieving independence and insisted that assimilation was merely another form of domination. In so doing he called for nothing less than a 'revolution' that would lead to decolonisation, though this was conceived not as full independence but as 'autogestion' or self-governance:

> So the Antillean 'revolution' is already underway. Peoples who are denied the right to govern themselves and denied the power to direct their destiny even to a very limited extent, who are even stripped of themselves, wake up to a new claim: that of their character and of self-governance.[2]

THE THEATRE OF DECOLONISATION 175

Césaire further explained his position in a speech at a press conference in Fort-de-France in April 1961, which was then printed in *Le Progressiste* in May, arguing that tensions would only be resolved if Martinicans could establish a new political status founded on self-governance together with solidarity with France. Citing the inequality in salaries and benefits for Martinicans in comparison with the metropole and the lack of investment in Martinican industry, he insisted that self-governance would work to the benefit of both Martinique and France. Just like the enslaved who take control of the ship at the end of the *Cahier*, the Antillean people are here 'standing up', though Césaire now artfully combines this powerful vocabulary of resistance with that of fraternity and solidarity with France in a utopian vision of a new kind of political status.[3]

While Césaire repeatedly articulated his claim for self-governance in Martinique at multiple forums, including the Assemblée Nationale, he kept a close eye on developments in Africa and other parts of the Caribbean, and decolonisation movements elsewhere fuelled his anticolonial vision at home. He openly supported Algerian independence, although he received death threats as a result early in 1962. He called on Martinicans to vote yes in the April 1962 referendum on the Évian accords that would grant self-determination to Algeria, arguing that this would be a vote in favour of peace, liberation, truth and cooperation. Later, in July 1968, he spoke at the Assemblée Nationale in favour of an amnesty for those convicted of crimes during the Algerian War and called for the amnesty to be extended to Martinicans and Guadeloupeans. In his speech, he clearly emphasised the connection between events in Algeria and unrest in France's wider colonial territories. Moreover, in 1963 Césaire participated in a conference of African heads of state in Addis Ababa, where he met figures such as Kwame Nkrumah and Ahmed Sékou Touré as well as old friends such as Senghor. Closer to home, changes in the status of British Caribbean colonies fuelled Césaire's anticolonial arguments in Martinique, as Trinidad and Tobago

176   THE THEATRE OF DECOLONISATION

and Jamaica both achieved independence in August 1962. Césaire attended the celebrations in Trinidad, though independence there would also fuel tensions in Martinique among young people eager to separate definitively from France.

In September 1962, young Martinicans frustrated with the stagnation of their political situation formed the *Organisation de la jeunesse anticolonialiste de la Martinique* (OJAM), calling for 'Martinique for Martinicans'. Although the group vented the same grievances as Césaire and the PPM, their pressure no doubt encouraged the development of Césaire's increasingly nationalist rhetoric. He went on to support members of OJAM on trial at the Palais de Justice in November 1963, defending their actions and sharing their disappointment in the face of the lack of change in the status of Martinique and the lack of improvement in living and working conditions. Speaking eloquently of the hope expressed by young people in Martinique, he used the forum to condemn once again the stifling of Martinican culture and the lack of opportunities for young people. He also, together with Leiris and Sartre, defended eighteen Guadeloupean protesters who were arrested in Pointe-à-Pitre in May 1967 at their trial in February 1968, making the point that the French Constitution gave them the right to express their claim for independence. As Gary Wilder points out in his analysis of Césaire and Senghor's visions for self-determination without state sovereignty in *Freedom Time*, however, Césaire's commitment to autonomy rather than full independence meant that he was somewhat out of touch with members of the younger generation who wanted a more radical solution.[4]

During the second half of the 1960s, Césaire nevertheless intensified his nationalist rhetoric even if he still stopped short of demanding independence. At a conference in Havana in January 1968, he spoke of national culture not as a static entity imposed from above but as emanating from the *genius loci*, created dynamically through a particular place out of its history and geography, though it is also significant that during his stay in Cuba he reaffirmed the important role Marxism

THE THEATRE OF DECOLONISATION   177

could play in the regeneration of underdeveloped countries.[5] In his speech in March 1968 for the tenth anniversary of the founding of the PPM, he renewed his call for autonomy but repeatedly insisted that Martinique and Guadeloupe were nations, and that it was as nations that they claimed the right to self-determination. He also notably reaffirmed his commitment to Communism despite the split from the PCF in 1956, arguing that his socialist and anticolonial goals were one and the same, and calling for an end to rivalries and for the collaborative pursuit of the liberation and regeneration of Martinique.[6]

Yet Césaire's nationalism during this period maintained a vague form, and he used a variety of terms to describe the proposed new status of Martinique, including 'autonomie', 'autogestion', 'autodétermination' and 'décentralisation'. Expressions of dissatisfaction towards the inequality of the status quo were mingled with more abstract evocations of a *genius loci*, and he never detailed what precise form this political and economic self-governance would take. Véron notes Césaire's ongoing fidelity to the philosophy of Spengler, who clearly influenced him during his youth, and whose vision of the evolution and decline of ethno-cultures in *The Decline of the West* can be detected in the vocabulary of the emergent *genius loci*.[7] At the same time, he struggled to shake off the conception held by the younger generation that he was the agent of the departmentalisation that had betrayed them. However, if in 1971 the PPM had allied itself with supporters of the independence movement 'La Parole au peuple', this led to a drop in support for Césaire, necessitating the reinforcement of his rhetoric in favour of autonomy as opposed to independence in his speech at the PPM Congress in July 1973. Césaire's conviction in the face of dissent among Martinicans is clear in the use of capitals in the print version of the speech published in *Le Progressiste* in September of that year:

After contradictory debate, the PPM has purely and simply REJECTED THE WATCHWORD INDEPENDENCE

178 THE THEATRE OF DECOLONISATION

> as inadequate, unrealistic, irresponsible and even dangerous in the sense that it could diminish the realisation that we are working for and harm the Martinican cause rather than serve it.
>
> Our position bears no equivocation: AUTONOMY, COMPLETE AUTONOMY AND NOTHING BUT AUTONOMY.[8]

A general strike in February 1974 further fuelled tensions and once again the authorities turned on protestors, killing one person and injuring several more. Césaire's response was furious, and he called at the Assemblée Nationale for an end to this politics of repression.

In supporting François Mitterrand in the elections of 1974 (which he lost), Césaire strengthened his connections with the Martinican Communist Party and the Socialist Federation of Martinique, but pressure from the right continued to derail his campaign for autonomy. In an interview with Marie-Thérèse Rouil for *Black Hebdo* in June 1976, he expressed his pessimism about the situation in Martinique, describing his work as *'the fight for the survival of Martinique'*.[9] Césaire struggled with other obstacles, moreover, in the lead-up to the municipal elections of March 1977, when he had to admit the dire financial situation in the local council, though he nevertheless went on to win the elections. In July of the same year, he again set out the objectives of the PPM at their seventh Congress, but admitted the various difficulties it was encountering: its failure to animate local organisations, difficulties in recruitment, as well as its exclusivism, groupthink and sentimentalism.[10] The Party needed to open to new voices and work more effectively with the community. Césaire's speech at the opening of the campaign for the legislative elections in February 1978 ambitiously set out the party's agenda for 'three ways and five freedoms' and provided greater detail on the form that autonomy in Martinique would take. The speech began with a series of incendiary accusations against the French government and the departmental regime for its political and economic failures. Mapping out the three options of departmentalisation, independence and autonomy, Césaire again insisted on autonomy, arguing that it would bring with it five new forms of freedom. These would include: freedom to decide on their own customs to protect local trade; commercial freedom, allowing Martinique to trade freely with its immediate neighbours in the Americas; economic freedom to manage their own industries; cultural freedom that would enable the development of Creole language and culture; and political freedom so that Martinique would be governed by Martinicans.[11] Véron comments on the vagueness of Césaire's proposals here, as it remains unclear how this autonomous state would also work as part of a federation with France.[12] Nevertheless, Césaire's impassioned rhetoric is on display in full force, testifying to his anger and frustration as well as to the heated climate in which he was working, which would be further intensified by the murder of a supporter of Michel Renard, a Communist standing against Césaire in the legislative elections of March 1978.

At the end of the 1970s, the situation in Martinique was in no way approaching resolution. In the wake of the elections in March 1978, the PPM joined together with the Martinican Socialist Party but in 1980 tensions resurfaced, and there was a wave of strike action across the country. Césaire's language began to shift further, as, when asked to choose between autonomy and independence in an interview with Laurence Masurel printed in *Paris Match* in March 1980 and in *Le Progressiste* in April, he replied: 'it is a false problem, sooner or later Martinique will be independent. Montesquieu knew that already. Colonies are like ripe fruit: when they are mature, they fall. I am sure that the Antilles will be independent soon'.[13] At the PPM Congress in July of the same year, however, he again rejected the term independence in favour of autonomy, though argued that the Martinican people had a right to independence. The speech is therefore somewhat obfuscatory on the question of whether independence may be the ultimate goal of autonomy and indicates Césaire's lack of precision on this

180 THE THEATRE OF DECOLONISATION

question. Rather than committing to independence as the end point of the pursuit of autonomy, Césaire significantly returns to Marx at the end of this speech, citing him to emphasise that it is the *emancipation* of the Martinican people that he pursues above all.[14]

If Césaire's political activities occupied much of his time during the 1960s and 70s, he nevertheless continued to celebrate the importance of culture as a form of anticolonial resistance. Whilst poetry was on the back burner for this period, his plays were a means to address the people directly, and alongside his political work he kept on attending conferences and discussing culture, art, and poetry as integral to the claim for freedom. As we saw in the previous chapter, at the Rome conference in 1959 Césaire spoke grandiosely about the responsibility of men of culture to articulate and give form to the national feeling of the people. Although in this speech the rhetoric hinted at a glorified image of the intellectual capable of speaking for the people, in an interview with Khalid Chraïbi in 1965, Césaire's language is closer to that of Fanon in its privileging the artist's immersion in his native land, his profound integration in the life of the people in order to be the very 'flesh of the people'.[15] And indeed commitment here is precisely not belonging to a political party but writing one's lived experience of suffering, shared by the people. Art, culture, commitment and politics come closer together here than ever. Just as Fanon argued in his own speech at the 1959 Rome conference, Césaire conceives creative activity as the people's source of life.[16]

Césaire's 'Discours sur l'art africain' delivered at the first *Festival mondial des arts nègres* in April 1966 makes a vibrant statement of support for the vitality of African art. The festival was a large-scale event attracting representatives from all over the world, and Césaire would speak at the end of the conference to celebrate the importance of art in resisting the reification and dehumanisation perpetuated by Western attempts at domination. Césaire redeploys here the

THE THEATRE OF DECOLONISATION   181

vocabulary of reification or 'thingification' he used in *Discours sur le colonialisme*, but this vilification now shifts quickly into an affirmation of the centrality of art to life itself. Moreover, whereas in 'Panorama', printed in *Tropiques* back in 1944, Césaire denounced the suffocation of Martinican culture by the Vichy regime using the metaphor of the breath, here he insists that the need for art and poetry is 'a truly vital need, in the sense that we say that air is vital to man'.[17] Art is a source of communication and participation that rehumanises the reified society created by colonialism, and poetry provides a way to access man's originary life force. In the wake of colonialism, moreover, Césaire argues that Africa needs more than ever to create its own art, not only because of the influence of European culture under colonialism but also because of the current demands of modernisation and economic and political development. This does not entail a movement backwards, to what Césaire observes Malraux conceived as the African culture of masks, but precisely the creation of a new vitality. African art will also emerge from the very body of the artist: *'African art is above all in the heart, the head, the stomach, and the pulse of the African artist'*.[18] The language throughout this discussion privileges vitality, corporeality and the senses in such a way as to position art at the very centre of the lived experience of freedom.

Césaire's 'Discours sur l'art africain' at the same time contains what appears to be something of a volte-face concerning the term negritude. As I noted in the Introduction, Césaire seems to voice a thinly veiled critique of Senghor (who was present at the conference) when he confesses: 'my dear friends, I must say straight away that no word irritates me more than "negritude"'.[19] Yet if Césaire is newly anxious about the word 'negritude' and its usage, he nevertheless emphasises its significance in the reinvention of black culture and the rebirth of Africa. If the term has been accused of reifying black identity, moreover, Césaire reminds his audience of negritude poetry's resistance to 'chosification' and to caricature. Negritude literature and poetry precisely set out to defy fixed stereotypes:

182 THE THEATRE OF DECOLONISATION

> The appearance of the literature and poetry of Negritude only caused such a shock because they disturbed the image that the white man created of the black man, which they marked with his qualities and faults, with his human burden, in the world of abstractions and stereotypes that the white man had until then unilaterally fabricated about him.[20]

At the same time, Césaire insists that if negritude is based on a notion of a particular identity, it also continually transcends the particular to open out to the universal. And whilst it may be punctuated with cries and demands, in the end it is above all a 'postulation of fraternity'.[21] In an interview with Depestre in Havana in 1968, printed in *Le Progressiste* as well as later, in 1980, in Depestre's *Bonjour et adieu à la négritude*, he defends the term negritude as 'a challenge-word'; it was the attempt to seize back that derogatory term and make it into a signifier of defiance.[22] Césaire is also keen to historicise the term in an interview with Michel Tétu in 1972, where he grounds it in the experiences of black intellectuals, alienated by the culture of assimilation in 1930s Paris.[23] Later, in an interview with Jean Mazel in a volume entitled *Présence du monde noir* in 1975, Césaire sums up the term negritude with three words: 'identity, fidelity, solidarity'.[24] Identity here does not mean shared characteristics, but the affirmation of belonging to the black race, whilst fidelity rests on connection with the motherland, and solidarity brings a sense of connection with black people across the world. Responding to Soyinka's ironic quip that the tiger does not proclaim his tigritude, Césaire aptly notes that tigers do not think and speak. His evocations of negritude carefully resist essentialism here; instead, he uses the term to signify resistance and relationality.

In 'Société et littérature dans les Antilles', first delivered at a conference at the Université Laval in Quebec in April 1972 and published in *Études littéraires* the following year, however, Césaire speaks not so much about negritude as about the importance of national culture in ways that complement his growing interest in forms of political nationalism. Here,

THE THEATRE OF DECOLONISATION   183

national culture is not so much the *genius loci* that Césaire describes as metaphysical, but rather the culture actively created by the people who make up the nation. Once again, his vocabulary emphasises both lived experience and dynamism, and indeed, this national culture in turn maintains its dynamism by contributing to and continually remodelling the universal. Césaire's reflections on national culture once again redeploy rhetorical features of the *Discours sur le colonialisme*, as he conjures in proliferating sentences the withering and destruction of Martinican culture under colonialism. Whilst education rates are high in Martinique, he argues that this in fact results in the suppression of local culture, and indeed, this continues in some nations that recently achieved independence, a phenomenon he defines as 'neocolonialism'. Césaire's language is again indebted to that of Fanon here, as he associates culture with revolution, and describes revolution as a live process. Antillean literature must also be deeply anchored in its connections with the land and the people, not stunted by an imposed culture or by a putative return to the past, but actively created and recreated through dialogue with both the human and the nonhuman environment: 'Antillean literature will be a deepening, a search, the deepening of a communion and re-establishment of man in his belonging and fundamental relations with his land, his country and his people'.[25]

Whilst Césaire's evocations of national culture during this period complement the parallel development in his political thought, the evocation of the alienation of Martinique and the call for integration with the land can be traced back to the aesthetics of *Tropiques* and the early poetry. It was in 1978 that the complete set of volumes of *Tropiques* was republished by Jean-Michel Place, prefaced with an interview with Jacqueline Leiner in which Césaire reflects on the explosive power of poetry as well as on the ways in which he drew on Frobenius to contemplate man's 'saisissement' by the world and the creation of culture out of that fundamental calling. In the 1979 essay 'La Martinique telle qu'elle est', moreover,

184   THE THEATRE OF DECOLONISATION

Césaire refers to Frobenius in conceptualising the migration of West African philosophy to the Caribbean and the ongoing influence of Bantu theories of the vital force. This life force fuels the dynamic movement of Martinican culture, where the people are seized by myth, allowing the reinvigoration of 'a living force for renewal, enrichment and fulfilment'.[26] Césaire may on the one hand be preoccupied with the political status of Martinique and the increasingly urgent demand for autonomy, but his vision for national culture also far exceeds his political programme. It retains a connection with his vision for an organic, living culture emerging out of man's dialogue with the environment while calling for a galvanising renewal appropriate to the demands of Martinique in the present.

The Drama of the Haitian Revolution: *Toussaint Louverture* and *La Tragédie du roi Christophe*

Bearing witness to independence movements in Africa, and intensifying his calls for autonomy in Martinique, Césaire was more and more preoccupied with politics during the 1960s and ever more committed to achieving practical political change. So it is perhaps not surprising that after publishing the politically explicit volume *Ferrements* in 1960, he turned to an art form that directly addressed the people: theatre. Césaire's plays of the 1960s are grounded in history and transparent in their representation of particular moments of emancipation and oppression. Wole Soyinka goes so far as to argue that the plays were for Césaire 'a clear agent of social transformation'.[27] They constitute a direct form of activism in their address to ordinary people and, while drawing on myth in portraying anticolonial leader figures, they address head-on the practical difficulties of decolonisation despite bearing traces of the author's visionary language of renewal. Césaire explains his desire to clarify the obscurity some readers found in his poetry:

THE THEATRE OF DECOLONISATION   185

This is the reason why for a while I have been engaged in theatrical activity. It seems to me to be the best way to make people become aware, especially people who do not read. Theatre can create a shock and it is an extraordinary force for awakening. Theatre allows a multiplication of poetic force, and that is what is essential for me.[28]

This does not mean that theatre completely relinquishes the language of poetry. Rather, it makes that language more accessible and more communicative. For Césaire, theatre is a way to 'bring poetry to the masses' and to achieve a form of political 'engagement'.[29] At the same time, he characterises his theatre as political because it tackles Africa's political problems and seeks to 'reactualise' black culture in the pursuit of a new revolutionary order where African culture could flourish.[30] It reflects on the past in order to shed light on the present and to envision a better future.

This politicisation and direct address to the people does not mean that the language of Césaire's plays is simple or transparent. Politically engaged theatre for Césaire is, on the contrary, artistically creative in its mixing of traditions, styles and idioms, to capture the cultural syncretism produced by creating anticolonial drama in French. Césaire is influenced by major European dramatists including Shakespeare and Brecht, as well as by Nietzschean philosophy, but blends these with references to Voodoo mythology, Creole and African traditions. Christophe, for example, is both a Nietzschean and a Shakespearean tragic hero transported to the turbulent years following the Haitian Revolution, whilst Brechtian addresses to the audience are coupled with music and dance invoking Voodoo gods. As Daniel Maximin observes, poetic language is brought to life through an oral delivery combining multiple registers and tones: 'the trivial, the popular, the epic, the political and the poetic, obscure omens, the grandiloquent speech of the leader, the suspicious humour of the peasants. And also, as in ancient tragedy, the choir's concerns towards the hero's overly solitary prophecy'.[31] Césaire also enriched

186 THE THEATRE OF DECOLONISATION

the French in his plays with Caribbean and African religious references, songs and idioms, challenging colonial hegemony in both content and form.[32]

Césaire's plays served no less than to inaugurate the production of an anticolonial theatre in French. They are a crucial reference for subsequent generations of Caribbean playwrights who follow Césaire's lead in using the stage as a form of activism to challenge colonialism and call for equal rights and emancipation. His impact on Caribbean theatre, however, exceeds the plays themselves, as he worked to promote cultural activity more broadly in Martinique. In 1971, Césaire established the Office Municipal d'Action Culturelle, succeeded by the Service Municipal d'Action Culturelle in 1975 directed for a long time by Jean-Paul Césaire, offering spaces and programming for visual and dramatic arts.[33] In 1972 Césaire also set up the Festival Culturel de Fort-de-France, an annual festival bringing together practitioners in the performing arts from across the world. *Une Tempête* was performed at the inaugural festival, directed by Yvan Labéjof, staged in the tradition of the oral culture of the *mornes*, using African music and clearly anchored in the Martinican landscape.[34] These initiatives led to the creation of further cultural centres and theatres in Martinique during this period, including the Centre Martiniquais d'Action Culturelle directed for a time by Manuel Césaire and the Théâtre de la Ville de Fort-de-France directed by Michèle Césaire. If Césaire's own plays are sweeping historical dramas, however, and raise large-scale questions of political governance and state sovereignty, the work of subsequent generations is highly diverse, and indeed his daughter Ina Césaire combines historical drama from a female perspective in *Rosanie Soleil* (1992) with a much more up-close and intimate portrait of two Creole mothers in *Mémoires d'isles* (1985).

Césaire's greatest and most celebrated play is *La Tragédie du roi Christophe*, first published in 1963, revised in 1970. The play takes the example of Haiti after independence in 1804 to reflect on African decolonisation as well as on the frustrations

THE THEATRE OF DECOLONISATION 187

of contemporary Martinique. The *Tragédie* should be understood as the culmination of Césaire's interest in Haiti, which can be traced back to the period he spent there in 1944, when he both marvelled at Haiti's history as the site of the first uprising of enslaved people leading to independence and lamented its economic difficulties and the estrangement of the ruling classes, personified by François Duvalier, from the masses.[35] Haiti was where 'la négritude se mit debout pour la première fois' ['negritude rose for the first time'] in the *Cahier* and it was the setting of the early 1943 version of *Et les chiens se taisaient*, where the Rebelle was actually named as the revolutionary Toussaint Louverture.[36] Despite the poor treatment of workers in contemporary Haiti, Césaire insists on the significance for him of its revolutionary history and its resonance for thinking about Africa: 'Haiti represented for me the heroic Antilles as well as the African Antilles. I saw a connection between the Antilles and Africa, and Haiti is the most African of all our Antilles'.[37] Raphael Confiant has objected to what he saw as Césaire's appropriation of Haitian history as a means to think about contemporary Africa, but it is important that if this crucial revolutionary claim for independence could be informative for Africa, Césaire nevertheless reads it as a pivotal moment in Caribbean history that speaks at the same time to the situation of contemporary Martinique.[38]

La Tragédie should be read against the background of Césaire's historical study *Toussaint Louverture: La Révolution française et le problème colonial* [*Toussaint Louerture: The French Revolution and the Colonial Problem*] published in 1961. A detailed account of the unfolding of the Haitian Revolution, Césaire's methodology in *Toussaint Louverture* reveals several important assumptions. First, the book's introduction evokes Saint-Domingue as 'an exemplary colony', the first to have lived through and challenged 'the colonial problem'.[39] It is also, despite its title, not a biography of Toussaint Louverture but a much wider account of the Haitian Revolution, based on extensive and meticulous research and comprising multiple quotations from sources and speeches from that period.

188 THE THEATRE OF DECOLONISATION

Toussaint Louverture both is and is not at the centre of the study; he is by turns conjured as the hero and driver of the revolution and as a cog in a larger dialectic. The text antici-pates Césaire's use of the historical figures of Christophe and Lumumba in *La Tragédie* and *Une Saison au Congo* respectively, in that he takes a tragic hero figure as the focus for a larger his-tory, and at once glorifies and questions the leader's solipsism. On the one hand, then, Toussaint Louverture is celebrated as a unique character capable of sophisticated strategising in his direction of enslaved people through the various stages of the revolution. Césaire cites his rousing rhetoric and eulogises his exceptional talent, noting for example not just his military prowess but his 'political mind', his understanding of the need to educate the people in order to forge the nation, and indeed his combination of multiple qualities: 'a man of thought, a man of action, a diplomat, an administrator'.[40] On the other hand, he notes Toussaint's mistakes, his failure to connect properly with the people, his championing of 'general free-dom', and, ironically anticipating Césaire himself, his failure to invoke independence as a means to catalyse the people.[41] Moreover, though Césaire is clearly compelled by Toussaint's leadership, Toussaint only appears after nearly two hundred pages in his study. His role is to take forward the last chapter in the revolution, following the revolt of the white planters and that of the mulattoes, so that he is at once the hero of the text and yet oddly decentred.

If the title's focus on Toussaint Louverture is in part mis-leading, so too is the subtitle 'the French Revolution'. It is surprising that Césaire designates the French Revolution rather than the Haitian Revolution, and if his aim is to show how the French Revolution indeed provided the backdrop for the uprising in Saint Domingue, he still emphasises the aegis of France. Césaire seems to want to avoid subordinating Saint Domingue to France by insisting: *'we must understand that there is no "French Revolution" in the French colonies. In each French colony there is a specific revolution, born at the same time as the French Revolution, connected to it, but unfolding according to*

THE THEATRE OF DECOLONISATION   189

its own laws and its own objectives.[42] And yet even this quotation suggests that the Haitian Revolution is part of the French Revolution, and Césaire at once tries to explore and to attenuate the connection with France. The three sections of the book, moreover, lay out a dialectical structure, foregrounding the links between the stages of the revolution and the political discourse around them in France, to create a complex narrative or even a drama in three acts rather than a celebratory linear history. The first section, detailing the frustrated claims of the white colonists in Saint Domingue against the bourgeoisie in France, precedes the representation of the abortive attempts of free people of colour to obtain full civil rights, which in turn gives way to the full blown 'negro revolution' spearheaded by Toussaint Louverture. Ultimately, independence is the result of multiple struggles, even as Toussaint's name in the title seems to give his actions a pre-eminent role.

Césaire's *Toussaint Louverture* shows Césaire thinking through the leader figure's problematic position in relation to France, to the Republican discourse of the rights of man, and to decolonisation. Césaire portrays Toussaint acting in the name of the enlightened ideals of liberty, equality and fraternity, and notes that, like himself, he never called for independence. Toussaint fought in the name of universal values, perhaps paying insufficient attention to the particular demands of the people in whose name he acted, but in calling for the recognition of the humanity of the slaves of Saint Domingue, Toussaint 'inscribes himself and the revolt of the black slaves of Saint Domingue in the history of universal civilisation'.[43] At the same time, however, although Toussaint was more driven by an abstract, universal idea of emancipation than by the particular experiences of his people, Césaire still affirms his significance for future generations. In setting Haitian history in motion, he is a 'Precursor', first of all anticipating subsequent leaders Dessalines and Christophe and later the contemporary Antillean context. His struggle for emancipation and for rights for Césaire clearly foreshadows that in which he himself is engaged in 1960s Martinique.[44]

190   THE THEATRE OF DECOLONISATION

Subsequent historians have expressed more reservations towards Toussaint's emancipatory role, as his biographers Forsdick and Hogsbjerg have observed, since it was discovered in the 1970s that Toussaint was himself a slave owner in the late 1770s, and his constitution for a self-governing Saint Domingue in 1801 could be seen as autocratic in its insistence on the power of a single governor.[45] Even C. L. R James notes Toussaint's inability to communicate with the people in his magisterial portrait of him in *The Black Jacobins* (published in 1938) and in later lectures he revised his narrative of the history of the Revolution so that Toussaint no longer occupied a central and heroic role.[46] Yet in his study Césaire clearly sees Toussaint at once as an aspirational role model and as a man struggling with comparable tensions and paradoxes to those he himself confronted.

La Tragédie du roi Christophe follows on directly from *Toussaint Louverture*, to the extent that Césaire's study of Toussaint has been seen as a long introduction to the play.[47] *La Tragédie* focuses not on the Revolution itself, however, but on its aftermath and on the new challenges facing leader figures, in this case King Henri Christophe, after decolonisation. Yet whereas Toussaint was driven by a vision for universal emancipation, Christophe worked specifically to establish the Haitian nation as it emerged out of colonial rule. And if for Césaire, Toussaint was flawed and yet heroic, Christophe is a more ambivalent figure; he is an inspirational visionary, yet the divorce between his visionary ideals and the real lives of the people he commands is disastrous. His project of nation-building finishes by brutalising the people who are enlisted to work for its construction. The play in this way tackles not just the moment of decolonisation but the contradictions of its aftermath in ways that resonated with the new African nations whose fates Césaire observed. The troubled portrayal of nation-building in Haiti after the Revolution served as a warning about the difficulties associated with the establishment of new regimes in recently decolonised African states. Whilst this connection between Haiti and Africa was clearly

THE THEATRE OF DECOLONISATION   191

crucial to Césaire, however, and he insisted on it several times in interviews during this period, the play could also be seen to reflect back on François Duvalier's dictatorship in Haiti, beginning in 1957. At the same time, James Arnold emphasises the play's broader Caribbean resonance, arguing that *La Tragédie* is, 'less the drama of the decolonisation of Africa than the tragedy of a generation of Afro-Caribbeans in the face of this decolonisation that escapes them'.[48] Christophe's journey is also one of a spiritual transformation, brought about by the invocation of African divinities, so the play should be seen as a profound cultural reflection and not limited to the question of state-building.

La Tragédie du roi Christophe is a major work in the history of theatre in French, and it made a significant impact on audiences from the start.[49] It was first performed under the direction of Jean-Michel Serreau at the Salzburg festival in the summer of 1964, and the production went on to tour in Vienna, Berlin, Innsbruck and eventually, in 1965, Paris. This production was revived again at the *Dakar Festival des arts nègres* in 1966, where, according to Serreau, several African dignitaries in the audience walked out, perhaps recognising in the play something of their own situation, an anecdote that reveals the play's contemporary social and political topicality.[50] Césaire reworked the play during this period, publishing a revised edition in 1970, in which Christophe's tyranny becomes clearer earlier and the staging of which was slightly simplified.[51] In 1973, it was taken up by the Senegalese Théâtre National Daniel-Sorano, who then brought it to Fort-de-France to coincide with a visit by Senghor. As Romuald Fonkoua insists, the significance of this staging should not be underestimated: an African theatre company brought the play to life before a Martinican public dissatisfied with their political status, and in so doing both informed them about political history and provoked them to consider alternative possibilities.[52] *La Tragédie* was also the first play by a black playwright to be staged at the Comédie-Française in Paris in 1991 and the first to be performed in the 'cour d'honneur' at the Avignon festival in

192   THE THEATRE OF DECOLONISATION

1996. Gregson Davis describes the play's 'exalted position within the Césairean theatrical corpus, comparable to that of the *Cahier* for his lyric œuvre'.[53] Nick Nesbitt goes even further in asserting that 'the appearance of *La Tragédie du roi Christophe* marks the inauguration of a monument in the history of the black Atlantic world'.[54]

The work speaks at once to the particular and to the universal, and draws on both history and myth, mixing a dizzying range of influences and styles. Césaire based his portrayal of Christophe on careful reading of historical sources, and some of Christophe's speeches in the play contain elements of original documents.[55] The play opens with the division of Haiti in 1806 between the republic led by Pétion in the south and Christophe's monarchy in the north, and it documents the King's reign from 1806 until his death in 1820. James Arnold notes inaccuracies in Césaire's version of this history, questioning in particular the sharp division between the 'mulâtres' in the south and the 'nègres' in the north, yet Césaire did conduct extensive historical research in preparing the script.[56] At the same time, *La Tragédie* is clearly steeped in myth and resonates on a universal level: Christophe is at once a Nietzschean and a Shakespearean tragic hero, a visionary whose hubris ultimately brings his downfall. The designation of the play as a 'tragédie' broadly references both Greek and Shakespearean traditions, and one could draw a more specific parallel between the scene of the assassinated archbishop Corneille Brelle's reappearance before Christophe and Macbeth's vision of Banquo. The gravity and scope of the tragedy, however, are eclectically mixed with comedy, with ridicule and farce. The clash between Pétion and Christophe is parodically anticipated by a cockfight in the opening scene, and Christophe's performances of his status often border on the ridiculous. Christophe's faithful advisor Vastey is mirrored by Hugonin the buffoon, a character reminiscent of King Lear's wise fool, whose ironic songs and comical responses to Christophe make a mockery of his inflated self-image. If Christianity is perniciously associated with colonialism in the play, moreover, the

THE THEATRE OF DECOLONISATION   193

ending enacts the triumph of Voodoo, as Hugonin is transformed into the loa Baron Samedi who presides over the dead, and Christophe is transmuted in death to the Yoruba god of thunder, Shango. Afro-Caribbean spiritualism emerges in revolt against Christophe's former tyranny, with Voodoo figures, music, chants and Creole language intervening in the tragedy to give it a dynamic new form representing the multifarious cultural contexts from which it emerges and to whom it is addressed.

The play tells the story of Christophe's increasing descent into tyranny as he seeks to rebuild Haiti after decolonisation. After the opening scene of the cockfight and an introduction to the play's historical setting by the Announcer-Commentator, Act I Scene 1 shows Christophe and Pétion in dispute: Pétion offers Christophe the presidency on the condition that he adopt a Constitution that limits his powers, and the latter refuses, claiming instead the monarchy of the northern province. Christophe vows to re-establish the dignity of former enslaved people by restoring their names and rejecting those imposed by the coloniser: 'de noms de gloire je veux couvrir vos noms d'esclaves / de noms d'orgueil nos noms d'infamie, / de noms de rachat nos noms d'orphelins!/ C'est d'une nouvelle naissance, Messieurs, qu'il s'agit!' ['I will cover your slave-names with names of glory, / Our names of disgrace with proud names, / Our orphaned names with names of redemption!'].[57] Already, however, there is an irony in Christophe's flamboyant embrace of the trappings of power, and this grandiose renaming is evidently at odds with the people's real needs. Soon it becomes evident that Christophe's reign is sliding into authoritarianism, as his vision for the new nation demands excessive work from the people, and he argues that blacks need to strive more than whites to rebuild themselves out of the destruction of the enslaved past. His exorbitant vision for the new nation is crystallised in his vision of a Citadel, a magnificent structure that for him would symbolise the creativity and strength of the people, but that in reality serves only to represent his glorification of his own power:

Je dis la Citadelle, la liberté de tout un peuple. Bâtie par le peuple tout entier, hommes et femmes, enfants et vieillards, bâtie pour le peuple tout entier! Voyez, sa tête est dans les nuages, ses pieds creusent l'abîme, ses bouches crachent la mitraille jusqu'au large des mers, jusqu'au fond des vallées, c'est une ville, une forteresse, un lourd cuirassé de pierre. . .

[I say the Citadel, the liberty of all the people. Built by the whole people, men and women, children and elders, built for the whole people! See how its head dreams towards the clouds, its feet plumb the abyss, while its mouths spit grape-shot as far as the open sea and the hollows of valleys; it is a city, a fortress, a massive breastplate of stone!][58]

As the drama unfolds, Christophe's power becomes increasingly tyrannical, as his vision for nation-building becomes a desire to refashion humanity itself. Peasants are beaten, forced to work through a storm, and the land is owned by the military rather than by those who toil upon it. Characters are put to death on a whim, such as when the French messenger Franco de Medina is condemned for not addressing Christophe correctly, and Archbishop Brelle is seen as a traitor for considering returning to France. As the King's inflated self-image grows ever more grotesque, the people are driven to revolt against him. He becomes more and more isolated, supported in the end only by the faithful Vastey, suffers a stroke and ends up committing suicide in his weakened state.

Christophe is a complex and intriguing figure, a successor to Toussaint in his vision for liberation and emancipation but a tyrant in his megalomaniacal claim for power. It is possible to perceive him at least in the earlier scenes as a precursor of negritude in his pursuit of a new order, and indeed, the critic Albert Owasu-Sarpong seeks to justify Christophe's violence more broadly as a means to galvanise the people and make them act.[59] Césaire himself explains Christophe's struggle with the demands of the independence effort and his love for his people, as if to emphasise the nobility of his goals even if their

THE THEATRE OF DECOLONISATION 195

execution was flawed.[60] He also articulates the core problems facing the leader of the new nation: the metaphysical question of race, the political problem of the construction of the new state and the human problem of the people's adaptation to the state.[61] Christophe struggles with these difficulties in such a way as to make clear the many challenges of the modern state in the wake of decolonisation. But Christophe's problem is his solipsism; he isolates himself from the people, fails to understand and communicate with them, and loses himself in his own grandiose and exorbitant vision of nation-building. His vision for the nation is an impossible ideal, and real people are subordinated to this ideal even as he maintains it in their name. As he becomes increasingly weakened, his self-image becomes monstrously exaggerated, as he blurs himself with the defiant structure of the Citadel: 'mon âme, sachez-le, / est debout, intacte, solide, comme notre Citadelle. / Foudroyé, mais inébranlé, l'image même / de notre Citadelle, Christophe' ['but know that my soul / stands upright, inviolate, sound, just like our Citadel / Stricken, yet unshaken, the very image / of our Citadel, is Christophe!'].[62] If Christophe speaks in the name of freedom, however, he becomes trapped by this exorbitant self-image, so that the play finishes by arguing, in Césaire's words, that 'il faut libérer l'homme nègre, mais il faut aussi libérer le libérateur' ['we need to liberate the black man, but also need to liberate the liberator'].[63]

If Christophe figures the danger of the role of the leader, other characters represent alternative attitudes to the pursuit of emancipation. One of these is Metellus, leader of the rebels during the civil war, who is killed on the battlefield and speaks rousingly about the liberation of black people in his parting words. Rejecting the tyranny of both Christophe and Pétion, he evokes the suffering of the battles for emancipation and the hope represented by Toussaint to vilify the betrayal by the new rival leaders. His idealistic rhetoric is reminiscent of that of the Rebelle in *Et les chiens se taisaient*, as he conjures, 'la Fille Espérance (les paumes de ses mains luisaient dans la nuit / de sa peau, comme la dorure au creux des / feuilles sombres du caïmitier)' ['the daughter, Hope / (the palms of her hands shone in the night / of her skin, like the gold in the dark hollows / of star-apple leaves)'].[64] He prefigures negritude in his utopian evocation of a land for all black people from around the world, a vision of a global black community that would eschew atavism and territorialism in favour of relationality and shared culture. Equally, Mme Christophe represents an ethical counter to Christophe, reminiscent of the Amante in *Et les chiens*, as she calls upon him to temper his megalomania and consider its consequences for the people and for future generations.

Césaire's depiction of female characters has caused controversy, as some critics object to his relegation of women to the sidelines. It is problematic that women feature only fleetingly in Césaire's theatre, and they are all subordinate to the male characters, occupying roles as advisors to the male tragic hero. Yet despite their minor roles, women such as Mme Christophe are sources of wisdom and poetry. Daniel Maximin recounts how he suggested to Césaire that he might in fact have seen himself not in the leader figures of Toussaint and Christophe but in Mme Christophe, as she, the Amante and Pauline Lumumba, are 'the three poteau-mitan women of his theatre, not timid bearers of fear, impediment or pusillanimity as is sometimes too easily said, but on the contrary lucid voices with a *vision* of the present confronting their lover's short-sighted *view* of the future'.[65] Mme Christophe's evocation, in the wake of Christophe's death, of a poor old woman hobbling through rain and dust and learning his name, is a powerful poetic antidote to Christophe's own self-aggrandising rhetoric.

Christophe's hubris is at the same time countered by non-human forces. His pursuit of nation-building crescendos into a claim to refashion the earth and to govern the water, to make of the Artibonite river the Nile of Haiti. One of the peasants laughs at his misguided methods, however, and more broadly, the power, the fluidity and movement of the river as it is captured by the Commentator at the opening of Act II signify a necessary organic dynamism that opposes the entrenchment

THE THEATRE OF DECOLONISATION   197

and rigidity of the Citadel.[66] As in *Et les chiens*, environmental and ecological forces serve to represent political movement. If Mme Christophe compares her husband to 'le gros figuier qui prend toute la végétation / alentour / et l'étouffe' ['the great fig tree that takes all the plants / Growing around it and strangles them'], Wilberforce's evocation of the organic growth of the nation, as opposed to its fabricated construction, cited at the beginning of this chapter, suggests a relational rather than oppressive process.[67] In Act III, moreover, the explosion of Voodoo and Yoruba spirituality signals the collapse of Christophe's power. The Christian Feast of the Assumption is interrupted by Voodoo divinities, as Christophe is haunted by the Archbishop Brelle whom he had condemned to death, and he suffers a stroke. He finally summons the loas or African gods and reconnects with his African heritage: 'Afrique de ta grande corne sonne mon sang! Et qu'il se déploie de toute l'envergure d'un vaste oiseau!' ['Africa, sound my blood from your great horn! And let it unfurl to the full wingspread of an enormous bird!'].[68] It is while summoning Africa, however, that Christophe shoots himself, as if to symbolise the defeat of the European model of power that he had persisted in enacting and to herald a process of spiritual transformation. His transmutation into the form of the Yoruba god Shango, representing thunder, lightning and fire, is captured in the African page's recitation of his funerary ritual in a speech that is rich in references to Ifa divination (palm oil, for example, is associated with religious sacrifice and the wind is a reference to the tradition of blowing into cowrie shells at the start of the divination process).[69] African religious tradition combines spirits with the elements to challenge both Christophe's assertion of sovereign power and his fabricated vision of the modern nation state.

Christophe's demise is a 'tragedy', as the play's title informs us, as his hubris takes him from visionary to tyrant, and the construction of the new nation leads only to the perpetuation of violence. Yet Césaire described his tragedies as optimistic and suggests that Christophe's failure could be the starting point for a different future.[70] Césaire also uses the imagery of standing, 'debout', featured in the *Cahier*, and if Vastey insists that Christophe's dead body be placed 'debout' at the end of the play, this could symbolise the survival of his idealistic dream even if its attempted realisation led only to disaster.[71] The hubristic tragic hero must fall, then, but the poet wants to retain something of his vision for emancipation and renewal.

If Césaire looks back to the past of the creation of the Haitian nation between 1806 and 1820 in this play, its language is persistently future-oriented. Ménil argues that 'it is not the past that we are invited to see in the attempted historical reconstruction but our future' and the play analyses processes of construction and invention in the new nation, though it remains open-ended in portraying these processes as dynamic and incomplete.[72] The resurgence of African spirituality at the end is at the same time not a conjuring of the past but a call for rebirth, as Vastey concludes the play with the image of 'oiseaux essaimeurs de pollens / dessinez-lui ses armes non périssables / d'azur au phénix de gueules couronné d'or' ['birds that scatter the pollen / design for him his immortal coat-of-arms: on an azure field, red phoenix crowned with gold'].[73] *La Tragédie* tells a story of struggle and failure but finishes by calling for political and spiritual renewal. The form of this renewal remains unknown, however, as Césaire laments the failings of decolonisation. The play leaves audiences uncertain about how a successful regime could come into being in the wake of the colonial presence.

Une Saison au Congo

Césaire's next play, *Une Saison au Congo* (1966), develops these questions of decolonisation, nation-building and leadership in the context of the period around independence in what is now the Democratic Republic of Congo. Césaire's interest in the Congo can be traced back to the 1943 edition of the *Cahier*, where the poet conjures a vibrant and defiant Congo lush with vegetation yet scarred by its history of enslavement. With *Une*

THE THEATRE OF DECOLONISATION 199

Saison au Congo, however, Césaire's focus is on the politics of independence and specifically on the inspirational figure of Patrice Lumumba, the first Prime Minister of the newly independent Republic of Congo between June and September 1960, who was assassinated in January 1961 by forces in the seceded province of Katanga. The play is based on careful research, mostly of published materials, but Césaire's Lumumba also deploys poetic rhetoric that allies the Congolese politician with the visionaries the Rebelle, Christophe and indeed the poet himself. In portraying Lumumba as a political visionary and poet, Césaire sought to rescue him from the negative portraits of him in the Western press and to explore his own vision for independence freed from a restrictive conception of national territoriality. The style is at once, as Gregson Davis suggests, 'far more down to earth' than that of previous works in its tracing of the sequence of events and machinations that led to Lumumba's assassination, and yet also characteristic of Césaire in its inclusion of rousing lyricism in Lumumba's idealised evocations of independence and freedom across Africa.[74]

The play depicts the attempts by Belgian officials to maintain power and influence after independence and their involvement in the secession of the resource-rich region of Katanga. Lumumba is dissatisfied with the vision for independence offered by the Belgians and seemingly accepted by Kasa-Vubu, the President of the Republic of Congo (renamed Kala Lubu by Césaire). As the new nation looks increasingly to be economically struggling and politically breaking down, Lumumba makes Mokutu (who is clearly based on the future President Mobutu) his Chief of the Army. When he turns to the United Nations, represented by Dag Hammerskjöld, for help, Lumumba is frustrated by the weakness of the latter's purportedly neutral stance. He continues to dream of an independent Congo that would work towards the liberation of all of Africa, but his rhetoric is increasingly at odds with the power struggles of Kala Lubu, Mokutu and also Tzumbi (based on Moise Tshombe, President of the State of Katanga), and he is ultimately killed by Katangan mercenaries. Césaire

200   THE THEATRE OF DECOLONISATION

continued to revise the play after its initial publication in 1966, and notably added a scene at the end of the 1973 version, in which Mokutu presides over the celebration of independence in 1966 and his soldiers open fire on crowds when Lumumba's name is cheered as a symbol of 'uhuru' or 'freedom', making clear the open brutality of Mobutu's regime.

It is perhaps not surprising that the play was highly controversial at the time of its publication and first performances, given its critique of Belgian officials and positive portrayal of Lumumba, who had been vilified in the Belgian press.[75] The Cold War features as the tense background to the play; when his plane is not permitted to land in Elizabethville, Lumumba asks for it to be diverted to Moscow, and the suggested association between Lumumba and the Soviet Union would have fuelled criticism of him in Europe. The United Nations, as figured by the somewhat feeble Hammerskjöld is also, as the critic Julie-Françoise Tolliver puts it, portrayed controversially as 'an easily perverted instrument'.[76] The Belgian theatre director Rudi Barnet set out to stage *Une Saison* in 1967, but no theatre would support it. He eventually gained financial support from artists and intellectuals and founded the Compagnie du Théâtre Vivant. The play was then performed in a world premiere at the Centre Intellectuel d'Anderlecht on 20 March 1967, and a review in *Le Soir* notes that it may have pleased black populations pursuing nationalism, but a European public would have difficulty accepting it.[77] In its wake, all of Barnet's contracts were terminated until 1969. Mobutu invited Barnet's Compagnie to stage the play in the Congo, but Barnet refused, and Césaire was clearly uncomfortable with the idea.[78] He produced a slightly revised version in 1967 that was less critical of Mokutu, which was staged by Serreau at the biennale in Venice and at the Théâtre de l'Est in Paris, but the response among young Congolese was still uneasy.[79]

There is clearly a continuity between *Une Saison au Congo* and *La Tragédie du roi Christophe*. Both plays explore the consequences of decolonisation and examine the struggles of the visionary leader to bring a successful and united new nation into existence. Both portray the conflicts created by territorial state power and reveal Césaire's simultaneous fascination with independence in Africa and his uncertainty towards models of nationhood based on territorial sovereignty. Both Christophe and Lumumba harbour ideas about the invention of the nation that ultimately distance them from the people for whom they set out to speak. Both are tragic heroes, prone to being carried away by their rhetoric and leaving their audiences behind as they pursue an ideal at odds with events unfolding around them. Césaire himself commented that, 'they are both poets cut off from most of the people, visionaries in advance of their people', and, 'they lose contact with an unforgiving reality'.[80] Both envisage a future with which reality cannot quite catch up, as in Act I Scene 8, Lumumba laments that others believe he is trying to move too quickly, when to him, history in the Congo is already progressing irrepressibly: 'le Congo est un pays où tout va vite. Une graine de terre aujourd'hui, et demain un buisson, que dis-je, une forêt!' ['Congo is a country where everything goes fast. Today a grain in soil, and tomorrow a bush – what am I saying! – a forest, rather!'].[81] Césaire is clearly compelled in both cases by this future-oriented vision and this pursuit of change, and yet Lumumba, like Christophe, allows his vision to lose touch with the political reality that surrounds him.

Yet if Christophe becomes a tyrant, Lumumba remains a much more seductive tragic hero. He represents an aspirational ideal for Africa and for negritude even if this ideal falters in the political tension and corruption that surrounds him. Christophe's idealism ultimately fuels a despotic pursuit of power, whereas for Lumumba it leads him rather to fall victim to the cynical power struggles of those around him. In *La Tragédie du roi Christophe*, it is clear from the title that the tragedy is that of the King himself and the fatal flaw that drives him to tyranny. In *Une Saison au Congo*, Lumumba's name is not in the title and the tragedy is that of this disastrous period in the history of the Congo as it emerges from colonial power.

Lumumba may have failed, moreover, but he remains captivating as a harbinger for the reinvention of Africa. Césaire described his portrayal of Lumumba as a symbol, as if the character transcended Lumumba the man to encapsulate the tension between the ideal and the reality of decolonisation: 'he is not just the man Patrice Lumumba; he is above all a symbol, a man who identifies with Congolese reality and with the Africa of decolonisation, an individual who represents the collective'.[82] Lumumba's vision for independence is one that would not compromise with the colonial powers but that would finally break all ties with the colonial period, that would end the alienation caused by centuries of oppression. In this, his vision is related to that of Césaire himself in 'L'homme de culture et ses responsabilités', where, as for Fanon, decolonisation requires a definitive rupture from colonial structures. Lumumba is also crafted as a prophet figure capable of envisioning a better future for all of Africa that would supersede all its ongoing political power struggles.

Lumumba's vision for freedom is complete and all-encompassing. At the ceremony for independence in Act 1 Scene 6, the Belgian King Basilio insists on singing the praises of Belgian colonialism in the Congo, and Kala-Lubu is happy to comply with this evocation and to envision an independent Congo continuing to work with the Belgians. Lumumba, however, interjects with an impassioned and inflammatory speech evoking a history of oppression: 'nous sommes ceux que l'on déposséda, que l'on frappa, que l'on mutila; ceux que l'on tutoyait, ceux à qui l'on crachait au visage' ['we are those who were dispossessed, struck, mutilated – those who were addressed as inferiors, whose faces were spat upon'].[83] The speech moves rousingly from an expression of outrage towards past injustices to a defiant reclaiming of the Congolese land, its rivers and vegetation, and a call to reclaim its customs and laws. Lumumba's extraordinary speech finishes with a vision of nothing less than a new temporality, suggesting a complete break with linear history so far and a Fanonian leap into 'le temps neuf!' ['the new times!']][84] His stance and his language contrast dramatically with those of Kala-Lubu, who comes across as weak and ineffectual. In Act I Scene 11, Lumumba denounces the ongoing 'Belgian plot' to maintain power and Tzumbi's declaration of the independence of Katanga, in league with the Belgians, this time denouncing the betrayal of the new nation in the name of freedom across all of Africa. He responds to Mokutu's seizing of power, moreover, with a prolonged reflection on the history of exploitation across Africa, insisting that independence must serve as an example for the liberation of all nations. As Césaire argued in *Tropiques*, the oppressed need to be able to breathe, and Lumumba prophesies uprising across the continent: 'elle serre les poings, et elle respire un peu mieux, l'Afrique! Déjà l'air de demain! l'air du large, sain et salé!' ['she clenches her fists, and she breathes a bit better, Africa! Already the air of tomorrow! The air of the open sea, hale and salty!'].[85] If Mokutu remains focused on maintaining order by means of his own power in the Congo, Lumumba speaks for an ideal of liberation for Africa as a whole.

Lumumba's greatest power is his poetry and rhetoric, however, as his visionary language allies him with the Rebelle and Christophe. Césaire explains that his linguistic skill is not so much that of a politician as that of a poet, conceived through Bantu philosophy as a man who creates through naming: 'he is a poet through the word. I am not referring to political rhetoric, as some people believe, but to Bantu philosophy, in which is embedded the magical power of the word, the power of *nommo*, the creative word'.[86] Lumumba's poetry intermittently interrupts the language of political machination and lifts the play into cosmic and spiritual time, as if liberation represents not just political independence but the complete transformation of people and landscape.

The image of Lumumba as a bird recurs through the play to crystallise this vision, as the bird symbolises at once prophesy and the freedom of flight, of the open air. In his long speech at the independence ceremony in Act I Scene 6, for example, Lumumba imagines, 'je voudrais être toucan, le bel oiseau, pour être à travers le ciel, annonceur, à races et à langues que Kongo nous est né, notre roi! Kongo, qu'il vive!' ['I want to be a toucan, the beautiful bird, to be all over the sky, to announce, to races and languages that Kongo is born to us, our king! Kongo, may he live!'].[87] When Mokutu seizes power over the Congo whilst Lumumba dreams of freedom for Africa at the end of Act II, the latter accuses him of slaughtering the great bird of freedom which promises rebirth. Later, when Lumumba refuses to wear the leopard-skin that would represent the trappings of power, he again envisages himself as a bird, further extending the metaphor that weaves through his poetry and through the play to figure his own stature and movement, as well as renewal. Drawing on a form of animist tradition, he figures himself as an ibis, which symbolises change, fertility and rebirth, alluding to the eye and the beak to conjure vision and speech, and again predicting a transition 'aux temps neufs!' ['to the new times!'].[88]

Yet Lumumba's idealism is also the cause of his downfall. He allows the military to choose Mokutu as their leader and fails to see both his corruption and that of his soldiers. It is his wife, Pauline, who sees through the plotting of Mokutu and the Belgian officials; like Mme Christophe and the Rebelle's Amante, she warns her husband not to lose himself in his vision. Whilst Lumumba tries to dismiss her fears, suggesting that women only ever see the worst, Pauline perceives the real power struggles that threaten him. Although she plays a fairly minor role in the play, she is (like Césaire's other female characters) an ethical voice that seeks to temper the hero's hubris. After she again points out the exorbitance of Lumumba's vision for Africa in Act III Scene 2, moreover, journalists remind him of the limits of his power and point out his disregard for the real situation in contemporary Congo. And if Lumumba's dreams put him out of touch with reality, it is also perhaps his rhetorical flights of fancy that exacerbate that distance. Gregson Davis points out his 'disproportionate faith in the power of words', and his self-characterisation as prophet suggests he believes his poetry can itself bring about change.[89] In the scene of his death, consisting of a stark stand-off with M'siri, a minister working with Tzumbi, Lumumba claims that he incarnates an indestructible idea and that he bears 'l'honneur de l'Afrique' ['the honour of Africa'] in his heart, but M'siri merely laughs before the fatal shot is fired.[90] It is at this moment that Lumumba's poetic ideal is most tragically shattered by the political corruption he fails to resist.

Whilst Christophe's vision for the new nation tipped into despotism, Lumumba's remains captivating to Césaire, the poet who also dreamed of freedom and emancipation in Africa and in his own land. *Une Saison au Congo* portrays Lumumba dreaming of freedom in a vocabulary that eschews state sovereignty, and this would resonate with Césaire seeking autonomy without full independence for Martinique. Both Lumumba and Césaire himself use poetry to envision alternative futures and engage with contemporary politics always with a view to looking beyond, to a new historical order beyond immediate temporality, figured as 'Grand Temps!' ['Great times!'].[91] The play shows Lumumba failing to reconcile poetry and politics, however, and his rhetoric is unable to undermine the ongoing power struggles that plague the new nation. Césaire himself continued to combine literary creation with day-to-day politics, but the play perhaps reflects his anxieties about the tensions involved in this dual endeavour. Like Lumumba, he still wants to believe in the power of the word, and yet his relinquishment of poetry during this period and use of drama to address the people show him striving to keep art in touch with contemporary lived reality. His appeals for autonomy in the name of freedom and emancipation betray something of Lumumba's idealism, and yet *Une Saison au Congo* suggests that he was all too aware of the difficulty of translating ideal into practice as colonial power continues to hold sway in both Africa and in the French Caribbean, albeit in very different ways.

Une Tempête

Une Tempête was conceived as the third play in a triptych: Césaire famously described the *Tragédie* as the Caribbean part, *Une Saison* as the African part, and *Une Tempête* as the American part.[92] The first version of the play was published in the journal *Présence Africaine* in 1968, with the book version published by Seuil following in 1969. Césaire had been eagerly researching events surrounding the Black Power movement in the US during this period and had been working on a play to be entitled *Un Été chaud* in 1967 directly referencing this context. He abandoned the project, however, instead acting on a suggestion by Serreau to write a response to Shakespeare's *The Tempest*, though Arnold notes that considerable work went into blending this interest in the American situation with the Elizabethan classic.[93] Having denounced Octave Mannoni's theory of the dependency complex based on Prospero and Caliban in *Discours sur le colonialisme*, with *Une Tempête*, Césaire conjured a ruthless Prospero driven by a will to power and a defiant Caliban, whose struggle was now the central focus of the drama. Whilst George Lamming had already used the figure of Caliban to analyse the linguistic alienation of the colonised in his 1960 study *The Pleasures of Exile*, Césaire gave Caliban a voice in which to assert his freedom and, as in the *Tragédie*, used Yoruba and Voodoo deities to disrupt and undermine the dominance of European culture. The play still references the US, however: Caliban's defiant resistance and reclaiming of his name with an 'X' points to Malcolm X, whilst Ariel's strategy of non-violent challenge echoes that of Martin Luther King. At the same time, the ending that leaves Prospero and Caliban still locked in combat on the island can be taken to represent Martinique and its status as a département seeking freedom and equality whilst remaining tied to France.

Une Tempête can be read as another performance of negritude revolt in its depiction of Caliban's rejection of Prospero's mastery and reclaiming of his own language and voice.

THE THEATRE OF DECOLONISATION   207

Following the Rebelle, Toussaint and Lumumba, Caliban pursues freedom and agency after a history of oppression, though the play again explores the difficulties of achieving and maintaining freedom rather than simply the act of revolution. This rewriting of Shakespeare was clearly highly provocative. *Une Tempête* was first performed under the direction of Serreau in August 1969 in Hammamet, Tunisia, but when the production travelled to the biennale in Venice and the Théâtre de l'Ouest Parisien it was met with criticism and was seen to lack the theatrical richness of the *Tragédie*.[94] The challenge to Shakespeare and to European culture would also have been uncomfortable for European audiences, though Césaire's play subtly draws out and uncovers questions of origins, belonging and power already present in Shakespeare and foregrounds a continuing ambivalence in the relationship between Prospero and Caliban rather than denouncing the original in order to herald a revolution.

The play can be seen as a development of negritude, moreover, by bringing together references to the oppression and revolt of black people across the world. Caliban's first word, 'Uhuru!', is the Swahili term for freedom or independence and was used frequently, as Steven Almquist notes, in East Africa during the early 1960s, whilst his assertion in English in Act II, 'Freedom now!', references the US Black Power movement.[95] The island setting seems to refer to Martinique and the continuing struggle for power between locals and the French government, though Almquist also notes that there are references to plants and trees suggestive of an African landscape rather than of the Caribbean. Césaire foregrounds racial identity, making clear the significance of negritude by subtitling the play 'adaptation for a black theatre' and describing Caliban and Ariel as a black slave and a mulatto slave respectively. Yet he also deliberately challenges racial essentialism, as the play is subversively introduced by the master of ceremonies, who hands out masks for actors to don as superficial signifiers of racial identity. The drunken butler Stephano also takes Caliban for a 'Zindien' in a reference to the significant population of Indian workers in the Caribbean, so that Caliban's racial identity comes across as somewhat confused whilst the comic characters' preconceptions about race are ironically mocked.[96] The play in this way challenges racial oppression and connects resistance movements in Africa, the Caribbean and the US whilst undermining reductive and ignorant conceptions of race.

Césaire reworks Shakespeare's *Tempest* to set the struggle between master and slave centre stage. If in Shakespeare, Prospero is the usurped and exiled duke with magical powers who at the end reclaims his rightful position, in Césaire his colonial ambitions are made explicit, as he explains his quest to take possession of other lands in a speech to his daughter Miranda in Act I Scene 2. He uses rationalism to plot the expansion of his power and to denigrate Caliban, whom he claims to have educated by teaching him language but whom he dehumanises as 'un barbare' ['a savage'] and 'une bête brute' ['a dumb animal'].[97] In Act II Scene 2, where Prospero mockingly offers a feast to the shipwrecked duke Antonio and his companions Alonso, the King of Naples and Gonzalo, whilst elves play with them by removing and then returning the food, he becomes frustrated when they refuse to eat because this affronts his will to power, and he monstrously insists, 'je suis la *Puissance*' ['I am Power'].[98] Prospero's attempts at mastery are at the same time, in Caliban's view, 'anti-Nature', and in his final stand-off with Caliban he reminds him of his control over all aspects of the island, comparing himself to an orchestral conductor, 'suscitant les voix, moi seul / et à mon gré les echaînant, / organisant hors de la confusion / la seule ligne intelligible' ['summoning voices, I alone, / and mingling them at my pleasure, / arranging out of confusion / one intelligible line'].[99] Césaire vilifies in Prospero this desire to own and manage the landscape like the plantation owners in the Caribbean, and Caliban's anticolonial stance demands a more respectful integration in the ecological environment. Whilst in Shakespeare, it is Prospero's plot to reclaim his title from his brother Antonio that is the main focus of the play, moreover,

THE THEATRE OF DECOLONISATION   209

in Césaire's play this part of the storyline is resolved at the end of Act II to place Prospero's pursuit of colonial mastery sharply into focus and clear the floor for Caliban's revolt.

Caliban's riposte to Prospero begins at the moment he enters with the cry 'Uhuru!' and with an invective reminiscent of the rebuff to authority introduced at the opening of the 1947 Bordas edition of the *Cahier*. Caliban deliberately corrupts the language Prospero bestowed upon him and greets him with bitterness: 'Bonjour. Mais un bonjour autant que possible de guêpes, de crapauds, de pustules et de fiente' ['But make that as froggy, waspish, pustular and dung-filled a "hello" as possible'].[100] Caliban also directly counters Prospero's claim to the island by remembering he inherited it from his mother Sycorax, who lives on in the landscape also in defiance of Prospero's attempts at mastery. Against Prospero's 'anti-Nature', then, Caliban represents a mode of living much closer to that of the 'homme-plante' of *Tropiques*. Caliban's rejection of Prospero as 'un écraseur, un broyeur' ['a crusher, a pulveriser'], moreover, contrasts with Ariel's non-violent complicity, as the latter dreams of harmony in terms strongly reminiscent of Martin Luther King: 'j'ai souvent fait le rêve exaltant qu'un jour, Prospero, toi et moi, nous entreprendrions, frères associés, de bâtir un monde merveilleux, chacun apportant en contribution ses qualités propres' ['I've often had this inspiring, uplifting dream that one day Prospero, you, me, we would all three set out, like brothers, to build a wonderful world, each one contributing his own special thing'].[101] Yet if Caliban rejects Prospero's mastery definitively, he does not himself use violence but recreates himself through language, revealing the falsity of Prospero's science and his fabricated image of the slave himself as savage. He creolises French through his invocations of the Yoruba god of thunder, Shango, by summoning him to move the elements in order to dwarf Prospero's power, and by offsetting rationalism with song: '*Shango est un secoueur de feu / chacun de ses pas ébranle le ciel / ébranle la terre / Shango Shango ho!*' ['Shango is a fire-bearer, / his steps shake the heavens / and the earth / Shango Shango, ho!'].[102] Caliban's use of Creole crystallises his rejection of the colonial language imposed upon him, his carnivalesque language anticipating at the same time Barbadian poet Kamau Brathwaite's 'Caliban', where the merging of the slave's name with the drum sound in the lines 'Ban Ban Caliban like to play pan at the Carnival' forms a subversive chant against the history of enslavement.[103] Prospero insists in return that he controls the éléments: 'j'ai déraciné le chêne, soulevé la mer, /ébranlé la montagne et bombant / ma poitrine contre le sort contraire, j'ai répondu à Jupiter foudre pour foudre' ['I have uprooted the oak and raised the sea, / I have caused the mountain to tremble / and have bared my chest to adversity. / With Jove I have traded thunderbolt for thunderbolt']. His claim that the island is 'muette' without him, however, rings hollow in the face of Caliban's invocation of the gods and spirits that infuse the land.

Caliban's appeal to Shango is juxtaposed with an interruption by the Yoruba trickster god Eshu, who subversively interrupts the festivities for the wedding of Miranda and Ferdinand. Shakespeare's masque scene is rudely debunked by this mocking figure, who undermines both the feebler gods and goddesses of the European tradition (Juno, Ceres and Iris) and Prospero's control over the ceremonies. Eshu's bawdy song disrupts Prospero's ritual and makes a mockery of his solemnity: '*Eshu est un Joyeux luron, / de son pénis il frappe / Il frappe / Il frappe. . .*' ['Eshu is a merry elf, / and he can whip you with his dick, / he can whip you, / he can whip you'].[104] Once again, language is reappropriated as the trickster god uses words to undermine colonial control, and, as in *La Tragédie*, Césaire diversifies his French not so much by using Creole words as by introducing these African figures, together with music, song and a bawdy register to subvert European cultural hegemony.

Yet Caliban's revolt never evolves into a complete overthrow of Prospero and the play's ending, like those of both *La Tragédie* and *Une Saison au Congo*, suggests an ambivalent future. In Act III, Caliban fraternises with Trinculo and

THE THEATRE OF DECOLONISATION   211

Stephano and they join in his song, '*La Liberté ohé! La Liberté!*' ['*Freedom hi-day! Freedom hi-day!*'], but the scene implies that he still needs European allies to support his attempts at resistance.[105] The final scene, moreover, with Prospero and Caliban remaining trapped together on the island, suggests they remain in deadlock, and despite his rejection of Prospero's authority, Caliban is in no way free of his oppressive presence. Time passes and Prospero is ultimately alone on the stage clinging to his defence of civilisation while inadvertently admitting that he at the same time depends on Caliban. Caliban again calls '*LA LIBERTÉ OHÉ, LA LIBERTÉ*' from off-stage, indicating his non-compliance, but neither character maintains the upper hand over the other.[106] Prospero dreams of civilisation and Caliban sings of freedom, but both remain suspended in an indeterminate limbo. Césaire makes of Caliban a figure for resistance but continues to ask where that resistance might lead and what form liberation would take. Freedom must be pursued, but this must be an ongoing process, as was devastatingly demonstrated in Césaire's other plays, so that, as Ojo-Ade argues, 'freedom is not yet attained, and if one thinks it has been achieved at all, it could only be the kind foisted on the Congo, far from being authentic, calling for another engagement'.[107] Like *La Tragédie* and *Une Saison*, *Une Tempête* portrays the quest for liberation and independence but reveals the poet's uncertainty about the process of achieving and maintaining independence, as he anxiously observes the decolonisation movements in Africa and continues to struggle to improve the status of his native Martinique.

Césaire's *Une Tempête* is one of the most famous recreations of Caliban but it would not be the last. Shakespeare's slave has been reappropriated by successive writers seeking to rehabilitate colonised culture from colonial and neocolonial dominance. The Cuban writer Roberto Fernandez Retamar's essay 'Caliban: Notes towards a Discussion of Culture in Our America', published in 1971, charts the progression from Shakespeare to Ernest Renan, whose Caliban is a savage

212 THE THEATRE OF DECOLONISATION

whose ignorance justifies the colonial mission, to Lamming and to Césaire's appropriation of Caliban as a symbol of resistance.[108] Retamar includes a long list of historical figures who enacted Caliban's revolt, among which notably can be found Toussaint, Césaire and Fanon, before detailing the contestatory vision of Cubans such as José Marti and Carlos Fuentes. In the francophone Caribbean context, Maryse Condé's volume of critical essays *L'Héritage de Caliban* again uses Caliban to symbolise the creation of a Caribbean culture and language in Martinican and Guadeloupean literature. But for all this Caliban remains a somewhat problematic figure in that, despite his revolt, he does not bring about significant change.[109] Indeed, postcolonial thinker Rob Nixon has noted that he ceased to be used as a symbol of resistance after the period of decolonisation, and if Shakespeare's play lacked a sixth act exploring a postcolonial era, so too does Césaire's lack a vision for a different future.[110]

Nixon also points out that, perhaps because in Shakespeare's original *Tempest* Caliban had no female counterpart, the writers reappropriating him seem to assume that 'heroic revolt is pre-eminently a male province'.[111] In Césaire's *Une Tempête*, there is no figure for female resistance, and the one female character, Miranda, plays a less significant role than in Shakespeare.[112] She may reveal her respectful attentiveness to the environment by teaching the names of plants and trees to Ferdinand, but she marries into royalty and remains complicit in that hierarchical system. Sycorax, moreover, is cherished by Caliban as a spirit that lives on in the landscape of the island, but she remains absent, and Césaire makes no attempt to reinvigorate either her character or the fusion with the environment she represents. In *La Tragédie* and *Une Saison au Congo*, Mme Christophe and Pauline Lumumba offer wise counsel and remind audiences of the ethical difficulties in their husbands' pursuit of freedom and independence. But there is perhaps in Césaire's writing of this period an association between revolution and masculinity and a blind spot when it comes to women's roles both in the struggle for freedom and in its aftermath. Césaire never fully addressed this lapsus in his writing, and yet his last poetic volumes will start to temper these portraits of poetic hubris with a quieter, mature aesthetics of humility and self-doubt.

6

Political and Poetic Disillusionment
'I inhabit a sacred wound'

The last decades of Césaire's career, the 1980s and 1990s, brought a sense of disillusionment and a marked shift in tone in both his political rhetoric and his poetry. This was a period during which Césaire found himself increasingly isolated, as he struggled to convince Martinicans of his vision for autonomy while also mourning the loss of dear friends and intellectual companions such as Senghor and Lam. The PPM was forced to change its tack with the realisation that autonomy was for the time being at least not a realistic possibility for Martinique, which Césaire argued was in desperate need of economic regeneration before any change in status could be contemplated. At the same time, Césaire's poetry volumes *moi, laminaire...* (published in 1982) and *Comme un malentendu de salut* [*Like a Misunderstanding of Salvation*] (published in 1994) articulate nothing of the incendiary revolt of earlier volumes and instead reveal the poet questioning his place in the world and the role of his poetry. In an interview published in *Le Journal guadeloupéen* in 1980, Césaire describes himself as '*un nègre marron*' ['*a runaway slave*'] to crystallise his continually rebellious stance, and he continues: 'I refuse to bow my head before anyone, I refuse big brothers, I refuse uncles, I refuse anyone showing me the way'.[1] Yet if the image of the 'marron' suggests defiance, it also connotes escape, a

POLITICAL AND POETIC DISILLUSIONMENT 215

resistance to established political structures, as well as freedom and mobility, perhaps capturing something of Césaire's uncertainty about his position during this period. 'Marronnage' has been used by recent activists such as Dénètem Touam Bona and Sylvie Chalaye as a figure for an improvised form of resistance, associated with nomadic existence and continual reinvention.[2] Césaire's institutional positions as Mayor of Fort-de-France and Deputy at the Assemblée Nationale may make him seem an unlikely 'marron' from this perspective, yet this self-designation perhaps reveals his unease towards his role and his sense of non-adherence to any established political agenda or social grouping.

In the French presidential elections in May 1981, Césaire and the PPM called for Martinicans to vote for François Mitterrand, the left-wing candidate who for Césaire represented democracy and a commitment to minority rights. Yet, although Mitterrand won the election overall, Martinicans ignored Césaire's call and voted overwhelmingly for Valéry Giscard d'Estaing, betraying their discontent about the situation in Martinique and lack of trust in the PPM. Césaire was disappointed and indignant, yet he insisted in a speech printed in *Le Progressiste* later that month that he understood that the vote was a response to the dire situation in which Martinicans were living. Martinicans were misguided, however, in turning in their unhappiness to the party that was its cause.[3] Conversely, for Césaire, Mitterrand would inaugurate a new era, one which he was convinced would bring improvements to the lives of people living in the DOM. He reminded Martinicans that Mitterrand's government intended to accord the same social benefits to the DOM as were available in the metropole. The new government also seemed to Césaire to provide a fresh opportunity for the Martinican situation to be properly addressed, so that soon after Mitterrand's election he called for a moratorium on autonomy while the country regained its health.

Césaire's speech declaring the moratorium indicates the difficult position he occupied. He points out at the beginning the

216 POLITICAL AND POETIC DISILLUSIONMENT

falsity of the idea that Martinicans were calling for secession and of the claim that France would cut its ties with Martinique. Yet if he recognises unease towards independence on both sides, he promises to suspend discussions of status while keeping open the idea that he will return to these at a future point. The moratorium was emphatically not an end but '*a provisional stopping*' or suspension, so that Césaire seemed both to be recognising the viewpoint of his compatriots and clinging to his own long-held vision for autonomy.[4] The speech at the same time betrays Césaire's own deep unease, as he describes Martinique as '*a great invalid*', but the personification suggests that he is also evoking his own sentiments having fought fruitlessly for autonomy for twenty years. His reference to fighting for more limited objectives hides undertones of bitterness and disappointment, and his assurance that he will wait for Martinicans to accept his view sounds somewhat patronising. The speech ends with his customary grandiose rhetoric, as he paints a devastating portrait of contemporary Martinique, 'a society of at once aggressive and frightened beggars'. This society can be replaced under Mitterrand by one of work and dignity, until a glimmer of hope becomes 'a great conflagration in the sky, which for us will be the dawn of the renewal of Martinique'.[5]

Césaire admits that his thought during this period was 'misunderstood both on the right and on the left', as well as within the PPM itself.[6] In the wake of the moratorium, he was accused of backing assimilationism, and he had to explain in a second speech in July 1981 that he had always believed and still believes in a Martinique for Martinicans, though his rhetoric here tends to remain a little vague. He explains to his colleagues in the PPM that it is important not to cling to doctrine, but that Martinique needs to be healed before a change in status can be considered. In subsequent interventions, he repeatedly appeals to notions of a 'rediscovered Martinican *personality*', allowing for some obfuscation of what that personality consists in and how it might be preserved.[7] If the PPM has suffered from ups and downs, he argues, this commitment to a Martinican personality remains constant, even if the means by which the party has combated assimilationists have had to evolve. In a much later interview looking back on the moratorium, he explains that he realised things had to move step by step, though if it was decided that a moratorium was needed, this was not his choice.[8] He comes across at once as committed to protecting the rights of Martinicans and as beleaguered in his position, adopting the moratorium as a compromise whilst struggling both to pursue his political ideals and to placate his dissatisfied compatriots.

In relinquishing his long-standing pursuit of autonomy, in the wake of Mitterrand's victory Césaire instead called for decentralisation, so that Martinique and the other DOMs would remain part of France but would attain more power to govern on local matters. In his intervention at the Assemblée Nationale on 27 July 1981, he noted that the decentralisation bill should make explicit reference to the DOMs, which had specific systems and needs that had to be addressed more precisely. Most notably, Martinique's inclusion in the European Common Market was problematic for Césaire, and he argued that the island needed to be able to trade more freely with closer neighbours rather than being subjugated to the status of 'a tropical sub-Europe'.[9] In December 1982, Césaire agreed to a new 'Conseil régional' for the DOM, with each département forming a region in a further push towards decentralisation. The aim of this regional council would be to accord more agency to the DOMs in governing their own affairs, as Césaire argued in his characteristically rousing terms: 'to allow people in the overseas departments to become agents of their own history by taking on new responsibilities instead of passively witnessing the unfolding of an uncontrollable destiny, as they have too often been invited to do in the past'.[10] Césaire would be the first to preside over this regional council, with Camille Darsières taking over in 1988. Initially the role of the new council remained unclear, and Césaire took the opportunity of his speech at its inauguration to reiterate his understanding of the political divisions among Martinicans and to affirm his

218   POLITICAL AND POETIC DISILLUSIONMENT

commitment to working collaboratively to improve living conditions without spelling out his economic position. He would continue to lobby for further decentralisation in the late 1980s and early 1990s, insisting in an interview in 1989 that decentralisation had not gone far enough, though he would want to further this while achieving consensus with people working from different political starting points.

Césaire's work on decentralisation continued alongside his endeavours as mayor, as he pursued multiple projects in the service of urban regeneration. In an interview printed in the 'Bulletin municipal' in the lead-up to the municipal elections in March 1983, he provides a clear outline of the urbanisation and modernisation achieved since he was elected back in 1945.[11] Areas such as Trénelle, Volga-Plage and Texaco were regenerated before he turned his attention to improvements in the electricity, water and sewer networks, as well as to schools, in the city centre. He goes on to insist on the importance of cultural regeneration too, quoting the activities of the Sermac (the Service Municipale d'Action Culturelle), for example, the founding of a new theatre group for unemployed young people. It is striking, however, that as Raphaël Confiant argues, Césaire and the PPM said little about a series of bomb attacks in Martinique, Guadeloupe, Guiana and France carried out by the Alliance révolutionnaire caraïbe in May 1983, preferring to continue to negotiate for improvements in Martinique rather than contemplate a more definitive protest against French colonialism.[12]

In January 1988, Césaire opened the new parking-silo Lafcadio Hearn, heralding the site as a heroic response to the challenge created by the marshy land on which the city of Fort-de-France was built: 'it is an invented space' and at the same time '*it is a conquered space*'.[13] If Césaire rather proudly sees himself here as an '*inventor of space*', moreover, this can be seen as a concrete legacy of the '*inventors of souls*' celebrated in the heady days of the *Deuxième congrès* in Rome in 1959. The echo reveals in stark terms the shift from Césaire's earlier visionary appeal to this later focus on practical achievements

POLITICAL AND POETIC DISILLUSIONMENT   219

while also showcasing the utopianism that, despite his disillusionment, continued to inflect his rhetoric in both the cultural and the political domain. A victorious rhetoric is also present in his 1993 opening of the new stadium in Fort-de-France, where the stadium is envisioned as an opportunity for Martinique fully to reach its potential.[14] This rhetoric nevertheless sits uneasily alongside high levels of dissatisfaction and unrest in Martinique concerning its ongoing status as a DOM.

During the 1990s, however, Césaire was slowly winding down his political activities even as he demonstrated his ongoing commitment to Martinican society. His interventions at the Assemblée Nationale were increasingly rare, until in 1993, at the age of 80, he announced his decision not to stand in the legislative elections, handing over the baton to Camille Darsières to avoid what he self-deprecatingly called 'gerontocracy'.[15] He insisted that he remained fully engaged in the concerns of the Martinican people, and that in any case he always considered himself as an 'awakener of consciousness' or a 'sower of ideas' more than as a politician.[16] Despite his age and his disillusionment, Césaire here still styled himself as a visionary, even as the relationship between his vision and the concrete demands of his people was increasingly fraught. In 2000, he went on to announce that he would not stand as mayor again in the municipal elections in the following year, celebrating his achievements in urbanising the city but noting the challenge remaining in building a *great community of free citizens*.[17] He would remain closely in touch with his successor as mayor, Serge Letchimy, and indeed it has been suggested that his retirement was never really a retirement, as he remained fully preoccupied with the future of Martinique.[18] He also continued to suffer in witnessing the ongoing difficulties after decolonisation in Africa, confessing he felt that, 'I am ill with Africa'.[19] He would continue to receive visitors in his office at the former city hall after his retirement and keep up with current affairs, commenting notably on the law establishing enslavement as a crime against humanity though opposing reparations because of the risk they imply that that history need no longer be discussed.[20]

It is notable that during this late stage in his career, Césaire frequently returns to the concept of negritude, despite the hesitations towards the term he expressed at the 1966 Dakar festival. His speech at the *Première conférence hémisphérique des peuples noirs de la diaspora en hommage à Aimé Césaire* in Miami in 1987 reclaims negritude as an active and dynamic term, a signifier of revolt and in no way an atavistic return to essentialism. The importance of the speech is recognised in its publication as 'Discours sur la négritude' alongside 'Discours sur le colonialisme' by Présence Africaine in 2004. Césaire insists at the outset that negritude is not a biological concept, nor a philosophy nor a metaphysics, but, in a nod to Fanon, a set of lived experiences and a shared history of marginalisation and oppression. Moreover, it is not a passive state or condition, and Césaire evokes its active force in a series of punchy statements:

> Negritude comes from an active and aggressive mental attitude.
> It is a jolt, and a jolt of dignity.
> It is a refusal, I mean a refusal of oppression.
> It is a struggle, a struggle against inequality.
> It is also a revolt.[21]

Echoing some of the acerbic critique articulated in 'Discours sur le colonialisme', this speech at the same time denounces the false universalism of European discourse which effectively alienates humanity from itself. Negritude served, Césaire goes on to insist, to set the stage for decolonisation in Africa, even as it originated in the revolutionary writing of the Black Renaissance in the US. If this speech revivifies the dynamism of early negritude, however, it is striking that here Césaire argues that the reclaiming of identity was always central. Whilst the more restrictive and normative 'Identique' was a force of oppression in the 'Nègreries' essays of *L'Étudiant noir* back in 1935, 'identity' here is celebrated as a signifier of 'the hard and irreducible kernel' out of which man's civilisation and singularity are constructed.[22] This identity is a reckoning with the past and an anticipation of the future, an antidote to alienation and an embrace of a larger fraternity. Whilst the negritude poems of the 1940s and 50s were less concerned with identity than with the explosive action of revolt, in his mature years Césaire reinvigorates identity, affirming its dynamism but reclaiming the anchoring it might nevertheless provide. Negritude is preserved as a source of identity in several interventions by Césaire during this late period, including for example in interviews conducted in 1984, and then in both 2003 and 2004. Again, this does not indicate a turn to essentialism but it perhaps suggests an awareness in the mature Césaire of contemporary discourses of identity politics and of the importance of shared culture and solidarity.

Césaire's defence of negritude during this period comes alongside scepticism towards the Créolité movement of the younger generation of Antillean writers. In 1989, Jean Bernabé, Patrick Chamoiseau and Raphaël Confiant produced a manifesto for Creole culture and language, *Éloge de la créolité* (of which Césaire was one of the dedicatees), and in which they recognised their debt to negritude while shifting the terms of the debate towards the celebration of Creole.[23] The Créolistes cast Césaire as a role model, insisting 'we are forever the sons of Aimé Césaire', but committed to capturing the authentic lived culture of contemporary Martinique rather than falling into what they see as the 'African illusion' with which Césaire replaced that of Europe.[24] In 1993, however, Raphaël Confiant published his vitriolic study *Aimé Césaire: une traversée paradoxale du siècle*, in which he vilified the Caribbean father of letters for what he saw as his broad failure properly to address the cultural and political situation of Martinique and specifically for his neglect of the Creole language and his Creole origins, including as an appendix a somewhat ironic version of the first pages of the *Cahier* written in Creole. Whilst not openly objecting to Confiant and the Créoliste movement to which he belonged, Césaire nevertheless qualified 'Créolité' as reductionist, in the sense that it focused specifically on the small area of the French Antilles whilst negritude celebrated the long and broad history of all of Africa. This difference in scope meant that, according to Césaire, 'Créolité is ok, but it is just a department of negritude'.[25] At the same time, he was happy to assert that he spoke Creole but his education was in French, and it is indeed somewhat paradoxical that the Créolistes use French to call for the rehabilitation of Creole. This ambivalence notwithstanding, Césaire emphasises the importance of preserving the Creole language and notes its historical situation as at once 'neo-French' and 'neo-African'. Creole is the spoken language of Martinicans but it has a history mixing French and African influences. Césaire is keen to underline that history rather than to see it only as a signifier of Martinican idiom in the present.

This tension surrounding the Créolité movement reveals Césaire's disengagement from the younger generation of Martinicans. Véron relates that he felt that younger writers did not match his talent, and that he was 'disappointed that his great cry of 1939 ended in social and political cacophony'.[26] The Créolistes may have agreed that he occupied the role of a father figure, but in so doing they at once acknowledged his extraordinary significance and positioned themselves as rebellious sons pursuing a new agenda for a different era. It is notable that Césaire did not engage in dialogue particularly actively with this younger generation; he was content for them to cite him but did not comment extensively on their work. Perhaps even more surprisingly, Césaire never discussed at length the work of Édouard Glissant, whose thinking on 'Antillanité' and Relation both in the Caribbean and across the globe is steeped in Césaire's thought but also fundamentally distinct in its orientation not towards Africa but towards the much larger web of interactions structuring and shaping Caribbean culture. Indeed, Véron notes that Césaire judged Glissant's thought to be too metaphorical, too 'deconstructed', even if there is a profound continuum between them.[27]

POLITICAL AND POETIC DISILLUSIONMENT   223

Glissant rethinks the 'Retour' of Césaire's *Cahier* not as a return to a single point of origin but instead as at once a 'Retour' and a 'Détour' or diversion, leading to a 'point of entanglement'.[28] The return of the *Cahier* could be read, from this perspective, as a complex, layered journey, as the point of origin becomes not an originary culture but the inauguration of Relation. The centrality of Africa in Césaire's thought can be read, through Glissant, alongside the multiple journeys undertaken in the *Cahier*, and in the rest of his poetry and thought, to anticipate the later philosopher's championing of Caribbean diversity. Négritude, too, should be conceived in this light as a harbinger of the forms of solidarity and dynamic reinvention crucial to Glissant's thought rather than an atavistic return from which subsequent thinkers would definitively depart. Despite these connections, however, Césaire during this late stage in his career seemed more preoccupied with his political work in Fort-de-France than with the younger writers coming to dominate Caribbean culture and thought.

Through the 1980s and 1990s, Césaire would lose many close relatives and friends. These losses would reinforce his sense of isolation, as well as the melancholic introspection found in *moi, laminaire. . . .* He had already lost Suzanne, from whom he had divorced in 1963 and who died in 1966 of a brain tumour, and it seems that his relationships with his children were strained in the wake of what they perceived as their father's mistreatment of their mother.[29] In *moi, laminaire. . .* he pays homage and laments the deaths of important interlocutors such as Wifredo Lam, Léon Gontran Damas and the Guatemalan poet and diplomat Miguel Angel Asturias. Throughout the volume, the lyric voice often seems an isolated one, even when he is not overtly mourning his intellectual companions. In 1987, Césaire also mourned Saint-Jean Perse and his former colleague on *Tropiques*, Gilbert Gratiant, paying homage by inaugurating the Avenue Saint-Jean Perse and the Place Gilbert Gratiant in Fort-de-France and praising in each case the writers' fidelity to the Caribbean despite living far away. Césaire's mother died in 1983, and he tragically lost

224   POLITICAL AND POETIC DISILLUSIONMENT

his son Francis in 1994 and his sister Denise in 1996. François Mittérand also died in 1996, and Césaire wrote a short text eulogising him as a humanist and a man of culture, 'the first statesman in France to have proclaimed the "right to difference" and called for respect for the fundamental identity of peoples'.[30] The frequent eulogies to lost colleagues in his later years perhaps crystallise a melancholy palpable in the poetry and latent in his political speeches and writings.

If Césaire's relationships with humans in *moi, laminaire. . .* testify to this sense of loss, the connection between the lyric voice and the ecological and cosmic environment is perhaps here closer than ever. Whilst Césaire's vision for the plant-human grew out of his dialogue with Suzanne Césaire as far back as *Tropiques* and was most affirmatively crystallised by the 'RENCONTRE BIEN TOTALE' of 'Corps perdu', the poet's blending and blurring with the ecosystem is most complete here, as he loses all traces of the demiurgic subject summoning the power of the elements to his will. If as far back as 'Les pur-sang', revolt was conceived through the mutual participation of human, animal and landscape, in those earlier poems the lyric subject intermittently occupied a position of power, even if that power was often distributed between the subject and the environment he enlisted in his rebellion. In *moi, laminaire. . .*, however, the lyric subject occupies a far more passive, humble position as he witnesses ecological and cosmic turmoil.

It is perhaps surprising that, given the increasing awareness of environmental destruction, Césaire nowhere commented on ecological issues from a political perspective during this period. The latest example of environmental devastation in Martinique which has come to light since Césaire's death is that of the scandal of the use of the pesticide chlordecone, a chemical used on banana plantations found in the 1970s to be carcinogenic, to cause problems in pregnancy and to affect early childhood development, but which continued to be used in Martinique and Guadeloupe until 1993. As Malcom Ferdinand writes in his ground-breaking study of decolonial

POLITICAL AND POETIC DISILLUSIONMENT 225

ecologies, the chemical was used on 20,000 hectares of land and has found its way into all ecosystems, and a 2018 study found that 90 per cent of inhabitants of Martinique and Guadeloupe had it in their blood.[31] The continued use of chlordecone years after it was known to be harmful testifies to the ongoing exploitation of the Martinican and Guadeloupean environment for economic profit at the expense of human and nonhuman life. Césaire would not have known about the risks associated with chlordecone, but his attention to ecological destruction and resistance throughout his poetry and most humbly in *moi, laminaire. . .* suggests that his poetry too could catalyse activist thinking even in areas where he remained politically silent. This late volume establishes a connection between human and nonhuman that clearly denounces the history of the colonial and neocolonial exploitation of both and which deliberately eschews hubristic and destructive claims for human mastery.

moi, laminaire. . .

moi, laminaire. . . was published in 1982, more than two decades after Césaire's last full poetic volume, *Ferrements*. A collection entitled 'Noria' had been published in 1976 in a volume of collected works comprising seventeen poems, some of which had been written during the 1950s and some of which would appear in *moi, luminaire. . .*, but the latter was his first major poetic work for twenty years. The volume was in part triggered by the death of Wifredo Lam, and includes a section devoted to Lam responding to a series of engravings by the artist begun in 1968 and published in *Annonciation* also in 1982. If Césaire was hesitant in publishing another poetic volume, moreover, the Guadeloupean writer Daniel Maximin encouraged him and promised to take charge of the editorial process. Césaire's political disillusionment is clearly detectable in the volume's tone, as we find nothing of the hubristic revolt of earlier volumes and a language and form

226   POLITICAL AND POETIC DISILLUSIONMENT

far more muted than the incendiary experiments of the 1940s. As Ba, Hénane and Kesteloot suggest, the sudden changes of rhythm, rhetorical questions and verbal violence give way here to 'a deliberate, generalised prosaicness that systematically contradicts enthusiasm and exaltation'.[32] Poetry now forms an 'outlet' for the politician's frustrations, and a 'lifebelt' to which he might cling in his uncertainty concerning his place in Martinican politics.[33]

Césaire first intended to entitle the volume *Gradient*, but changed his mind and came up with *moi, laminaire...*, a title rich in meaning whose various layers capture the preoccupations expressed in the poems. 'Laminaria' is a form of algae that both stretches out for miles into the sea and adheres tightly to the rock from which it grows. The poet figures the 'moi' or self as this vegetal form, implying a fusion between plant and human, and at once an attachment to the land and a sort of nomadism. The humble, exploratory, horizontal form of the seaweed also contrasts directly with the affirmative and rebellious uprightness of the trees in Césaire's earlier corpus, such as the majestic Kaïlcédrat royal, a type of mahogany tree native both to Senegal and to Martinique conjured in the *Cahier*. Jean Khalfa notes that 'laminaria' is also 'a thin, ribbon-like regime of the flow of winds', so that the image is suggestive of elemental forces, captured here not so much as rebellious cosmic powers but as a series of restless, connective movements.[34] Moreover, the term 'laminaire' contains echoes of Lam, and the poet's coupling of the 'moi' with the 'Lam' of 'laminaire' pays homage to his relationship with the painter. And 'laminaire' echoes with the 'lagunaire' of the volume's opening poem, 'calendrier lagunaire', suggesting the slower rhythmic temporality of the lagoon protected from the open sea while gesturing towards the 'lacunaire' or lacunary, the impression that there will always be something missing from the poems' expressive forms. Finally, the lower-case letters and ellipsis deliberately eschew any sense of mastery or completion. These multiple layers in the volume's title perform the poetic project as an opening out of meaning, whilst the

POLITICAL AND POETIC DISILLUSIONMENT   227

resonances together capture the volume's rich tonality conjuring the human as vegetal, as well as the poet's self-questioning and wandering in the Martinican landscape. *moi, laminaire. . .* attempts a new aesthetic, one where the 'moi' is at once sought after and diffuse, and the poet no longer celebrates his rebellious power but reflects rather on his struggles and his disappointments: 'between the *Cahier* and *moi, luminaire. . .* there is quite simply a whole life, they are fifty years apart', and the later volume reflects, 'man confronting harsh reality and taking stock'.[35]

moi, laminaire. . . opens with a short preface, a piece of poetic prose that sets up the aesthetic of the volume. This preface establishes two different but superposed temporalities: '*le non-temps impose au temps la tyrannie de sa spatialité*' ['*non-time imposes on time the tyranny of its spatiality*'].[36] The ordinary progression of linear time is from this perspective overlaid and expanded by 'non-time', a clinging to 'spatiality' or to the land in the wake of the devastating historical rupture created by the slave trade. This non-time could also, however, be related to a much larger cosmic temporality evoked in 'sentiments et ressentiments des mots' as 'Grand Temps' ['Great Time'], the time of elemental and geological movement that far supersedes human history.[37] Throughout the collection, colonial history will be set against these larger movements, and human agency is often dwarfed by environmental phenomena that belittle human endeavour – both that of the oppressor and that of the poet. Secondly, the preface sets up a series of oppositions, '*l'inégale lutte de la vie et de la mort, de la ferveur et de la lucidité, fût-ce du désespoir et de la retombée, la force aussi de regarder demain*' ['*the unequal struggle of life and death, of fervor and lucidity, albeit one of despair and collapse, the strength as well to face tomorrow*'].[38] Although the poetic persona does not speak in the first person here, the lines betray his ambivalence, his oscillation between hope and disillusionment, and the swing between idealism and compromise detectable in both his poetry and his political rhetoric. The poems in the collection, too, will contain moments of optimism while

228 POLITICAL AND POETIC DISILLUSIONMENT

frequently conveying a sense of stasis and powerlessness. This binary pattern is mimicked by the elements and the landscape, '*entre soleil et ombre, entre montagne et mangrove, entre chien et loup, claudiquant et binaire*' ['*between sun and shadow, between mountain and mangrove, between dawn and dusk, stumbling and binary*'].[39] Here, day and night determine human experience, with the sun a symbol of energy against darkness, whilst the hills provide refuge and the mangrove swamp a stifling presence, and throughout the poet is shaped by the environment rather than triumphantly calling elements and landscape to his aid. Finally, the volume promises to '*régler leur compte à quelques fantasmes et à quelques fantômes*' ['*settle the score with several fantasies and a few phantoms*'] in a reference to Césaire's own past ideals both political and poetic, regretfully conjured here as ghostly fantasies in which he has lost faith but which continue to haunt him.[40]

The opening poem, 'calendrier lagunaire', is among Césaire's most famous, perhaps because it is printed on his tombstone. The poem is structured by the stubborn anaphora 'j'habite' ['i inhabit'], as the poet evokes his dwelling in both human and cosmic history, and the verb reinforces a passive succumbing, far removed from the intermittently commanding 'je' of earlier volumes. The opening lines, 'j'habite une blessure sacrée / j'habite des ancêtres imaginaires' ['i inhabit a sacred wound / i inhabit imaginary ancestors'] portray the poetic voice steeped in the wounds of history, determined more specifically as the history of enslavement with the reference in line seven to 'une guerre de trois cents ans' ['a three-hundred-year war'].[41] The destruction of the Martinican landscape by the plantation system and its subsequent exoticisation in the French imaginary is suggested by 'une version du paradis absurdement ratée' ['an absurdly botched version of paradise'], whilst the landscape's revolt is conjured by a tidal wave of lava running upstream. Amid the fury of the volcano and the whirlwind, the poetic subject here no longer joins the revolt but is figured as rootless, suffering and nomadic: 'j'habite de temps en temps une de mes plaies / chaque minute je change

POLITICAL AND POETIC DISILLUSIONMENT   229

d'appartement / et toute paix m'effraie' ['i inhabit from time to time one of my sores / each minute i change apartments / and all peace frightens me']. As Carrie Noland argues, this inhabiting is at once suggestive of the poet's unsettled search for rootedness and belonging, and of a looser sense of his 'haunting' or animating the landscape, as he dwells in it in a state of passive and uncertain fusion with its movements rather than conceiving it as a background to suit his own purposes.[42] As the poet tracks his participation in the struggles of the natural world in the wake of its destruction and in its ongoing stagnation, the poem gradually progresses towards a greater sense of despair. The poet's project no longer seems worth it, as he laments, 'frère n'insiste pas / vrac de varech' ['brother drop it / wrack rubbish'] and evokes 'mon néant' ['my nothingness'] in the face of the vigorous movement of the elements. Both atmospheric and historic pressure – or cosmic and linear time – weigh on the poet's suffering, though the poem ends with a reference to his words made 'sumptuous' by this pain. Perhaps nothing is left of his quest for revolt other than the words of the poem, though if poetry ultimately remains valuable it is unclear now how it could break the cycle of suffering.

This opening poem provides a rich introduction to Césaire's new aesthetic, conveying disillusionment but also his passive and humble presence in the landscape, as if the poet's voice resonates alongside it rather than commanding it, tracking both human and nonhuman suffering. In 'j'ai guidé du troupeau la longue transhumance', the poetic subject is even less pronounced, as the anaphora this time consists of the repetition of the verb 'marcher' with no 'je' despite his presence in the title. Yet the poem clearly alludes to the poet's earlier self-styling as the voice of negritude in the *Cahier*, where he triumphantly portrayed himself speaking for those unable to speak for themselves and crafted himself as a poetic leader. The 'troupeau' are the Martinican people and the 'transhumance' is the long history he purported to guide them through. Yet the landscape through which the poetic voice imagines he guides the people is one of lethargy and decay, where cyclones slumber, cities sleepwalk, districts are plundered, and the stars that used to spark and guide the poet's revolt have gone astray. As in many of the poems of *moi, laminaire. . .*, the rhythm of 'j'ai guidé' also seems prosaic and pedestrian, the effervescent explosions of *Soleil cou coupé* have here died out to leave a melancholy, uneven wandering through a dejected and deflated landscape. The human figure that appears in the last stanza, moreover, seems lost, inactive and uncertain:

> marcher en se disant qu'il est impossible
> que la surtension atmosphérique
> captée par les oiseaux parafoudres
> n'ait pas été retransmise quelque part
> en tout cas quelque part un homme est qui l'attend

> [to walk telling oneself that it is impossible
> that the atmospheric hypertension
> picked up by thunder-rod birds
> may not have been retransmitted somewhere
> at all events somewhere there is a man waiting for it][43]

The closing image of 'une belle parade de trochilidés' ['a beautiful parade of trochildae'] (the 'trochildae' is another word for the hummingbird family) appears to herald a resurgence of vibrant life, though in the final line this turns out to be fleeting, 'le ventre flammé d'un beau temps récessif' ['the flambé / belly of receding fair weather']. The melancholic tone of this poem, directly undermining the poet's previous pretensions, is intensified in poems such as 'condition mangrove', where the mangrove swamp connotes oppressive stagnation, an impasse that forecloses change and revolt. Whilst in Glissant's work, the mangrove represents the relational network of Caribbean identity, culture and ecology, in Césaire it is the opposite of marronnage and freedom, which are in turn associated with the 'mornes' or hills. The imagery in these poems clearly undermines the poet's earlier visionary poetic power.

POLITICAL AND POETIC DISILLUSIONMENT 231

Yet *moi, laminaire. . .* still contains traces of Césaire's vision-ary pursuit at once of transformation in the ecosystem and of linguistic alchemy. In 'annonciations', creatures undergo metamorphosis and different elements in the environment are connected as if in an expression of agency and rebellion. Stick insects become foliage and form autonomous forests in an image of solidarity and defiant reconstruction. A cur-rent seems to connect the sun with the salamanders that keep watch over tunnels from which butterflies emerge, as if this solar energy triggers a relational force that provokes rebirth. And once again, these transformations are punctuated with volcanoes spewing out their lava to create new lakes in their craters in a direct assertion of agency. Césaire's imagery in this way captures the environment as a vast interplay of energies, in which interdependency is a starting point for continual renewal. The poetic 'je' appears only late in the poem, moreo-ver, as these movements lead him to assert: 'poussants mon fol élan / feuillants ma juste demeure / racines ma survie' ['growings my mad surge / leafings my just dwelling / roots my survival']. Poetic energy appears blurred here with that of the volcano and the forest, as the poetic subject gathers energy from the elements to find his place at home in the land. This land is still scarred by the memory of past devastation, how-ever, as 'une goutte de sang monte du fond' ['a drop of blood rises from the depths'], and the poet seeks both to establish a new sense of belonging in this transforming landscape and to record its traumatised past.

In 'sentiments et ressentiments des mots', however, the poet's attention to cosmic time and to ecological transforma-tion generates an energy that is crystallised in words, as the names of various creatures come to him and voice their defi-ant presence. The poem opens with the archangels of Great Time emerging out of what seems to be a military environ-ment to keep vigil over the 'cheminement d'un lendemain naissant' ['approach of a nascent tomorrow'].[44] This larger cosmic temporality seems to enable a vision of change that transcends the relentless progression of colonial history. Next,

232   POLITICAL AND POETIC DISILLUSIONMENT

the poet's words join this summoning of energy in the quest for renewal:

il y a aussi les capteurs solaires du désir
de nuit je les braque: ce sont mots
que j'entasse dans mes réserves
et dont l'énergie est à dispenser
aux temps froids des peuples

[there are too the solar captors of desire
by night i aim at them: they are words
that i amass in my stockroom
whose energy is to be dispensed
during the cold times of peoples]

Words here are akin to weapons that can be deployed when people need them. They seem to work with the 'archangels' referenced at the beginning to disrupt oppression, their sensory properties emerging rebelliously as the poem forms into a list of powerful creatures:

le mot oiseau-tonnerre
le mot dragon-du-lac
le mot strix
le mot lémure
le mot touaou
    couresses que j'allaite

[the word thunderbird
the word dragon-of-the-lake
the word strix
the word lemur
the word touaou
    couresses that i nurse].

It is as if the utterance of the word produces this defiant procession, including the strix (a mythological bird of ill omen

POLITICAL AND POETIC DISILLUSIONMENT   233

capable of metamorphosis), the 'touaou' or bridled tern native to the Caribbean, and the 'couresse' or grass snake that hides from danger. As in 'mot macumba', words are like voodoo spirits taking different animal forms and acquiring their properties, and their incantation becomes a performance of a rebellious spiritual power.

This vision of transformation, renewal and spiritual linguistic power is developed further in Césaire's poem dedicated to the Guatemalan poet Miguel Angel Asturias, printed as a section of its own within *moi, laminaire.* ... As Gregson Davis observes, Asturias was fascinated by Mayan mythology, and this 'quest for authenticity' bears striking resemblance to Césaire's search for an originary negritude culture in Africa.[45] Davis also notes that Asturias was a precursor for magic realism, which has parallels with what he calls Césaire's 'francophone surrealism'. In keeping with other poems in *moi, laminaire...*, however, the poem opens with imagery testifying to the power of Asturias's words. Whereas earlier in the volume, Fanon was the 'guerrier silex' (or flint warrior) who breaks down barriers with his words, Asturias is a 'batteur de silex' (or flint striker), his words like golden grain flung into the dark night of the mind.[46] The poem then proceeds by anaphora, repeating 'Michel Angel' only to conjure each time a new image of the poet's incantatory power, or later his metamorphosis. These images again repeatedly fuse human and elemental, animal and plant forms, as Césaire evokes the blurring of the poet and of his craft with the ecosystem to envision transformation in dialogue with the land rather than seeking a position of sovereignty. Miguel Angel's pen, for example, 'caressait / la grande calotte des vents et le vortex polaire' ['caressed / the great skullcap of winds and the polar vortex'], whilst he also 'allumait de pins verts / les perroquets à tête bleue de la nuit' ['ignited with green pines / the blue-headed parrots of the night']. Poetry here brings species together to generate elemental movement, illumination and metamorphosis in a powerful release of energy. Later in the poem, Miguel Angel's death reveals the poet not lying down but stretching tall from the bottom of a lake towards the light, an image that prefaces his transformation from the animal to the elemental and his ultimate fusion with the landscape:

> Miguel Angel immergea sa peau d'homme
> et revêtit sa peau de dauphin

> Miguel Angel dévêtit sa peau de dauphin
> et se changea en arc-en-ciel

> Miguel Angel rejetant sa peau d'eau bleue
> revêtit sa peau de volcan

> et s'installa montagne toujours verte
> à l'horizon de tous les hommes

> [Miguel Angel immersed his human skin
> and donned his dolphin skin
> Miguel Angel took off his dolphin skin
> and changed into a rainbow

> Miguel Angel discarding his blue-water skin
> donned his volcano skin

> and settled an ever green mountain
> on the horizon of all men]

These lines crystallise Césaire's vision of the blending of human, animal, plant and cosmos, as if Miguel Angel's poetry speaks with the ecosystem as his body fuses and is reborn in the landscape.

The following series in *moi, laminaire...* is dedicated to Wifredo Lam, and the poems are less eulogies like those to Asturias, Damas or Fanon than syntheses of the poet's and the artist's aesthetic visions. Unlike many of Césaire's earlier compositions, these are all brief reflections, expressed in much simpler, more pared down language, and the poet's

POLITICAL AND POETIC DISILLUSIONMENT 235

subject position is effaced as he instead conjures visions apparent in both his own writing and Lam's painting. The opening poem, entitled 'Wifredo Lam', is replete with imagery typical of Césaire's own output. It begins with a kingdom under siege but moves towards an affirmation of artistic form as he addresses the 'récitant de macumbas' ['reciter of macumbas'] who searches through forests full of horns, hooves, wings, and horses.[47] The speaker recognises the 'armes enchantées' of the artist in a clear echo of his own 'armes miraculeuses'. The following poem picks up on the citation from Lam praising his Afro-Cuban godmother, Mantonica Wilson, a healer and Santeria priestess, and again seems to blur the voice of poet and addressee to summon orishas and loas affirming life against oppression and cheating death. Many of the poems invoke actions and processes in the landscape rather than expressing any kind of poetic will, however, as 'façon langagière' gives agency not so much to the lyric voice as to 'le territoire sacré mal luminai par des feuilles' ['the sacred territory reluctantly conceded by the leaves'].[48] 'Rabordaille', conversely, is a brutal evocation of the destruction of the landscape created by the colonial regime, figured by the advent of man as 'un homme stylet / un homme scalpel' ['a stiletto man / a scalpel man'].[49] Arnold and Eshleman explain that the title refers to a type of drum, played with a rapid rhythm as in a boarding attack, as if the poem should incite resistance.[50] Finally, in 'nouvelle bonté', elements in the natural world conspire to predict the coming of a new order, 'une nouvelle bonté ne cesse de croître à l'horizon' ['a new bounty increases ceaselessly on the horizon'].[51] Despite the disillusionment more broadly expressed in Césaire's later years, the volume ends on this expression of hope.

Comme un malentendu de salut

Césaire's very last volume of poetry, *Comme un malentendu de salut*, was published with the encouragement of Daniel

236   POLITICAL AND POETIC DISILLUSIONMENT

Maximin in 1994, and included just twenty-two poems for the most part continuing with a similar tone to *moi, laminaire*. . . . Several of the poems again express disillusionment, sometimes with clear reference to the poet's pursuit of negritude or departmentalisation during the 1940s, as if he is standing back and taking stock of his career with all its hopes and frustrations. The collection includes eulogies to Senghor and to Alioune Diop (who founded the journal *Présence africaine* in 1947 as well as the associated publishing house in 1949), commemorating in 'Dyali' Senghor's use of the African griot tradition, and praising Diop's ambition in 'Stèle obsidienne pour Alioune Diop'. Otherwise, however, many of the poems capture the poet's sense of humility and tend to sideline the lyric subject in favour of evocations of agency in the landscape. The title *Comme un malentendu de salut* foregrounds uncertainty, as salvation is no longer heralded through poetry or through political action but instead merely generates misunderstanding. Arnold and Eshleman note the ambiguity in the title, pointing out that Smith and Thomas's translation *Like a Misunderstood Salvation* suggests that salvation is still possible but has been misunderstood, whereas their own *Like a Misunderstanding of Salvation* places the very possibility of salvation in doubt.[52] This later translation also captures the idea that the visionary project of negritude and indeed of departmentalisation may have been misunderstood all along, so that the volume portrays not only the mature poet unsure of his place but also his awareness of the difficulties that hampered him throughout his career.

Several of the poems in *Comme un malentendu de salut* allude to past mistakes, and imagery conjuring stasis or discontent in the environment is interspersed with allusions to more concrete steps or missteps taken by Césaire during his career. 'Passage', for example, starts with the poet rejecting what seems to be an implacable, unproductive movement, 'une rumination de jusants / l'inventaire aussi de la longueur des sécheresses' ['a rumination of ebb tides / the inventory as well as the length of droughts'].[53] Later in the poem, the

POLITICAL AND POETIC DISILLUSIONMENT   237

poetic subject openly admits responsibility for previous misguided decisions, as he laments, 'je sais qu'il m'appartient /
pour l'impatience d'un printemps de grandes erres fourvoyé'
['I know that I am responsible / for the impatience of a spring-
time of mistaken tracks']. A sense of hindrance or lack of
progress in this way becomes crystallised by this clear statement of personal regret. In 'Vertu des lucioles', the poet begins
by expressing respect for fireflies, recommending patience
and warning against trying to capture their light. Again, in
the second half of the poem, he alludes more directly to his
own difficulties, as he confesses his struggles to make himself
understood: 'la communication par hoquets d'essentiel' ['communication via essential hiccups'].[54] The poem ends with the
poet's realisation that progress is never smooth and communication always halting, as if to question and undermine his
former claims to speak for the people. In 'Comme un malentendu de salut', the poet looks back on his career, 'de grief
en grief / de souvenance en rémanence' ['from one grievance
to the next / from remembrance to remanence'], figuring the
shifts and changes of his life as movements through different
forms of landscape.[55] By the end, these movements peter out,
until 'bavure' ['bungle'] and 'bévue' ['blunder'] each drift alone
in a line, giving way to the 'malentendu de salut' ['misunderstanding of salvation'] that closes the poem. The evocation of
these movements or actions as fading also suggests not a clear
denouement but a slow build-up of frustrations that gradually
erode the poet's self-belief.

In 'Dérisoire', Césaire reflects critically on the hubristic
imagery of his earlier negritude poetry and of *Et les chiens
se taisaient*. The poem opens with the poet distancing himself from the Promethean hero previously incarnated by the
Rebelle: 'Je ne suis pas cloué sur le plus absurde des rochers /
Aucune prouesse ailée ne me visita jamais' ['I am not nailed to
the most absurd of rocks / No winged feat of valor ever visited me'].[56] Moreover, the poetic subject is not welcomed by a
chorus of cheers, but is met only by 'le hoquet d'un cargaison
de naufragés' ['the occasional hiccup of a cargo of castaways'].

He addresses only those who too are adrift, and they do not communicate with him but only tentatively stutter their suffering. This dejected Promethean imagery is followed by a more concrete rejection of his earlier preoccupation with civil status, presumably here referencing departmentalisation and its fraught and contested legacy. The poet suggests that his difficulty in looking back is coupled with a broadening of his vision in the present, not so much with renewed certainty, however, as with a mature admission of his limits. Insisting that 'Je ne broute pas la panique / Je ne rumine pas le remords' ['I do not browse panic / I do not ruminate on remorse'], he adopts a steady, humble position, accepting his limitations rather than railing against them in regret. In a muted 'PS', composed of even shorter lines than the main body of the poem, the poet suggests that if the elements do not conspire with him to bring broader change then perhaps his silence alone will provide him with energy, 'la jubilation mal déchiffrée d'un / magma solitaire / Cavalier du temps et de l'écume' ['the ill-deciphered jubilation of a / solitary magma / Rider of time and spume']. This closing image is a revealing recasting of the 'Peléen' poet with his volcanic temperament, this time not commanding elemental revolt but merely riding, confused and alone, the undirected movements of time and molten rock.

The final poem in the volume, 'Configurations', is addressed to the critic Jacqueline Leiner and notably taken by Kora Véron as the title of her biography. This is the longest poem in the collection and captures a range of moods, juxtaposing the stagnation of the mangrove with the energy of the volcano while suggesting that, out of the poet's uncertainty there nevertheless emerges a belief at least in the power of language. The poem is an apt testimonial in its succinct combination of the different kinds of landscapes seen across his poems and in its final affirmation not so much of concrete change but of poetry itself. It opens with a reference to the mangrove with its associated 'mustiness' and to seeds by turns flying in the wind or anchored in a tortured land, as if to evoke the difficulty of establishing roots in a land that has been ravaged. This

POLITICAL AND POETIC DISILLUSIONMENT   239

first section describing an uncertain landscape is followed by a second, in which the poetic subject becomes the focus. Here the poet is at first 'tout montagne' ['all mountain'], associated with verticality and with the incendiary Mount Pelée, but then he attaches himself to the Martinican Caravelle peninsula, adopting a horizontal position more akin to the laminaria.[57] The peninsula stretches into 'un océan d'huile fausse et de fli-buste' ['an ocean of false oil and of freebooting'], in a clear reference to the colonial sapping of environmental resources. It is in the third section that language occupies centre stage, as if after all his political tribulations the poet finds solace instead in poetry: 'rien ne délivre jamais que l'obsurité du dire / Dire de pudeur et d'impudeur / Dire de la parole dure' ['Nothing ever frees but the obscurity of the word / The word of modesty and immodesty / The word of hard speech'].[58]

Language here can be assertive and direct ('hard speech') but its power also comes from the potential openness of its meaning, as if this obscurity is an effective form of liberation from dogmatism and overdetermination. Language can also be a 'sursaut' ['burst of energy'] and can 'briser la boue' ['break the muck'], as if the poet is reclaiming the visionary explosive-ness of his earlier poetry, though notably the energy here takes the form of brief flashes rather than complete destruction and reinvention. The final section of the poem suggests that the attempt at rapid change figured by the image of volcanic lava needs to give way to Time, the capital suggesting again cosmic time, a greater set of forces beyond everyday human life. The poem configures multiple images and tonalities from Césaire's wider poetic work, culminating at once in an affirmation of poetic power and in a relinquishment of any claim for poetic or political mastery.

Césaire's tireless work in improving living conditions in Martinique would continue until his resignation from the office of mayor in 2001, yet his achievements during this period were accompanied by frustration and by an increasing sense of disconnection from younger generations. The poems of *moi, laminaire. . .* and *Comme un malentendu de salut* reflect

240   POLITICAL AND POETIC DISILLUSIONMENT

this disillusionment, together with a sense of uncertainty towards past decisions, and often portray human activity as fruitless and paltry compared with the greater forces at work in the landscape and the cosmos. This reminder of the agency of the landscape, however, should be read as highly significant for subsequent generations as our awareness of the disastrous effects of our hubristic manipulation of the land and its resources grows. The humility of the poetic subject in these poems can be seen as an important lesson for contemporary environmentalism. Above all, Césaire insists that, even if his earlier poetic vision was too grandiose, poetry can bring freedom and is still vital to him even if it no longer has the rousing and far-reaching power he originally attributed to it. The poet no longer commands the landscape, but his writing provides a space for accepting his contingent place in the wider forces of the ecosystem. The lyric voice also no longer speaks for the masses and accepts his uncertain position in the world, confessing to his solitude and understanding his limits. In *moi, laminaire. . .* poetry can trigger transformation, as words work their magic to evoke the blurring of humans, plants and animals, whilst in *Comme un malentendu de salut*, it is a space of reckoning and its open-endedness is potentially a form of freedom. This is a very different form of poetic power from that seen in the *Cahier*, but these late works still attest to a belief in language as a convincing force for change.

Afterword

Césaire died on 17 April 2008, and his mourning was a national event. It was briefly suggested that his body be transferred to Paris and interred at the Panthéon alongside France's most illustrious writers and historical figures, but it was quickly apparent that this was not appropriate. Césaire himself had chosen the cemetery he wanted to be buried in, in Martinique. His funeral, however, was attended by President Sarkozy and an array of other ministers in recognition of his long and remarkable career, even though Césaire himself had refused to meet Sarkozy just three years previously when the President had visited Fort-de-France. Pierre Aliker, a long-standing colleague, gave a moving homage, before the body was transferred to La Joyau cemetery just outside Fort-de-France. Césaire had also himself chosen 'Calendrier lagunaire' for the plaque on his tombstone, a poem evoking at once the poet's sense of anchoring in the landscape and a broader, universalised communion with the elements, as if poet and cosmos are blurred in their expression of resistance. Césaire is also commemorated with a plaque at the Panthéon, displaying the five opening lines of 'Calendrier lagunaire' as well as the bold affirmation from the *Cahier* of the poet's aspiration to be 'la bouche des malheurs qui n'ont point de bouche' ['the mouth of those calamities that have no mouth'], together with

242 AFTERWORD

the hope expressed in *moi, laminaire...* in the line 'la force de regarder demain' ['the strength to face tomorrow']. These lines foreground his fidelity to history, referenced through connection with the ancestors in 'Calendrier lagunaire', together with his assumption of leadership in the present, and his aspiration for a better future. The plaque records his resonance across time and connects his reflectivity and his actions with a universalised pursuit of forward movement.

Beyond the immediate adulation for Césaire following his death, however, his legacy includes a range of highly varied responses, as colleagues, readers and activists remember him in different ways. On the one hand, Césaire can be recognised as a successful and long-standing statesman, holding his office as mayor for fifty-six years and his position as Deputy at the Assemblée Nationale for forty-eight years. He should be remembered as a public figure, a leader and spokesman, tirelessly campaigning for improvements in the lives of Martinicans in his political work and denouncing historical injustices in his poetry and theatre. On the other hand, as we saw at the beginning of Chapter 6, Césaire described himself as a 'nègre marron', rebellious, subversive, critical of institutions that perpetuate inequality and championing revolt over orthodoxy. His cultural and poetic vision reaches heights of revolutionary fervour while his everyday politics cast him as a moderate, continuing to work with the French state rather than against it, and seeking to negotiate autonomy rather than to demand independence. The anticolonial thrust of *Discours sur le colonialisme*, moreover, presents him as an angry militant, pointing out the violence and hypocrisy at the heart of French culture and history, and yet in his political role Césaire was committed to working with the French government rather than rejecting it.

Césaire's political legacy has been construed in different lights by different commentators. In his discussion of the mass general strikes in Guadeloupe and Martinique in 2009, in which activists from a variety of milieus came together in an alliance against profiteering or 'lyannaj kont pwofitayson',

AFTERWORD 243

the francophone Caribbean scholar Adlai Murdoch draws a link between the more recent protest against social and political inequalities and that of Césaire in the first years of his disappointment towards departmentalisation.[1] Césaire's immediate protest, at the very moment of departmentalisation, against the passing of a law allowing for differentiation in salaries between the metropole and the DOM, and his continued campaigning for equal rights over the following decades, anticipates the protests of 2009 and shows how little progress has been made. The causes for which Césaire fought tirelessly, his commitment to working towards social and economic equality for Martinicans, were still alarmingly relevant in 2009 and continue to be so today. Moreover, Césaire's relevance for militant activism in France is signalled by Houria Bouteldja, spokesperson for the controversial movement Indigènes de la République, created in response to the law of 23 February 2005 according to which the positive effects of colonialism should be taught in schools, and denouncing the structural racism of French society. In *Les Blancs, les Juifs et nous: vers une politique révolutionnaire*, Bouteldja cites *Discours sur le colonialisme* several times to highlight the complicity between colonialism and Nazism, a complicity that she argues lives on in new forms of imperialism.[2] Bouteldja has been associated with anti-Semitic views, however, and Césaire should not be seen as a precursor for her work or for the Indigènes movement. More broadly, scholar and activist Frieda Ekotto has insisted on the connections between Césaire's work and that of Black Lives Matter, arguing that Césaire's focus on the history of blackness crucially supplements the current movement's focus on present forms of brutality.[3]

Yet while Césaire fought the same battles as Martinicans, and perhaps of black people around the world, in the present, he remained a political negotiator rather than an activist, and his struggles took place at the Assemblée Nationale rather than on the streets. In Confiant's censorious study *Aimé Césaire: Une traversée paradoxale du siècle*, in which, as we saw in Chapter 6, he vilifies Césaire's obfuscation of Creole language

244   AFTERWORD

and culture, the author also identifies four key moments of upheaval in Martinique in response to which Césaire failed to act decisively. The first of these moments was the riots of December 1959, when police clamped down on protesters, and Césaire merely insisted that the local council was not responsible. The second was at the time of the revolt of the Organisation de la jeunesse anticolonialiste de la Martinique in 1962–3, when Confiant objects that Césaire did not take the opportunity to push for independence. The third relates to the PPM's failure to demand a proper investigation into the violent repression of striking workers at the Habitation Chalvet in February 1974. Finally, Confiant criticises Césaire's refusal to offer support to the Alliance révolutionnaire Caraïbe in 1983–4. Césaire was (in Confiant's view) an assimilationist in spite of himself who failed to ally himself with Martinican activists at moments of crisis when they most needed support.

If there is some uncertainty around Césaire's political legacy, however, his cultural legacy has generally been more positively celebrated, despite his ambivalent reception by the Créolistes. Whilst Césaire never closely engaged with the work of Édouard Glissant, his imprint can be seen in many of Glissant's works. Glissant included his own version of a poem entitled 'Le Grand midi' in *Le Sel noir*, published in 1960, though the poem seems both to acknowledge the significance of Césaire as father figure and to express some disillusionment towards his rhetorical grandeur. More recently, various twentieth- and twenty-first-century writers and artists have reinvigorated his poetry and signalled its relevance in the present. Daniel Maximin's writing is steeped in Césaire, and not only did Maximin publish a full-length homage to Césaire with *Aimé Césaire, frère volcan* in 2013, as well as editing the Seuil volume of Suzanne Césaire's *Le Grand Camouflage: Écrits de dissidence 1941–1945* in 2009, but also his novel *L'Isolé soleil* published in 1987 explores the history of the *Tropiques* generation.[4] The Haitian writer Dany Laferrière's moving work *L'Enigme de retour*, published in 2009, is also heavily influenced by Césaire, as the narrator reflects on his return to Haiti after

AFTERWORD

the death of his father with repeated references to the *Cahier*.[5] At the same time, Césaire's influence is exhibited beyond the literary sphere in both film and music. In 2013, marking the centenary of his birth, the French writer of Martinican origin Fabienne Kanor, together with her sister Véronique Kanor, made a documentary entitled *Retour au Cahier*, in which they explore the composition and haunting resonance of Césaire's most famous poem. In reflecting on the subject matter for the film, Véronique Kanor encapsulates Césaire's significance for her generation, insisting:

> The *Notebook* formed us, it allowed us to grow and to find a position in the world. It allowed us to know who we were in relation to enslavement and colonisation, in relation to our colour. This book helped us to be standing and free. This poem has accompanied us since adolescence.[6]

Véronique Kanor notes at the same time, however, that for the most part it is not Martinicans who have taken the *Cahier* as a symbol of their own journey, but other cultural groups, particularly in Africa, who have read the work as emblematic of their call for liberation. Césaire's significance has also been registered by the music industry, as a vast poster with his photograph and the line 'la force de regarder demain' overlooked the 'Rencontres urbaines' hip hop festival at the Grande Halle de la Villette in 2008.[7] In 2012 French singer Arthur H set some of his lines to music, together with some poems by Depestre and Glissant, in 'L'Or noir'. In 2018, the French rapper of Congolese descent known as Youssoupha paid homage to Césaire in 'Rendons à Césaire', alluding to the controversy surrounding negritude but denouncing the oppression of black people and affirming solidarity. Notably, Youssoupha asserts, 'J'ai pas grandi avec le rap mais avec la rumba zaïroise' ['I didn't grow up with rap but with Zairean rumba'], using and reinventing a French form to capture a different cultural heritage, just as Césaire did with Caribbean and negritude culture in his poetry.

Whilst Césaire's cultural influence is far-reaching, however, his writing cannot be seen unproblematically to represent a particular cultural community. He worked closely with local colleagues on *Tropiques* and maintained dynamic dialogues with a wide range of international writers and artists particularly during the earlier part of his career. But his poetry and theatre do not speak directly for Martinicans; later volumes such as *moi, laminaire...* rather cast the poet as an isolated figure with an uneasy sense of rootedness. Negritude was for Césaire never a label for a determined group of writers with a shared identity, and his literary influence is diffuse and transcultural. The Créolistes testify to the ambivalence of the next generation of Martinican writers towards Césaire, the father figure from whom they learned but from whom they also seek to escape. He is strikingly depicted by Patrick Chamoiseau in *Texaco* as irrevocably solitary, 'j'ai toujours le sentiment d'une solitude sans fin' ['I always have the impression of an endless solitude'], and certainly at a distance from the emergent, dynamic, Creole community of Texaco represented in the novel.[8] Romuald Fonkoua's biographical study of Césaire concludes with a chapter figuring him as 'alone and splendid', despite his many political and literary meetings and connections.[9] When the Faculty Council at the Free University of Brussels decided in 2006 to nominate him for the Nobel Peace Prize, he turned down the proposal, perhaps demonstrating his discomfort with public life. Readers from around the world reference and redeploy his writing for its resonance in different contexts, but despite his monumental importance in Martinican culture and politics, his writing forges less a local identity than a universalised voice of revolt that is at the same time internally conflicted and grappling with its uneasy belonging.

Césaire's universalising vocabulary is not without difficulties, and despite his commitment to Martinican society, he pays little attention to particular or personal experiences within the broader frame of colonial oppression. I mentioned the virile imagery recurrent in the *Cahier* in Chapter 1, as well as the ambivalence towards Césaire among feminist thinkers (who have criticised *Une Tempête*, for example, for failing to take the opportunity to afford more space to female characters). More broadly, there is no doubt that Césaire remained troublingly silent on the specific difficulties faced by black women. Women writers such as Maryse Condé and Fabienne Kanor have celebrated his revolutionary influence, and yet if Césaire was already uneasy about his capacity to represent the Martinican people, he nowhere addresses the struggles of Martinican women. Female figures feature often in the poetry, yet they are rarely subjects with agency but rather part of the landscape of suffering and oppression, their bodies part of the ecological environment rather than instigators of action or change. Fleeting references to the poet's female companion reveal his desire for complicity, as in 'Chevelure' in *Soleil cou coupé*, for example, he conjures the woman's hair as a 'crinière paquet de lianes espoir fort des naufrages' ['mane bundle of lianas stubborn hope of the shipwrecked'].[10] Here, her hair like the liana vine represents organic growth and connection, as poet, plant and woman are woven together to generate solace and hope. Nevertheless, it is the poet who provides the solid home and anchoring for this relationship, and the woman remains in a passive state as he entreats her, 'dors doucement au tronc méticuleux de mon étreinte ma femme / ma citadelle' ['sleep softly in the meticulous trunk of my embrace my woman / my citadel']. Although we might take this as a signifier of the importance of Suzanne Césaire in the poet's visionary universe, it is also perhaps notable that he nowhere writes explicitly about her intellectual work.

Césaire's achievements in both poetry and politics are nevertheless monumental, despite the difficulties he experienced in reaching parts of the population for whom he wanted to speak. Ultimately, as I noted in the Introduction and as is testified by my readings of his speeches and poems, the reason for his success is perhaps his extraordinary mastery of language, which he deployed with visionary power in his speeches, his poems and his plays. Césaire's own belief in the

248   AFTERWORD

transformative potential of language is evident as far back as 'Panorama', published in *Tropiques* in February 1944, and in which, as we saw in Chapter 2, he insists that revolution happens in the name of bread, but also in the name of air and poetry.[11] Inspiration is respiration, and freedom comes with the liberation of the lungs, enabling self-expression. The most erudite scholars of Césaire tend to agree that it is his poetry that will be the most lasting. Gregson Davis argues that it is Césaire the 'extraordinary verbal artist' who will be remembered for posterity.[12] Véron's biography similarly concludes that, whilst Martinique's political and economic problems are far from resolved, Césaire's legacy lies elsewhere, in his poetry and in his capacity for inventive thinking of all kinds.[13] James Arnold finds Césaire's leadership in his words, his 'miraculous weapons', as if to suggest that his political achievements are above all the result of his true talent in mastering poetic language. Césaire's poetry will no doubt outlive the contingency of his political activities in its revolutionary and imaginary vision that transforms past and present injustices into a timeless call for change. His political activities exemplify his relentless commitment to practical improvements as well as to liberatory ideals, but it is his incendiary language that performs creative transformation both for the moment and for a liberated and egalitarian future still to come.

Notes

Introduction

1 Aimé Césaire, 'Hommage à Victor Schoelcher', *Écrits politiques: 1935–1956* (Paris: Nouvelles Éditions Jean-Michel Place, 2016), pp. 85–9 (p. 86).

2 Aimé Césaire, 'Relier Schoelcher', *Écrits politiques: 1957–1971* (Paris: Nouvelles Éditions Jean-Michel Place, 2016), pp. 55–6 (p. 55).

3 Aimé Césaire, 'Jusques à quand ?', *Écrits politiques: 1957–1971*, pp. 65–6 (p. 66).

4 Aimé Césaire, 'L'homme de culture et ses responsabilités', *Écrits politiques: 1957–1971*, pp. 95–101 (p. 97).

5 Ibid., pp. 100–1.

6 Aimé Césaire, 'Réponse de *Tropiques* à M. le lieutenant de vaisseau Bayle, chef du service d'information', *Écrits politiques: 1935–1956*, p. 41.

7 Aimé Césaire, 'Culture et colonisation', *Écrits politiques: 1935–1956*, pp. 357–72.

8 Daniel Maximin, *Aimé Césaire, frère volcan* (Paris: Seuil, 2013).

9 Thomas Hale and Kora Véron, 'Is there unity in the writings of Aimé Césaire', *Research in African Literatures* 41.1 (2010): 46–70 (p. 57).

10 James Arnold notes an article in *Le Progressiste* on 18 June 2008 using the quotation 'je suis un nègre marron' from an undated interview in the Guadeloupian press. See A. James Arnold, 'Césaire is Dead! Long live Césaire!', *French Politics, Culture and Society* 27.3 (2009): 9–18 (p. 12).

11 Raphaël Confiant, *Aimé Césaire, une traversée paradoxale du siècle* (Paris: Stock, 1993).

NOTES TO PP. 9–18

12 M. a M. Ngal, *Aimé Césaire, un homme à la recherche d'une patrie* (Dakar, Abidjan: Les Nouvelles Editions Africaines, 1975) 21. See also Romuald Fonkoua, *Aimé Césaire* (Paris: Perrin, 2013), p. 30.

13 See Aimé Césaire, '1er Séance du 12 Mars 1946', *Écrits politiques: Discours à l'Assemblée Nationale 1945–1983* (Paris: Nouvelles Éditions Jean Michel Place, 2013), pp. 27–37.

14 Ibid., p. 37.

15 Aimé Césaire, 'Contre le sabotage de l'assimilation', *Écrits politiques: 1935–1956*, pp. 197–9.

16 Ibid., p. 198.

17 Aimé Césaire, 'Nègreries: Conscience raciale et révolution sociale', *Écrits politiques: 1935–1956*, pp. 32–33 (p. 33).

18 Aimé Césaire, *Cahier d'un retour au pays natal*, *The Complete Poetry of Aimé Césaire*, trans. James Arnold and Clayton Eshleman (Middletown: Wesleyan University Press, 2017), pp. 42–3.

19 Léopold Sédar Senghor, 'Ce que l'homme noir apporte', *Liberté I: Négritude et humanisme* (Paris: Seuil, 1964), pp. 22–38 (p. 24).

20 Aimé Césaire, 'Discours sur l'art africain', *Écrits politiques: 1957–1971*, pp. 217–24 (p. 219).

21 Ibid., p. 220.

22 See https://blacklivesmatter.com/about

23 Wole Soyinka, *The Burden of Memory, the Muse of Forgiveness* (Oxford: Oxford University Press, 1999), p. 123.

24 F. Abiola Irele, 'Introduction', *Cahier d'un retour au pays natal/Journal of a Homecoming*, trans. Gregson Davis (Durham: Duke University Press, 2017), p. 51.

25 Aimé Césaire, 'Discours de Miami: Première conférence hémisphérique des peuples noirs de la diaspora en hommage à Aimé Césaire', *Écrits politiques 1972–1988*, p. 524.

26 Jean Khalfa, *Poetics of the Antilles: Poetry, History and Philosophy in the Writings of Perse, Césaire, Fanon and Glissant* (Oxford: Peter Lang, 2017), p. 5.

27 See A. James Arnold, *Modernism and Negritude: The Poetry and Poetics of Aimé Césaire* (Cambridge, Massachusetts: Harvard University Press, 1981); Carrie Noland, *Voices of Negritude in Modernist Print: Aesthetic Subjectivity, Diaspora and the Lyric Regime* (New York: Columbia University Press, 2015).

28 See Aimé Césaire, 'Pour la transformation de la Martinique en région dans le cadre d'une Union française fédérée', Rapport présenté au congrès constitutif du PPM, 22 mars 1958, *Écrits politiques: 1957–1971*, pp. 17–28.

29 'Entretien avec Aimé Césaire: propos recueillis par Jacqueline Sieger', *Écrits politiques: 1957–1971*, pp. 156–61 (p. 161).

NOTES TO PP. 19-28

30 Mireille Rosello, 'The "Césaire Effect": Or, How to Cultivate one's Nation', *Research in African Literatures* 32.4 (2001): 77–91 (p. 81). On this question see also H. Adlai Murdoch, '*Ars poetica, ars politica:* The Double Life of Aimé Césaire', *Research in African Literatures* 41.1 (2010): 1–13.

31 Thomas Hale and Kora Véron, 'Is there unity in the writings of Aimé Césaire?', *Research in African Literatures* 41.1 (2010): 46–70.

32 Cited from *L'Express*, 13 September 2001, in Thomas Hale and Kora Véron, 'Is there unity in the writings of Aimé Césaire?', p. 67.

33 Euzhan Palcy, *Aimé Césaire, une parole pour le XXIème siècle*, 1994, 2006.

34 See Condé's comments in Euzhan Palcy's documentary, *Aimé Césaire, une parole pour le XXIème siècle*, 1994, 2006.

35 Fred Constant, 'Aimé Césaire et la politique: Sept leçons de leadership', *French Politics, Culture and Society* 27.3 (2009): 34–43.

36 Ann M. Simmons and Jaweed Kaleen, 'Q&A: A founder of Black Lives Matter answers a question on many minds: where did it go?', *Los Angeles Times*, 25 August 2017, quoted in Elvira Basevich, *W. E. B. Du Bois: The Lost and the Found* (Cambridge: Polity, 2021), p. 105.

Chapter 1

1 Aimé Césaire, 'Nègreries: Conscience raciale et révolution sociale', *Aimé Césaire: Écrits politiques 1935–1956*, pp. 32–33 (p. 32).

2 Aimé Césaire, *Cahier d'un retour au pays natal, The Complete Poetry of Aimé Césaire*, pp. 60–1.

3 Frantz Fanon, *Pour la révolution africaine, Œuvres* (Paris: La Découverte, 2011), p. 708; *Toward the African Revolution*, trans. Haakon Chevalier (New York: Grove Press, 1967), p. 21.

4 Paulette Nardal, 'Guignol Ouolof', *L'Étudiant noir* 1 (1935), pp. 4–5 (p. 4).

5 Cited in Romuald Fonkoua, *Aimé Césaire* (Paris: Perrin, 2010), p. 49.

6 Alain Locke, 'Foreword', *The New Negro: Voices of the Harlem Renaissance*, ed. Alain Locke (New York: Touchstone, 1999), pp. 24–6 (p. 26).

7 Aimé Césaire, *Cahier d'un retour au pays natal, The Complete Poetry of Aimé Césaire*, pp. 56–7.

8 See Brent Hayes Edwards, *The Practice of Diaspora: Literature, Translation and the Rise of Black Internationalism* (Cambridge, Massachusetts: Harvard University Press, 2010), p. 16.

9 Ibid., p. 26.

10 From Lamine Senghor, 'Le Mot *nègre*', quoted by Christopher

L. Miller, *Nationalists and Nomads: Essays on Francophone African Literature and Culture* (Chicago: University of Chicago Press, 1998), pp. 33–6. See Miller also for an extended analysis of Senghor's article.

11 Frantz Fanon, 'Antillais et Africains', *Pour la révolution africaine*, *Œuvres* (Paris: La Découverte, 2011).

12 Louis-Thomas Achille, 'Preface', *Revue du monde noir* 1 (1931): vii–xvii (p. viii).

13 Kora Véron, *Aimé Césaire: Configurations* (Paris: Seuil, 2021), p. 75.

14 Editorial 'Ce que nous voulons faire', *Revue du monde noir* 1 (1931): xviii.

15 Aimé Césaire, *Nègre je suis, nègre je resterai: Entretiens avec Françoise Vergès* (Paris: Albin Michel, 2005), p. 25.

16 Kora Véron, *Aimé Césaire: Configurations*, p. 74.

17 Étienne Léro, 'Misère d'une poésie', *Légitime Défense* (Paris: Jean-Michel Place, 1979), pp. 10–12 (p. 10).

18 See René Ménil's Introduction, *Légitime Défense*, p. 3.

19 Cited from an interview with Thomas Hale in Kora Véron and Thomas Hale (eds.), *Les Écrits d'Aimé Césaire: Biobibliographie commentée* 1 (Paris: Honoré Champion, 2013), p. 15.

20 Aimé Césaire, 'Nègreries: Jeunesse noire et assimilation', *Aimé Césaire: Écrits politiques 1935–1956*, pp. 29–31 (p. 30).

21 Aimé Césaire, 'Nègreries: Conscience raciale et révolution sociale', *Aimé Césaire: Écrits politiques 1935–1956*, p. 33.

22 Léopold Sédar Senghor, 'L'Humanisme et nous: René Maran', *L'Étudiant noir* 1 (1935): 4.

23 Gilbert Gratiant, 'Mulâtres: pour le bien et le mal', *L'Étudiant noir* 1 (1935): 5–7.

24 M. a M. Ngal, *Aimé Césaire: un homme à la recherche d'une patrie*, p. 67.

25 Kora Véron, *Aimé Césaire: Configurations*, p. 68.

26 Ibid., p. 68.

27 See Leo Frobénius, *Histoire de la civilisation africaine*, trans. D. H. Back and D. Ermont (Paris: Gallimard, 1936).

28 See Léopold Sédar Senghor, 'Ce que l'homme noir apporte', *Liberté* I (Paris: Seuil, 1964), pp. 22–38.

29 Lilyan Kesteloot, 'Entretien avec Aimé Césaire', in Lilyan Kesteloot and Barthélemy Kotchy, *Aimé Césaire, l'homme et l'œuvre* (Paris: Présence Africaine, 1973), pp. 227–43 (p. 236).

30 Véron, *Aimé Césaire: Configurations*, p. 88.

31 Cited in Roger Toumson and Simonne Henry-Valmore, *Aimé Césaire: Le Nègre inconsolé*, p. 40.

32 Kora Véron, *Aimé Césaire: Configurations*, pp. 138–9.

NOTES TO PP. 37–43

33 Ibid., p. 139.

34 Ibid., p. 143.

35 Cited in M. a M. Ngal, *Aimé Césaire: un homme à la recherche d'une patrie*, p. 64.

36 Aimé Césaire, 'Introduction à la poésie nègre américaine', *Aimé Césaire: Écrits politiques 1935–1956*, pp. 35–38 (p. 37).

37 Cited in M. a M. Ngal, *Aimé Césaire: un homme à la recherche d'une patrie*, p. 69.

38 André Breton, 'Un grand poète noir', *Cahier d'un retour au pays natal* (Paris: Présence Africaine, 1971), pp. 16, 17.

39 Jean-Paul Sartre, 'Orphée noir', in Léopold Sédar Senghor (ed.), *Anthologie de la nouvelle poésie nègre et malgache de langue française* (Paris: Presses universitaires de France, 1948), pp. ix–xliv (p. xxvi); 'Black Orpheus', *The Massachusetts Review* 6.1 (1964–65): 13–52 (p. 33).

40 For more on the circumstances of the publication of the *Cahier* with *Volontés*, see Carrie Noland, *Voices of Negritude in Modernist Print: Aesthetic Subjectivity, Diaspora, and the Lyric Regime*.

41 A. James Arnold, *Aimé Césaire: Poésie, Théâtre, Essais et Discours* (Paris: CNRS Editions, 2013), p. 65.

42 Christopher Miller, 'Editing and Editorializing: The New Genetic Criticism of Aimé Césaire', *The South Atlantic Quarterly Review* 115.3 (2016): 441–55 (p. 450).

43 Aimé Césaire, 'Nègreries: Conscience raciale et révolution sociale', p. 33.

44 A. James Arnold outlines these four sections similarly in his Introduction to his translation, together with Clayton Eshelman, of *The Original 1939 Notebook of a Return to My Native Land* (Middletown: Wesleyan University Press, 2013), though again he foregrounds the spiritual resonances of this process more prominently. Dominique Combe also divides the text into sections, though he is working with the 1956 version and brings the second and third together as one. For Combe, the three sections are characterised by 'haine' ['hatred'], 'introspection et souvenirs' ['introspection and memory'] and 'révolte sociale' ['social revolt']. See Dominique Combe, *Aimé Césaire* (Paris: Presses universitaires de France, 1993).

45 For the rest of this section, references to the *Cahier* are from the 1939 version, in *The Complete Poetry of Aimé Césaire*.

46 Aimé Césaire, *Cahier d'un retour au pays natal*, *The Complete Poetry of Aimé Césaire*, pp. 12–27.

47 Ibid., pp. 18–19.

48 Ibid., pp. 14–15.

254 NOTES TO PP. 43–56

49 Aimé Césaire, 'Nègreries: Conscience raciale et révolution sociale', p. 32.

50 Aimé Césaire, *Cahier d'un retour au pays natal/Notebook of a Return to the Native Land*, *The Complete Poetry of Aimé Césaire*, pp. 22–3.

51 Ibid., pp. 24–5.

52 Ibid., pp. 26–7.

53 Ibid., pp. 28–9.

54 Ibid., pp. 28–9.

55 Ibid., pp. 32–3.

56 Ibid., pp. 34–5.

57 Ibid., pp. 36–7.

58 Ibid., pp. 38–9.

59 Ibid., pp. 42–3.

60 See A. James Arnold, 'Beyond Postcolonial Césaire: Reading *Cahier d'un retour au pays natal* historically', *Forum for Modern Language Studies* 44.3 (2008): 258–79; Brent Hayes Edwards, 'Aimé Césaire and the Syntax of Influence', *Research in African Literatures* 36.2 (2005): 1–18.

61 Aimé Césaire, *Cahier d'un retour au pays natal*, *The Complete Poetry of Aimé Césaire*, pp. 44–5.

62 Ibid., pp. 44–5.

63 Ibid., pp. 46–7.

64 Ibid., pp. 48–9.

65 Ibid., pp. 50–1.

66 See Arnold's Introduction to *The Original 1939 Notebook of a Return to the Native Land*, p. xiv.

67 Aimé Césaire, *Cahier d'un retour au pays natal*, *The Complete Poetry of Aimé Césaire*, pp. 50–1.

68 Ibid., pp. 52–3.

69 Ibid., pp. 52–3.

70 Ibid., pp. 52–3.

71 Ibid., pp. 58–9.

72 Ibid., pp. 58–9.

73 Ibid., pp. 60–1.

74 Ibid., pp. 60–1.

75 See Carrie Noland, *Voices of Negritude in Modernist Print*, p. 40.

76 Aimé Césaire, *Cahier d'un retour au pays natal*, *The Complete Poetry of Aimé Césaire*, pp. 60–1.

77 Ibid., pp. 14–15. See also Hedy Kalikoff, 'Gender, Genre, and Geography in Aimé Césaire's *Cahier d'un retour au pays natal*', *Callaloo* 18.2 (1995): 492–505.

78 See Mireille Rosello, 'Introduction', *Cahier d'un retour au pays natal / Notebook of a Return to My Native Land*, trans. Mireille Rosello with

NOTES TO PP. 59–67   255

Annie Pritchard (Newcastle-upon-Tyne: Bloodaxe Books, 1995), p. 38.

Chapter 2

1 For a more detailed historical analysis of this period see Kristen Stromberg Childers, *Seeking Imperialism's Embrace: National Identity, Decolonization, and Assimilation in the French Caribbean* (Oxford: Oxford University Press, 2016).
2 Aimé Césaire, 'Panorama', *Tropiques 10* (1944): 7–10 (p. 7).
3 Ibid., pp. 9–10.
4 Aimé Césaire, *Cahier d'un retour au pays natal, The Complete Poetry of Aimé Césaire*, pp. 44, 45.
5 Frantz Fanon, *Peau noire, masques blancs, Œuvres* (Paris: La Découverte, 2011), p. 247; *Peau noire, masques blancs*, trans. Richard Philcox (London: Penguin, 2008), p. 201.
6 M. a M. Ngal, *Aimé Césaire: un homme à la recherche d'une patrie*, p. 94.
7 Aimé Césaire in 'Entretien avec Jacqueline Leiner', *Tropiques* (Paris: Jean-Michel Place, 1978), vi–xxiv (p. xxi).
8 Ibid., p. xxi.
9 Ibid., p. xi.
10 Aimé Césaire, 'Présentation', *Tropiques* I (1941): 5–6 (p. 5).
11 René Ménil, 'Pour une lecture critique de *Tropiques*', *Tropiques* (Paris: Jean-Michel Place, 1978): xxv-xxxv (p. xxvi).
12 Aimé Césaire, 'Présentation', *Tropiques* I, p. 6.
13 Ibid., p. 6. See also *Cahier d'un retour au pays natal, The Complete Poetry of Aimé Césaire*, pp. 46–7.
14 Aimé Césaire and René Ménil, 'Introduction au folklore martiniquais', *Tropiques* 4 (1942): 7–11 (p. 7).
15 Suzanne Césaire, 'Le Grand camouflage', *Tropiques* 13–14 (1945): 267–273 (p. 269); 'The Great Camouflage', in *The Great Camouflage: Writings of Dissent (1941–1945)*, ed. Daniel Maximin, trans. Keith Walker (Middletown: Wesleyan University Press, 2012), pp. 39–46 (p. 41).
16 Ibid., p. 271, p. 44.
17 Suzanne Césaire, 'Leo Frobenius et le problème des civilisations', *Le Grand camouflage: Écrits de dissidence 1941–1945* (Paris: Seuil, 2009); Suzanne Césaire, 'Leo Frobenius and the Problem of Civilisations', *The Great Camouflage: Writings of Dissent (1941–1945)*, pp. 3–10 (p. 5).
18 Suzanne Césaire, 'Malaise d'une civilisation', *Le Grand camouflage: Écrits de dissidence (1941–1945)*, pp. 67–75 (pp. 74–5); 'The Malaise of

Civilization', *The Great Camouflage: Writings of Dissent (1941–1945)*, pp. 28–33 (pp. 32–3).

19 See Donna V. Jones, *The Racial Discourses of Life Philosophy: Negritude, Vitalism, and Modernity* (New York: Columbia University Press, 2010), p. 173.

20 Aimé Césaire, 'Poésie et connaissance', *Tropiques* 12 (1945): 157–170 (p. 162).

21 Ibid., p. 163.

22 Aimé Césaire, 'Fragments d'un poème', *Tropiques* 1 (1941): 9–23 (p. 9).

23 Arthur Rimbaud, 'Lettre à Paul Demeny', *Poésies* (Paris: Gallimard, 1999), p. 88.

24 Aimé Césaire, 'Maintenir la poésie', *Tropiques* 8–9 (1943): 7–8 (p. 8).

25 For more on refugees travelling from France to Martinique during the Second World War, see Eric T. Jennings, *Escape from Vichy: The Refugee Exodus to the French Caribbean* (Cambridge, Massachusetts: Harvard University Press, 2018).

26 Aimé Césaire, 'Entretien avec Aimé Césaire par Jacqueline Leiner', p. vi.

27 Suzanne Césaire, 'André Breton, poète', *Le Grand camouflage: Écrits de dissidence (1941–1945)*, 54–62 (p. 59); 'André Breton, Poet', *The Great Camouflage: Writings of Dissent (1941–1945)*, pp. 19–24 (p. 22).

28 Suzanne Césaire, '1943: Le Surréalisme et nous', *Le Grand camouflage: Écrits de dissidence (1941–1945)*, 76–83 (p. 78); '1943: Surrealism and Us', *The Great Camouflage: Writings of Dissent (1941–1945)*, pp. 34–38 (p. 35).

29 Aimé Césaire, 'En guise de manifeste littéraire', *Tropiques* 5 (1942): 7–12 (p. 7).

30 For a more extensive discussion of the complex use of the unconscious in *Tropiques*, see Celia Britton, *Race and the Unconscious: Freudianism in French Caribbean Thought* (Oxford: Legenda, 2002).

31 Aimé Césaire, 'En guise de manifeste littéraire', p. 11.

32 'Lettre du Lieutenant de Vaisseau Bayle, chef du service d'information, au directeur de la revue *Tropiques*', Documents-Annexes, *Tropiques*, pp. xxxvii–xxxviii (p. xxxvii).

33 Aimé Césaire, 'Georges-Louis Ponton, Gouverneur de la Martinique', *Tropiques* 12 (1945): 153–156 (p. 153).

34 Aimé Césaire, 'Hommage à Victor Schoelcher', *Tropiques* 13–14 (1945): 229–235 (p. 235).

35 See A. James Arnold, *Aimé Césaire: genèse et transformations d'une poétique* (Würzburg: Verlag Königshausen & Neumann, 2020), p. 76.

NOTES TO PP. 74–84

36 See Kora Véron, 'Césaire at the Crossroads in Haiti: Correspondence with Henri Seyrig', *Comparative Literature Studies* 50.3 (2013): 430–44.

37 See A. James Arnold, *Aimé Césaire: genèse et transformations d'une poétique*, p. 90.

38 Aimé Césaire, *Cahier d'un retour au pays natal*, *The Complete Poetry of Aimé Césaire*, pp. 28–9.

39 M. a M. Ngal, *Aimé Césaire: l'homme à la recherche d'une patrie*, p. 97; Roger Toumson and Simonne Henry-Valmore, *Aimé Césaire: Le nègre inconsolé*, p. 79.

40 Jacqueline Leiner, 'Entretien avec Aimé Césaire: Paris, 1982', Jacqueline Leiner, *Aimé Césaire: le terreau primordial* (Tubingen: Gunter Narr Verlag, 1993), pp. 129–143 (p. 137).

41 M. a M. Ngal, *Aimé Césaire: un homme à la recherche d'une patrie*, p. 106.

42 René Hénane, Les Armes miraculeuses *d'Aimé Césaire: Une lecture critique* (Paris: L'Harmattan, 2008), p. 202.

43 Aimé Césaire, 'Avis de tirs', *The Complete Poetry of Aimé Césaire*, p. 66, p. 67.

44 René Hénane, Les Armes miraculeuses *d'Aimé Césaire: Une lecture critique*, p. 43.

45 Aimé Césaire, 'Les pur-sang', *The Complete Poetry of Aimé Césaire*, pp. 68–69.

46 Ibid., pp. 78–79.

47 Ibid., pp. 82–83.

48 Aimé Césaire, 'Le Grand midi', *The Complete Poetry of Aimé Césaire*, pp. 138–9.

49 Ibid., pp. 140–141.

50 Ibid., pp. 150–1.

51 Aimé Césaire, 'Conquête de l'aube', *The Complete Poetry of Aimé Césaire*, pp. 120–1.

52 Ibid., pp. 123–4.

53 Ibid., pp. 123–4.

54 Aimé Césaire, 'Les Armes miraculeuses', *The Complete Poetry of Aimé Césaire*, pp. 104–5.

55 Ibid., pp. 104–5. See also René Hénane, Les Armes miraculeuses *d'Aimé Césaire: Une lecture critique*, p. 150.

56 Ibid., pp. 106–7.

57 Aimé Césaire, 'Batéké', *The Complete Poetry of Aimé Césaire*, pp. 96–7.

58 See Aliko Songolo, *Aimé Césaire: une poétique de la découverte* (Paris: L'Harmattan, 1985).

59 Aimé Césaire, 'Batouque', *The Complete Poetry of Aimé Césaire*, pp. 162–3.

258   NOTES TO PP. 85–94

60 Aimé Césaire, 'L'Irrémédiable', *The Complete Poetry of Aimé Césaire*, pp. 110–111.
61 See A. James Arnold, *Aimé Césaire: Genèse et transformations d'une poétique*, pp. 108–9.
62 See Kora Véron, *Aimé Césaire: Configurations*, p. 253.
63 Interview with François Beloux, 'Un poète politique: Aimé Césaire', *Le Magazine littéraire* 34 (1969): 27–32 (p. 30).
64 Aimé Césaire, *Et les chiens se taisaient*, *The Complete Poetry of Aimé Césaire*, pp. 170–171.
65 Gregson Davis, *Aimé Césaire*. Cambridge: Cambridge University Press, 1997, p. 129.
66 Aimé Césaire, cited in Rodney E. Harris, *L'Humanisme dans le théâtre d'Aimé Césaire* (Ottawa: Editions Naaman, 1973), p. 28.
67 A. James Arnold, *Aimé Césaire: Genèse et transformations d'une poétique*, pp. 120–121.
68 Aimé Césaire, letter to Breton, cited in Kora Véron and Thomas Hale, *Les Écrits d'Aimé Césaire: Biobibliographie commentée (1913–2008)* (Paris: Honoré Champion, 2013), p. 102.
69 A. James Arnold, *Poésie, Théâtre, Essais et Discours*, p. 228.
70 Romuald Fonkoua, *Aimé Césaire*, p. 267; see also Rodney Harris, *L'Humanisme dans le théâtre d'Aimé Césaire*, p. 69.
71 Aimé Césaire, *Cahier d'un retour au pays natal*, *The Complete Poetry of Aimé Césaire*, pp. 26–7. See also Carrie Noland, *Voices of Negritude in Modernist Print: Aesthetic Subjectivity, Diaspora, and the Lyric Regime* p. 62.
72 Aimé Césaire, *Et les chiens se taisaient*, *The Complete Poetry of Aimé Césaire*, pp. 192–3.
73 Ibid., pp. 202–3.
74 Ibid., pp. 224–5.
75 Ibid., pp. 204–5.
76 Jacqueline Leiner, 'Entretien avec Aimé Césaire: Paris, 1982', Jacqueline Leiner, *Aimé Césaire: le terreau primordial*, p. 141.
77 Aimé Césaire, *Et les chiens se taisaient*, *The Complete Poetry of Aimé Césaire*, pp. 168–9.
78 Jackqueline Frost, '"The Red Hour": Poetic Violence and the Time of Transformation in Aimé Césaire's *Et les chiens se taisaient*', *The Global South* 11.1 (2017): 57–81.
79 Aimé Césaire, *Et les chiens se taisaient*, *The Complete Poetry of Aimé Césaire*, pp. 232–3.
80 Ibid., pp. 214–5.
81 Ibid., pp. 174–5.
82 Ibid., pp. 190–1.
83 Ibid., pp. 234–5.

NOTES TO PP. 94–102   259

84 See Carrie Noland, *Voices of Negritude in Modernist Print: Aesthetic Subjectivity, Diaspora, and the Lyric Regime*.

85 Aimé Césaire, *Et les chiens se taisaient*, *The Complete Poetry of Aimé Césaire*, pp. 230–1.

86 Ibid.

87 See for example pp. 256–7 and pp. 264–5.

88 Ibid., pp. 224–5.

89 Ibid., pp. 302–3.

90 Ibid.

91 Aimé Césaire, in 'Entretien avec Aimé Césaire: Paris 1982', Jaqueline Leiner, *Aimé Césaire: le terreau primordial* (Tubingen: Gunter Narr Verlag, 1993) 129–143 (p. 139).

92 Femi Ojo-Ade, *Aimé Césaire's African Theater: Of Poets, Prophets and Politicians* (Trenton, New Jersey and Asmara, Eritrea: Africa World Press, 2010), p. 62.

93 Aimé Césaire, *Cahier d'un retour au pays natal*, Brentano's 1947, A. James Arnold, *Poésie, Théâtre, Essais, Discours*, p. 111; translation from Mireille Rosello's translation of the 1956 version, *Notebook of a Return to My Native Land* (Newcastle-upon-Tyne: Bloodaxe, 1995), pp. 85–7.

94 Ibid., p. 119, p. 95.

95 Ibid., p. 120, p. 93.

96 Ibid., p. 122, p. 99.

97 Ibid., p. 120; this line is not in the 1956 edition.

Chapter 3

1 Quoted in Kora Véron, *Aimé Césaire: Configurations*, p. 264.

2 Aimé Césaire, 'Pourquoi je suis communiste', *Écrits politiques 1935–1956*, p. 99.

3 Aimé Césaire, 'Corps perdu', *The Complete Poetry of Aimé Césaire*, pp. 498–499.

4 Nick Nesbitt, *Caribbean Critique: Antillean Critical Theory from Toussaint to Glissant* (Liverpool: Liverpool University Press, 2013), p. 87.

5 Kristen Stromberg Childers discusses the few dissenters in *Seeking Imperialism's Embrace: National Identity, Decolonization and Assimilation in the French Caribbean* (Oxford: Oxford University Press, 2016).

6 Quoted in Kora Véron, *Aimé Césaire: Configurations*, p. 287.

7 Aimé Césaire, 1ère séance du 12 mars 1946, *Écrits politiques: Discours à l'Assemblée nationale 1945–1983* (Paris: Jean-Michel Place, 2013), p. 27.

8 Ibid., p. 34.

260 NOTES TO PP. 103–14

9 Aimé Césaire, 2e séance du 18 septembre 1946, *Écrits politiques: Discours à l'Assemblée nationale 1945–1983*, p. 46.
10 Aimé Césaire, 'Aimé Césaire demande le rappel du préfet Trouillé', *Écrits politiques: 1935–1956*, p. 171.
11 Aimé Césaire, 'Commémoration du centenaire de l'abolition de l'esclavage, 27 avril 1848 – 27 avril 1948: Discours de la Sorbonne', *Écrits politiques: 1935–1956*, p. 159.
12 Kora Véron, *Aimé Césaire: Configurations*, p. 312.
13 Aimé Césaire, 'L'impossible contact', *Écrits politiques: 1935–1956*, p. 165.
14 Ibid., p. 169.
15 Aimé Césaire, Séance du 4 juillet 1949, *Écrits politiques: Discours à l'Assemblée nationale 1945–1983*, p. 59.
16 Aimé Césaire, Séance du 15 mars 1950, *Écrits politiques: Discours à l'Assemblée nationale 1945–1983*, p. 77.
17 René Hénane, 'Aimé Césaire, une parole incandescente', *Écrits politiques: Discours à l'Assemblée nationale 1945–1983*, pp. 7–16.
18 Kora Véron, *Aimé Césaire: Configurations*, p. 282.
19 Aliko Songolo explores this polysemy surrounding the figure of the sun in *Aimé Césaire: une poétique de la découverte* (Paris: L'Harmattan, 1985), p. 112.
20 René Hénane, *Ma conscience et son rythme de chair: Aimé Césaire, une poétique* (Paris: Orizons, 2018), p. 112.
21 Aimé Césaire, 'Wifredo Lam aux Antilles', cited in Kora Véron and Thomas Hale, *Les Écrits d'Aimé Césaire: Biobibliographie commentée (1913–2008), Volume I* (Paris: Honoré Champion, 2013), p. 112.
22 Cited in Anne Egger, 'Rencontre du Volcan et du Minotaure', *Césaire et Picasso*: Corps Perdu, *Histoire d'une rencontre* (Paris: HC Editions, 2011), pp. 9–23 (p. 12).
23 Kora Véron, '*Corps perdu* d'Aimé Césaire et de Pablo Picasso, un recueil de guerres et de paix', *Continents manuscrits* 18 (2022): 1–13 (p. 6).
24 A. James Arnold, '*Cahier d'un retour au pays natal* (première édition française, Bordas, Paris, 1947)', *Aimé Césaire: Poésie, Théâtre, Essais et Discours*, pp. 149–150 (p. 150).
25 Aimé Césaire, *Cahier d'un retour au pays natal*, première édition française, Bordas, Paris 1947, *Aimé Césaire: Poésie, Théâtre, Essais et Discours*, p. 151. Translations are from Mireille Rosello's *Notebook of a Return to My Native Land* (Newcastle-upon-Tyne: Bloodaxe Books, 1995), p. 73.
26 Ibid., p. 176, p. 133.
27 Ibid., p. 177, p. 133.
28 Ibid., p. 161, p. 97.

NOTES TO PP. 116–24

29 See A. James Arnold, *Modernism and Negritude: The Poetry and Poetics of Aimé Césaire*, p. 192; Roger Toumson and Simonne Henry-Valmore, *Aimé Césaire: Le nègre inconsolé*, p. 108.

30 Aimé Césaire, 'Magique', *The Complete Poetry of Aimé Césaire*, pp. 310–11.

31 Aimé Césaire, 'Jugement de la lumière', *The Complete Poetry of Aimé Césaire*, pp. 474–5.

32 Aimé Césaire, 'Lynch I', *The Complete Poetry of Aimé Césaire*, pp. 314–15.

33 Ibid.

34 Aimé Césaire, 'Lynch II', *The Complete Poetry of Aimé Césaire*, pp. 374–5.

35 A. James Arnold, *Modernism and Negritude: The Poetry and Poetics of Aimé Césaire*, p. 197.

36 Aimé Césaire, 'Le coup de couteau dans le dos de villes surprises', *The Complete Poetry of Aimé Césaire*, pp. 346–7.

37 Ibid.

38 Ibid.

39 Aimé Césaire, 'Défaire et refaire le soleil', *The Complete Poetry of Aimé Césaire*, pp. 382–3.

40 Aimé Césaire, 'Demeure antipode', *The Complete Poetry of Aimé Césaire*, pp. 456–7.

41 Aimé Césaire, 'Couteaux midi', *The Complete Poetry of Aimé Césaire*, pp. 418–19.

42 Ibid.

43 Ibid.

44 See Pierre Laforgue, 'A l'Afrique d'Aimé Césaire: un poème dans l'histoire (variations génétiques)', *Présence Africaine* 184 (2011): 221–43. Laforgue also discusses the differences between the versions, drawing attention to the cuts Césaire made to the idealised imagery of the original opening and the increased coherence of the apocalyptic vision of the version printed in *Soleil cou coupé*.

45 Aimé Césaire, 'A l'Afrique', *The Complete Poetry of Aimé Césaire*, pp. 408–9.

46 A. James Arnold, *Modernism and Negritude: The Poetry and Poetics of Aimé Césaire*, p. 214.

47 Aimé Césaire, 'A l'Afrique', *The Complete Poetry of Aimé Césaire*, pp. 408–9.

48 Ibid., pp. 410–11.

49 Ibid.

50 Aimé Césaire, 'Barbare', *The Complete Poetry of Aimé Césaire*, pp. 464–5.

51 A. James Arnold, *Aimé Césaire: Genèse et transformations d'une poétique*, p. 186.

262   NOTES TO PP. 126–37

52 Aimé Césaire, 'Mot', *The Complete Poetry of Aimé Césaire*, pp. 480–1.
53 Ibid., pp. 482–3.
54 Ibid.
55 Ibid.
56 Ibid.
57 Clayton Eshleman, 'Aimé Césaire's lost, found, scattered body', *Callaloo* 31.4 (2008): 983–6 (p. 986).
58 Bernadette Cailler explores this use of nouns as verbs and links this with Léopold Sédar Senghor's comments about this practice in African languages, in particular Wolof. See Bernadette Cailler, *Proposition poétique: une lecture de l'œuvre d'Aimé Césaire* (Sherbrooke, Québec: Éditions Naaman de Sherbrooke, 1976), p. 101.
59 Aimé Césaire, 'Corps perdu', *The Complete Poetry of Aimé Césaire*, pp. 496–7.
60 Ibid., pp. 496–9.
61 Ibid., pp. 498–9.
62 Ibid.
63 Aimé Césaire, 'Dit d'errance', *The Complete Poetry of Aimé Césaire*, pp. 516–17.
64 Ibid.
65 Ibid., pp. 518–19.

Chapter 4

1 Roger Toumson and Simonne Henry-Valmore, *Aimé Césaire: Le Nègre inconsolé*, p. 119.
2 See Romuald Fonkoua, *Aimé Césaire* (Paris: Perrin, 2010), p. 148.
3 A. James Arnold, *Aimé Césaire: Poésie, Théâtre, Essais et Discours*, p. 1446.
4 Cited in M. a M. Ngal, *Aimé Césaire, un homme à la recherche d'une patrie*, pp. 212–13.
5 Aimé Césaire, *Discours sur le colonialisme*, *Aimé Césaire: Essais Politiques 1935–1956*, 303–329 (p. 303); Aimé Césaire, *Discourse on Colonialism*, trans. Joan Pinkham (New York: Monthly Review Press, 2000), p. 31.
6 Aimé Césaire, *Discours sur le colonialisme*, *Aimé Césaire: Essais Politiques 1935–1956*, p. 305; Aimé Césaire, *Discourse on Colonialism*, p. 36.
7 Ibid., p. 308, p. 41.
8 See Michael Rothberg, *Multidirectional Memory: Remembering the Holocaust in the Age of Decolonization* (Stanford: Stanford University Press, 2009).
9 Aimé Césaire, *Discours sur le colonialisme*, *Aimé Césaire: Essais Politiques 1935–1956*, p. 315; Aimé Césaire, *Discourse on Colonialism*, p. 55.

NOTES TO PP. 137–50   263

10 Roger Toumson and Simonne Henry-Valmore, *Aimé Césaire: Le Nègre inconsolé*, p. 115.

11 See Véronique Corinus, *Aimé Césaire* (Paris: Presses universitaires de France, 2019), p. 93.

12 Aimé Césaire, Séance du 10 juin 1953, *Écrits politiques: Discours à l'Assemblée Nationale 1945–1983* (Paris: Jean-Michel Place, 2013), p. 93.

13 Aimé Césaire, 'La mort aux colonies', *Aimé Césaire: Écrits Politiques 1935–1956*, p. 345.

14 Aimé Césaire, 'Préface à *Végétations de Clarté*', *Aimé Césaire: Écrits Politiques 1935–1956*, p. 248.

15 René Depestre, quoted by Kora Véron, *Aimé Césaire: Configurations*, p. 383.

16 The poem was originally published in *Présence Africaine*, but I cite it here from Arnold and Eshleman's *The Complete Poetry of Aimé Césaire*, pp. 806–7.

17 Aimé Césaire, 'Sur la poésie nationale', *Aimé Césaire: Écrits Politiques 1935–1956*, p. 333.

18 René Depestre, 'Réponse à Aimé Césaire (Introduction à un art poétique haïtien)', *Présence Africaine* 4 (1955): 42–62.

19 See Romuald Fonkoua, *Aimé Césaire*, p. 182.

20 Roger Toumson and Simonne Henry-Valmore, *Aimé Césaire: Le Nègre inconsolé*, p. 132.

21 See 'À Moscou, Aimé Césaire reçu par Maurice Thorez', *Aimé Césaire: Écrits Politiques 1935–1956*, p. 273.

22 See Romuald Fonkoua, *Aimé Césaire*, pp. 216–23.

23 Aimé Césaire, 'Lettre à Maurice Thorez, secrétaire général du Parti communiste français', *Aimé Césaire: Écrits Politiques 1935–1956*, p. 391.

24 For more on Césaire's commitment to Marxism, see Nick Nesbitt, *The Price of Slavery: Capitalism and Revolution in the Caribbean* (Charlottesville and London: University of Virginia Press, 2022).

25 Ibid., p. 396.

26 Kora Véron, *Aimé Césaire: Configurations*, p. 414.

27 Aimé Césaire, 'Discours de la Maison du sport', *Aimé Césaire: Écrits Politiques 1935–1956*, p. 399.

28 Ibid., p. 413.

29 Aimé Césaire, 'Introduction à *Les Antilles décolonisées* de Daniel Guérin', *Aimé Césaire: Écrits Politiques 1935–1956*, p. 339.

30 See Gary Wilder, *Freedom Time: Negritude, Decolonization, and the Future of the World* (Durham and London: Duke University Press, 2015), p. 172.

31 See Aimé Césaire, 'Contre la ratification des traités instituant la CEE', *Aimé Césaire: Écrits Politiques 1957–1971*.

264 NOTES TO PP. 150–57

32 Aimé Césaire, 'Pour la transformation de la Martinique en région dans le cadre d'une Union française fédérée', *Aimé Césaire: Écrits Politiques 1957–1971*.

33 Ibid., p. 28.

34 Aimé Césaire, 'L'enjeu des élections cantonales: Lettre-circulaire aux électeurs et électrices', *Aimé Césaire: Écrits Politiques 1957–1971*, p. 31.

35 Aimé Césaire, 'Tenir le pas gagné', *Aimé Césaire: Écrits Politiques 1957–1971*, p. 75.

36 A. James Arnold, *Aimé Césaire: Genèse et transformations d'une poétique*, p. 222.

37 Kora Véron, *Aimé Césaire: Configurations*, p. 404.

38 Aimé Césaire, 'Culture et colonisation', *Aimé Césaire: Essais Politiques 1935–1956*, p. 372.

39 Some of the responses to Césaire's speech are collected in 'Débats autour de l'intervention d'Aimé Césaire au premier congrès des écrivains et artistes noirs, 19–22 Septembre 1956', *Aimé Césaire: Écrits Politiques 1935–1956*.

40 Aimé Césaire, 'L'homme de culture et ses responsabilités', *Aimé Césaire: Écrits Politiques 1957–1971*, p. 98.

41 Ibid., p. 99.

42 Ibid., p. 101.

43 A. James Arnold, *Aimé Césaire: Genèse et transformations d'une poétique*, p. 209.

44 In addition to James Arnold's genetic edition of the various versions in *Poésie, Théâtre, Essais, Discours* and his analysis in *Aimé Césaire: Genèse et transformations d'une critique*, Lilian Pestre de Almeida lists and analyses the changes made to the successive versions in her *Cahier d'un retour au pays natal* (Paris: L'Harmattan, 2012).

45 Aimé Césaire, *Cahier d'un retour au pays natal*, Bordas Edition, in A. James Arnold, *Aimé Césaire: Poésie Théâtre, Essais et Discours*, p. 159. The line from the Présence Africaine edition can be found in the same volume, p. 194, or with the English translation, in Aimé Césaire, *Cahier d'un retour au pays natal/Notebook of a Return to My Native Land*, trans. Mireille Rosello (Newcastle-upon-Tyne: Bloodaxe Books, 1995), pp. 92–3.

46 Aimé Césaire, *Cahier d'un retour au pays natal*, Bordas Edition, in A. James Arnold, *Aimé Césaire: Poésie Théâtre, Essais et Discours*, p. 159.

47 Aimé Césaire, *Cahier d'un retour au pays natal/Notebook of a Return to My Native Land*, trans. Mireille Rosello, pp. 92–3.

48 Aimé Césaire, *Cahier d'un retour au pays natal*, Bordas Edition, in A. James Arnold, *Aimé Césaire: Poésie Théâtre, Essais et Discours*, p. 169, p. 173.

NOTES TO PP. 157–65   265

49 Aimé Césaire, *Cahier d'un retour au pays natal/Notebook of a Return to My Native Land*, trans. Mireille Rosello, pp. 120–1.

50 Ibid., pp. 122–3.

51 For a discussion of the paratextual elements of other editions of the *Cahier*, see Richard Watts, *Packaging Post/coloniality: The Manufacture of Literary Identity in the Francophone World* (Lanham: Lexington, 2005), pp. 99–115.

52 The blurb is reproduced and discussed in Lilian Pestre de Almeida's study of the *Cahier* and its editions, Lilian Pestre de Almeida, *Cahier d'un retour au pays natal*, pp. 36–7.

53 See James Arnold's discussion of the revised version of *Et les chiens se taisaient* in *Aimé Césaire: Genèse et transformations d'une poétique*, pp. 214–19.

54 Gregson Davis, *Aimé Césaire* (Cambridge: Cambridge University Press, 1997), p. 125.

55 Nick Nesbitt, *Voicing Memory: History and Subjectivity in French Caribbean Literature* (Charlottesville: University of Virginia Press, 2003), p. 110.

56 For more on Césaire and negritude in the context of the Cold War, see Christopher T. Bonner, *Cold War Negritude: Form and Alignment in French Caribbean Literature* (Liverpool: Liverpool University Press, 2023).

57 Aliko Songolo, *Aimé Césaire: Une poétique de la découverte*, p. 136.

58 See *The Complete Poetry of Aimé Césaire*, p. 527.

59 Christopher T. Bonner, 'The Ferrements of Poetry: The Geopolitical Vision of Aimé Césaire's Cold War Poems', *International Journal of Francophone Studies* 19.3–4 (2016): 275–300.

60 Aimé Césaire, 'Ferrements', *The Complete Poetry of Aimé Césaire*, pp. 528–9.

61 Aimé Césaire, 'Ferment', *The Complete Poetry of Aimé Césaire*, pp. 588–9.

62 Aimé Césaire, 'Spirales', *The Complete Poetry of Aimé Césaire*, pp. 534–5.

63 Gregson Davis, *Aimé Césaire*, p. 118.

64 Aimé Césaire, 'Spirales', *The Complete Poetry of Aimé Césaire*, pp. 534–5.

65 Aimé Césaire, 'Salut à la Guinée', *The Complete Poetry of Aimé Césaire*, pp. 536–7.

66 Aliko Songolo, *Aimé Césaire: une poétique de la découverte*, p. 143.

67 Aimé Césaire, 'Bucolique', *The Complete Poetry of Aimé Césaire*, pp. 586–7.

68 Aimé Césaire, 'Le Temps de la liberté', *The Complete Poetry of Aimé Césaire*, pp. 598–9.

266 NOTES TO PP. 166–78

69 Aimé Césaire, 'Mémorial de Louis Delgrès', *The Complete Poetry of Aimé Césaire*, pp. 610–11, pp. 614–15.
70 Ibid., pp. 616–17.
71 Gary Wilder also discusses how Césaire would have been particularly compelled by Delgrès' resistance to the reinstatement of slavery as a movement backwards, just as the reassertion of the colonial status of Martinique as a department seemed to be a movement backwards when juxtaposed with decolonisation in Africa. See Gary Wilder, *Freedom Time: Negritude, Decolonization and the Future of the World*, p. 185.
72 Aimé Césaire, '. . . sur l'état de l'Union', *The Complete Poetry of Aimé Césaire*, pp. 624–5.
73 Aimé Césaire, 'Pour saluer le tiers monde', *The Complete Poetry of Aimé Césaire*, pp. 634–5.
74 Ibid.
75 Aimé Césaire, '. . . mais il y a ce mal', *The Complete Poetry of Aimé Césaire*, pp. 554–5.
76 Ibid.

Chapter 5

1 Aimé Césaire, *La Tragédie du roi Christophe* (Paris: Présence Africaine, 1963), p. 57. This text is in fact the revised version of 1970; *The Tragedy of King Christophe*, trans. Paul Breslin and Rachel Ney (Evanston: Northwestern University Press, 2015), p. 36.
2 Aimé Césaire, 'Crise dans les départements d'outre-mer ou crise de le départementalisation' *Écrits politiques 1957–1971*, p. 140.
3 Aimé Césaire, 'À la croisée des chemins', *Écrits politiques 1957–1971*, p. 153.
4 Gary Wilder, *Freedom Time: Negritude, Decolonization and the Future of the World*, p. 242.
5 See Kora Véron, *Aimé Césaire: Configurations* (Paris: Seuil, 2021), p. 525.
6 Aimé Césaire, 'Xe anniversaire du PPM: Plus d'efforts! Plus de travail constructif! Plus d'enthousiasme! Plus de discipline! Plus d'initiatives aussi!', *Écrits politiques 1957–1971*, pp. 265–72.
7 Kora Véron, *Aimé Césaire: Configurations*, p. 531.
8 Aimé Césaire, 'Fermes et résolus', *Écrits politiques: 1972–87* (Paris: Nouvelles éditions Jean-Michel Place, 2018), pp. 59–60.
9 Aimé Césaire, 'Entretien avec Marie-Thérèse Rouil: "Il n'y a pas de solution pour les Antilles dans le système départemental"', *Écrits politiques: 1972–1987*, p. 125.

NOTES TO PP. 178–85   267

10 Aimé Césaire, 'Le PPM est un outil, le meilleur outil du peuple martiniquais', *Écrits politiques: 1972–1987*, p. 152.

11 Aimé Césaire, 'Discours *dit* des Trois voies ou des cinq libertés', *Écrits politiques: 1972–1987*, pp. 184–96.

12 Kora Véron, *Aimé Césaire: Configurations*, p. 588.

13 Aimé Césaire, 'Autonomie? Indépendance? C'est un faux problème', *Écrits politiques: 1972–1987*, pp. 248–9.

14 Aimé Césaire, 'La lutte du PPM est une lutte pour la reconnaissance de la personnalité collective du peuple martiniquais', *Écrits politiques: 1972–1987*, pp. 260–7.

15 Aimé Césaire, 'Il est bien plus difficile d'être un homme libre que d'être un esclave', *Écrits politiques: 1957–1971*, p. 213.

16 Frantz Fanon, 'Fondement réciproque de la culture nationale et des luttes de libération', *Présence Africaine* 24–25 (1959): 82–9. The text of the speech was expanded and printed as 'Sur la culture nationale' in *Les Damnés de la terre* (Paris: Maspéro, 1961) and translated by Richard Philcox as 'On National Culture', *The Wretched of the Earth* (London: Grove Press, 2004).

17 Aimé Césaire, 'Discours sur l'art africain', *Écrits politiques: 1957–1971*, p. 218.

18 Ibid., p. 223.

19 Ibid., p. 219.

20 Ibid., p. 220.

21 Ibid., p. 221.

22 Aimé Césaire, 'Entretien d'Aimé Césaire avec René Depestre', *Écrits politiques: 1957–1971*, p. 253.

23 Aimé Césaire, 'Entretien de Césaire à l'Université Laval avec Michel Tétu', *Écrits politiques: 1972–1987*, pp. 20–2. This interview was then printed in Lilyan Kesteloot's *Césaire et Senghor, un pont sur l'Atlantique* (Paris: L'Harmattan, 2006).

24 Aimé Césaire, 'Entretien avec Jean Mazel', *Écrits politiques: 1972–1987*, p. 89.

25 Aimé Césaire, 'Société et littérature dans les Antilles', *Écrits politiques: 1972–1987*, p. 39.

26 Aimé Césaire, 'La Martinique telle qu'elle est', *Écrits politiques: 1972–1987*, p. 242.

27 Wole Soyinka in *Aimé Césaire, le legs: nous sommes de ceux qui disent non à l'ombre* ed. Annick Thébia-Melson (Paris: Argal Editions, 2009), p. 8.

28 Aimé Césaire, cited in Thomas Hale and Kora Véron, *Les Écrits d'Aimé Césaire: Biobibliographie commentée, 1913–2008, 1*, p. 356.

29 Aimé Césaire, 'Il est bien plus difficile d'être un homme libre que d'être un esclave', *Écrits politiques: 1957–1971*, p. 212.

30 Cited in Bathélemy Kotchy, 'Le théâtre de Césaire', in Lilyan Kesteloot and Barthélemy Kotchy, *Aimé Césaire: L'homme et l'œuvre* (Paris: Présence Africaine, 1973), pp. 129–136 (p. 136).

31 Daniel Maximin, *Aimé Césaire, frère volcan*, p. 50.

32 See Aimé Césaire, 'Mon théâtre c'est le drame des nègres dans le monde moderne', *Écrits politiques: 1957–1971*, pp. 246–7.

33 See Stéphanie Bérard, 'Panorama sur l'archipélisme théâtral de la Caraïbe', *Émergences Caraïbe(s): une création théâtrale archipélique*, ed. Sylvie Chalaye and Stéphanie Bérard, *Africultures* 80–1 (Paris: L'Harmattan, 2012), pp. 14–23.

34 Cited in Kora Véron, *Aimé Césaire: Configurations*, p. 561. The 'mornes' are the hills where runaway slaves took refuge.

35 Aimé Césaire, *Nègre je suis, nègre je resterai: Entretiens avec Françoise Vergès* (Paris: Albin Michel, 2005), p. 56.

36 Aimé Césaire, *Cahier d'un retour au pays natal, The Complete Poetry of Aimé Césaire*, pp. 28–9.

37 Aimé Césaire in René Depestre, *Bonjour et adieu à la Négritude* (Paris: Robert Laffont, 1980), p. 76.

38 Raphael Confiant, *Aimé Césaire: une traversée paradoxale du siècle*, p. 89.

39 Aimé Césaire, *Toussaint Louverture: La Révolution française et le problème colonial* (Paris: Présence Africaine, 1981), p. 24.

40 Ibid., p. 205, p. 228, p. 234.

41 Ibid., p. 305.

42 Ibid., p. 24.

43 Ibid., p. 344.

44 Ibid., p. 345.

45 Charles Forsdick and Christian Hogsbjerg, *Toussaint Louverture: A Black Jacobin in the Age of Revolutions* (London: Pluto Press, 2017), p. 25, p. 95.

46 C. L. R. James, *The Black Jacobins: Toussaint Louverture and the San Domingo Revolution* (London: Penguin, 1938), p. 195.

47 Gérard Cogez, *Aimé Césaire* (Lausanne: Ides et Calendes, 2018), p. 47.

48 A. James Arnold, 'De l'Haiti à l'Afrique: *La Tragédie du roi Christophe* d'Aimé Césaire', *Revue de littérature comparée* 60.2 (1986): 1–16 (p. 16).

49 Axel Artheron, *Le Théâtre révolutionnaire afro-caribéen au XXe siècle: Dramaturgies révolutionnaires et enjeux populaires* (Paris: Honoré Champion, 2018), p. 9.

50 Ibid., p. 411.

51 For more on the changes made to the 1970 edition, see James Arnold's 'Présentation', *La Tragédie du roi Christophe* in *Poésie, Théâtre, Essais, Discours*, pp. 988–1000.

NOTES TO PP. 191–200 269

52 Romuald Fonkoua, *Aimé Césaire (1913–2008)*, p. 315.

53 Gregson Davis, *Aimé Césaire*, p. 137.

54 Nick Nesbitt, *Voicing Memory: History and Subjectivity in French Caribbean Literature* (Charlottesville: University Press of Virginia, 2003), p. 144.

55 Aimé Césaire, 'Il est bien plus difficile d'être un homme libre que d'être un esclave', *Écrits politiques: 1957–1971*, p. 208.

56 See A. James Arnold, 'Présentation', *La Tragédie du roi Christophe* in *Poésie, Théâtre, Essais, Discours*, pp. 988–9.

57 Aimé Césaire, *La Tragédie du roi Christophe*, p. 37; *The Tragedy of King Christophe*, p. 22.

58 Ibid., pp. 62–3, p. 40.

59 Albert Owasu-Sarpong, *Le temps historique dans l'œuvre théâtrale d'Aimé Césaire* (Sherbrooke: Éditions Naaman, 1986).

60 Aimé Césaire, 'Il est bien plus difficile d'être un homme libre que d'être un esclave', *Écrits politiques: 1957–1971*, p. 209.

61 From an interview quoted in M. a M. Ngal, *Aimé Césaire: un homme à la recherche d'une patrie*, p. 220.

62 Aimé Césaire, *La Tragédie du roi Christophe*, pp. 130–1; *The Tragedy of King Christophe*, p. 81.

63 Aimé Césaire, *Nègre je suis, nègre je resterai*, p. 63.

64 Aimé Césaire, *La Tragédie du roi Christophe*, p. 42; *The Tragedy of King Christophe*, p. 25.

65 Daniel Maximin, *Aimé Césaire, frère volcan*, p. 58.

66 See Shane Gordon, 'It cancels the slave ship! Africa, slavery, and the Haitian Revolution in Langston Hughes's *Emperor of Haiti* and Aimé Césaire's *Tragedy of King Christophe*', *Modern Drama* 62.4 (2019): 458–82.

67 Aimé Césaire, *La Tragédie du roi Christophe*, p. 60, p. 57; *The Tragedy of King Christophe*, p. 38, p. 36.

68 Ibid., p. 143, p. 90.

69 See Femi Ojo-Ade, *Aimé Césaire's African Theater: Of Poets, Prophet and Politicians*, p. 138.

70 Aimé Césaire, 'Mon théâtre c'est le drame des nègres dans le monde', *Écrits politiques: 1957–1971*, p. 245.

71 Aimé Césaire, *La Tragédie du roi Christophe*, p. 151; *The Tragedy of King Christophe*, p. 96.

72 René Ménil, 'Le romanesque et le réalisme dans "La Tragédie du roi Christophe"', *Antilles déjà jadis, précédé de Tracées* (Paris: Jean-Michel Place, 1999), pp. 180–6 (p. 181).

73 Ibid., p. 153, p. 97.

74 Gregson Davis, *Aimé Césaire*, p. 151.

75 See Julie-Françoise Tolliver, 'Césaire/Lumumba: A Season of Solidarity', *Journal of Postcolonial Writing* 50.4 (2014): 398–409.

NOTES TO PP. 200–9

Tolliver evokes how Lumumba was characterised in the press as a devil.

76 Ibid., p. 401.

77 See A. James Arnold, 'Présentation', *Une Saison au Congo*, in *Poésie, Théâtre, Essais, Discours*, p. 1106.

78 See Kora Véron, *Aimé Césaire: Configurations*, p. 503.

79 Gregson Davis, *Aimé Césaire*, p. 151.

80 Cited in Roger Toumson and Simonne Henry-Valmore, *Aimé Césaire: le nègre inconsolé*, p. 195.

81 Aimé Césaire, *Une Saison au Congo* (Paris: Seuil, 1973), p. 39; *A Season in the Congo*, trans. Gayatri Chakravorty Spivak (London: Seagull Books, 2020), p. 39.

82 Aimé Césaire, 'Mon théâtre c'est le drame des nègres dans le monde moderne', p. 246.

83 Aimé Césaire, *Une Saison au Congo*, p. 30; *A Season in the Congo*, p. 29.

84 Ibid., p. 32, p. 31.

85 Ibid., p. 92, p. 104.

86 Aimé Césaire, 'Mon théâtre c'est le drame des nègres dans le monde moderne', p. 246.

87 Aimé Césaire, *Une Saison au Congo*, p. 31; *A Season in the Congo*, p. 30.

88 Ibid., p. 105, p. 122.

89 Gregson Davis, *Aimé Césaire*, p. 155.

90 Aimé Césaire, *Une Saison au Congo*, p. 124; *A Season in the Congo*, p. 144.

91 Ibid., p. 32, p. 31.

92 Aimé Césaire, 'Mon théâtre c'est le drame des nègres dans le monde moderne', p. 247.

93 James Arnold, 'Présentation', *Une Tempête, Poésie, Théâtre, Essais, Discours*, p. 1200.

94 See Kora Véron, *Aimé Césaire: Configurations*, p. 542.

95 Aimé Césaire, *Une Tempête* (Paris: Seuil, 1969), p. 24, p. 36. See also Steven M. Almquist, 'Not quite the gabbling of a thing most brutish: Caliban's Kiswahili in Aimé Césaire's *A Tempest*', *Callaloo* 29.2 (2006): 587–607.

96 Aimé Césaire, *Une Tempête*, p. 58; *A Tempest*, trans. Richard Miller (New York: TCG Translations, 2002), p. 41.

97 Ibid., p. 25, p. 17.

98 Ibid., p. 44, p. 32.

99 Ibid., p. 90, p. 64.

100 Ibid., p. 24, p. 17.

101 Ibid., p. 38, p. 27.

NOTES TO PP. 210–16

102 Ibid., p. 89, p. 63.

103 Kamau Brathwaite, 'Caliban', *The Arrivants: A New World Trilogy* (Oxford: Oxford University Press, 1967), p. 192.

104 Aimé Césaire, *Une Tempête*, p. 70; *A Tempest*, p. 49.

105 Ibid., pp. 64–5, p. 45.

106 Ibid., p. 92, p. 66.

107 Femi Ojo-Ade, *Aimé Césaire's African Theater: Of Poets, Prophet and Politicians*, p. 293.

108 Roberto Fernandez Retamar, 'Caliban: Notes towards a Discussion of Culture in our America', *The Massachusetts Review* 15.1/2 (1974): 7–72.

109 Maryse Condé (ed.), *L'Héritage de Caliban* (Pointe-à-Pitre: Éditions Jasor, 1992).

110 Rob Nixon, 'Caribbean and African Appropriations of *The Tempest*', *Critical Inquiry* 13.3 (1987): 557–78.

111 Ibid., p. 577.

112 There are several lively feminist critiques of Césaire's *Une Tempête*, including Sylvia Wynter, 'Afterword: Beyond Miranda's Meanings: Un/Silencing the "Demonic Ground" of Caliban's "Woman"', in Carole Boyce Davies and Elaine Savory Fido (eds.), *Out of the Kumbla: Caribbean Women and Literature* (Trenton, New Jersey: African World Press, 1990), pp. 355–70; Jyotsna G. Singh, 'Caliban versus Miranda: Race and Gender Conflicts in Postcolonial Rewritings of *The Tempest*', in Anne McClintock (ed.), *Dangerous Liaisons: Gender, Nation, and Postcolonial Perspectives* (New York: Routledge, 1995), pp. 205–23; Jonathan Goldberg, *Tempest in the Caribbean* (Minneapolis: University of Minnesota Press, 2003).

Chapter 6

1 Aimé Césaire, 'Je suis un nègre marron', *Écrits politiques 1972–1987* (Paris: Nouvelles Éditions Jean-Michel Place, 2018), p. 253.

2 See for example Dénètem Touam Bona, *Fugitif où cours-tu ?* (Paris: Presses universitaires de France, 2016); Sylvie Chalaye, *Corps marron: les poétiques de marronnage des dramaturgies afro-contemporaines* (Paris: Passages, 2018).

3 Aimé Césaire, 'Je crois que la Martinique se ressaisira', *Écrits politiques 1972–1987*, pp. 268–272.

4 Aimé Césaire, 'Discours du moratoire', *Écrits politiques 1972–1987*, p. 275.

5 Ibid., p. 277.

6 Aimé Césaire, 'Second discours du moratoire: L'heure de la victoire,

272 NOTES TO PP. 216–23

c'est aussi l'heure de la responsabilité', *Écrits politiques 1972–1987*, p. 301.

7 Aimé Césaire, 'Le PPM a 25 ans: l'heure du bilan', *Écrits politiques 1972–1987*, p. 385.

8 Aimé Césaire, 'Entretien avec Jean-Marc Party et Rudy Rabathaly: Le monde est à reconstruire', *Écrits politiques 1988–2008* (Paris: Nouvelles Éditions Jean-Michel Place, 2018), p. 167.

9 Aimé Césaire, 'Séance du 27 juillet 1981', *Écrits Politiques: Discours à l'Assemblée Nationale 1945–1983*, p. 234.

10 Aimé Césaire, 'La creation du conseil régional: un projet acceptable', *Écrits politiques 1972–1987*, p. 343.

11 Aimé Césaire, 'Élections municipales de mars 1983: Entretien avec Aimé Césaire', *Écrits politiques 1972–1987*, pp. 361–8.

12 Raphaël Confiant, *Aimé Césaire, une traversée paradoxale du siècle*.

13 Aimé Césaire, 'Fort-de-France ville de défi', *Écrits politiques 1988–2008*, p. 18.

14 Aimé Césaire, 'Inauguration du stade d'honneur de Fort-de-France', *Écrits politiques 1988–2008*, pp. 132–5.

15 Aimé Césaire, 'Il faut que le peuple se soude derrière Camille Darsières, et je serai à ses côtés', *Écrits politiques 1988–2008*, p. 124.

16 Ibid., p. 125.

17 Aimé Césaire, 'C'est mon dernier mandat', *Écrits politiques 1988–2008*, p. 212.

18 Roger Toumson and Simonne Henry-Valmore, *Aimé Césaire: le nègre inconsolé*, p. 224.

19 Ibid., p. 224.

20 Kora Véron, *Aimé Césaire: Configurations*, pp. 684–5.

21 Aimé Césaire, 'Discours de Miami: Première conférence hémisphérique des peuples noirs de la diaspora en hommage à Aimé Césaire', *Écrits politiques 1972–1988*, p. 524.

22 Ibid., p. 526.

23 Jean Bernabé, Patrick Chamoiseau, Raphaël Confiant, *Éloge de la Créolité* (Paris: Gallimard, 1989).

24 Ibid., p. 20.

25 Aimé Césaire, 'Entretien avec Frédéric Bobin', *Écrits politiques 1988–2008*, p. 156.

26 Kora Véron, *Aimé Césaire: Configurations*, p. 682.

27 Ibid., p. 597.

28 Édouard Glissant, *Le Discours antillais* (Paris: Gallimard, 1997), p. 57; *Caribbean Discourse: Selected Essays*, trans. J. Michael Dash (Charlottesville: University of Virginia Press, 1989), p. 26.

29 Kora Véron, *Aimé Césaire: Configurations*, p. 480.

NOTES TO PP. 224–35

30 Aimé Césaire, 'Réaction d'Aimé Césaire au décès de François Mittérand', *Écrits politiques 1988–2008*, p. 179.

31 Malcom Ferdinand, *Decolonial Ecology: Thinking from the Caribbean World*, trans. Anthony Paul Smith (Cambridge: Polity, 2022), pp. 109–11. Ferdinand explicitly links the chlordecone scandal with the history of enslavement, as 'it stems mainly from the colonial inhabitation of the Earth that transforms the world into a Plantation' (p. 110).

32 M. Souley Ba, René Hénane, Lilyan Kesteloot, *Introduction à moi, laminaire... d'Aimé Césaire: une édition critique* (Paris: L'Harmattan, 2011), p. 29.

33 Aimé Césaire, 'Aimé Césaire, poète rebelle', *Écrits politiques 1972–1987*, p. 312.

34 Jean Khalfa, *Poetics of the Antilles: Poetry, History, and Philosophy in the Writings of Perse, Césaire, Fanon, and Glissant*.

35 Aimé Césaire, 'Entretien avec Daniel Maximin: Poésie, la parole essentielle', *Écrits politiques 1972–1987*, p. 396.

36 Aimé Césaire, *moi, laminaire... The Complete Poetry of Aimé Césaire*, pp. 650–1.

37 Aimé Césaire, 'sentiments et ressentiments des mots', *The Complete Poetry of Aimé Césaire*, pp. 668–9.

38 Aimé Césaire, *moi, laminaire... The Complete Poetry of Aimé Césaire*, pp. 650–1.

39 Ibid.

40 Ibid.

41 Aimé Césaire, 'calendrier lagunaire', *The Complete Poetry of Aimé Césaire*, pp. 652–3.

42 Carrie Noland, *Voices of Negritude in Modernist Print: Aesthetic Subjectivity, Diaspora and the Lyric Regime*, pp. 207–8.

43 Aimé Césaire, 'j'ai guidé du troupeau la langue transhumance', *The Complete Poetry of Aimé Césaire*, pp. 692–3.

44 Aimé Césaire, 'sentiments et ressentiments des mots', *The Complete Poetry of Aimé Césaire*, pp. 668–9.

45 Gregson Davis, *Aimé Césaire*, p. 173.

46 Aimé Césaire, 'quand Miguel Asturias disparut', *The Complete Poetry of Aimé Césaire*, pp. 764–5.

47 Aimé Césaire, 'Wifredo Lam', *The Complete Poetry of Aimé Césaire*, pp. 772–3.

48 Aimé Césaire, 'façon langagière', *The Complete Poetry of Aimé Césaire*, pp. 780–1.

49 Aimé Césaire, 'rabordaille', *The Complete Poetry of Aimé Césaire*, pp. 784–5.

50 James Arnold and Clayton Eshleman, 'Notes to the Poems', *The Complete Poetry of Aimé Césaire*, p. 911.

274 NOTES TO PP. 235–46

51 Aimé Césaire, 'nouvelle bonté', *The Complete Poetry of Aimé Césaire*, pp. 790–1.
52 See A. James Arnold, *Aimé Césaire: Genèse et transformations d'une poétique*, p. 302.
53 Aimé Césaire, 'Passage', *The Complete Poetry of Aimé Césaire*, pp. 820–1.
54 Aimé Césaire, 'Vertu des lucioles', *The Complete Poetry of Aimé Césaire*, pp. 826–7.
55 Aimé Césaire, 'Comme un malentendu de salut', *The Complete Poetry of Aimé Césaire*, pp. 852–3.
56 Aimé Césaire, 'Dérisoire', *The Complete Poetry of Aimé Césaire*, pp. 844–5.
57 Aimé Césaire, 'Configurations', *The Complete Poetry of Aimé Césaire*, pp. 864–5.
58 Ibid., pp. 866–7.

Afterword

1 H. Adlai Murdoch, 'Introduction: Non-Sovereignty and the Neoliberal Challenge: Contesting Economic Exploitation in the Eastern Caribbean', in H. Adlai Murdoch (ed.), *The Struggle of Non-Sovereign Caribbean Territories: Neoliberalism Since the French Antillean Uprisings of 2009* (New Brunswick, Newark, and London: Rutgers, 2021), pp. 1–49 (p. 11).
2 Houari Bouteldja, *Les Blancs, les Juifs et nous: vers une politique de l'amour révolutionnaire* (Paris: La Fabrique, 2016), p. 21, p. 28, p. 58.
3 Frieda Ekotto, 'Aimé Césaire in the Era of Black Lives Matter', in Ken Seigneurie (ed.), *A Companion to World Literature* (Oxford: Wiley Blackwell, 2019), pp. 1–9 (p. 7).
4 Daniel Maximin, *Aimé Césaire, frère volcan*; Suzanne Césaire, *Le Grand Camouflage: Écrits de dissidence 1941–1945*; Daniel Maximin, *L'Isolé soleil* (Paris: Seuil, 1987).
5 Dany Laferrière, *L'Enigme du retour* (Paris: Grasset et Fasquelle, 2009).
6 Philippe Triay, 'Un documentaire sur Aimé Césaire bientôt sur les écrans, réalisé par Fabienne et Véronique Kanor', *France Info* Un documentaire sur Aimé Césaire bientôt sur les écrans, réalisé par Fabienne et Véronique Kanor – Outre-mer la 1ère (francetvinfo.fr) consulted 12.10.23.
7 See Felicia McCarren, *French Moves: The Cultural Politics of le Hip Hop* (Oxford: Oxford University Press, 2013), p. 25.
8 Patrick Chamoiseau, *Texaco* (Paris: Gallimard, 1992), p. 454.
9 Romuald Fonkoua, *Aimé Césaire (1913–2008)*.

10 Aimé Césaire, 'Chevelure', *The Complete Poetry of Aimé Césaire*, pp. 368–9.
11 Aimé Césaire, 'Panorama', *Tropiques* 10, Février 1944, pp. 7–10 (p. 9).
12 Gregson Davis, *Aimé Césaire*, p. 183.
13 Kora Véron, *Aimé Césaire: Configurations*, p. 694.

Bibliography

Works by Césaire

Collected Poetry and Essays

Toussaint Louverture: La Révolution française et le problème colonial. Paris: Présence Africaine, 1981.

Cahier d'un retour au pays natal / Notebook of a Return to My Native Land. Trans. Mireille Rosello with Annie Pritchard. Newcastle-upon-Tyne: Bloodaxe Books, 1995.

Nègre je suis, nègre je resterai: Entretiens avec Françoise Vergès. Paris: Albin Michel, 2005.

Aimé Césaire: Poésie, Théâtre, Essais et Discours. Ed. A. James Arnold. Paris: CNRS Editions, 2013.

Aimé Césaire: Écrits politiques, Discours à l'Assemblée Nationale 1945–1983. Paris: Nouvelles Éditions Jean-Michel Place, 2013.

Aimé Césaire: Écrits politiques 1935–1956. Paris: Nouvelles Éditions Jean-Michel Place, 2016.

Aimé Césaire: Écrits politiques 1957–1971. Paris: Nouvelles Éditions Jean-Michel Place, 2016.

The Complete Poetry of Aimé Césaire, trans. A. James Arnold and Clayton Eshleman. Middletown: Wesleyan University Press, 2017.

Aimé Césaire: Écrits politiques 1972–1987. Paris: Nouvelles Éditions Jean-Michel Place, 2018.

Aimé Césaire: Écrits politiques 1988–2008. Paris: Nouvelles Éditions Jean-Michel Place, 2018.

Bibliography

Plays

Et les chiens se taisaient. Paris: Présence Africaine, 1956.
La Tragédie du roi Christophe. Paris: Présence Africaine, 1963.
Une Tempête. Paris: Seuil, 1969.
Une Saison au Congo. Paris: Seuil, 1973.

Essays not printed in collected volumes

'Fragments d'un poème', *Tropiques* 1 (1941): 9–23.
'Présentation', *Tropiques* 1 (1941): 5–6.
'Introduction au folklore martiniquais' (with René Ménil) *Tropiques* 4 (1942): 7–11.
'Maintenir la poésie', *Tropiques* 8–9 (1943).
'Panorama', *Tropiques* 10 (1944): 7–10.
'Poésie et connaissance', *Tropiques* 12 (1945): 157–170.
'Georges-Louis Ponton, Gouverneur de la Martinique', *Tropiques* 12 (1945): 153–156.
'Hommage à Victor Schoelcher', *Tropiques* 13–14 (1945): 229–235.
'Entretien avec Jacqueline Leiner', *Tropiques*. Paris: Jean-Michel Place, 1978, pp. vi–xxiv.

Translations cited not presented in bilingual editions

Discourse on Colonialism. Trans. Joan Pinkham. New York: Monthly Review Press, 2000.
A Tempest. Trans. Richard Miller. New York: TCG Translations, 2002.
The Tragedy of King Christophe. Trans. Paul Breslin and Rachel Ney. Evanston: Northwestern University Press, 2015.
A Season in the Congo. Trans. Gayatri Spivak. London: Seagull Books, 2020.

Other Works

Achille, Louis-Thomas. 'Preface', *Revue du monde noir* 1 (1931): vii–xvii.
Allen-Paisant, Jason. *Engagements with Aimé Césaire: Thinking with Spirits.* Oxford: Oxford University Press, 2004.
Almquist, Steven M. 'Not quite the gabbling of a thing most brutish: Caliban's Kiswahili in Aimé Césaire's *A Tempest*', *Callaloo* 29.2 (2006): 587–607.
Arnold, A. James. *Modernism and Negritude: The Poetry and Politics of Aimé Césaire.* Cambridge, Massachusetts: Harvard University Press, 1981.

Arnold, A. James. 'De l'Haiti à l'Afrique: *La Tragédie du roi Christophe* d'Aimé Césaire', *Revue de littérature comparée* 60.2 (1986): 1–16.

Arnold, A. James. 'Beyond Postcolonial Césaire: Reading *Cahier d'un retour au pays natal* historically', *Forum for Modern Language Studies* 44.3 (2008): 258–279.

Arnold, A. James. 'Césaire is dead! Long live Césaire!', *French Politics, Culture, and Society* 27.3 (2009): 9–18.

Arnold, A. James. *Aimé Césaire: Genèse et transformation d'une poétique.* Würzburg: Königshausen and Neumann, 2020.

Artheron, Axel. *Le Théâtre révolutionnaire afro-caribéen au XXe siècle: Dramaturgies révolutionnaires et enjeux populaires.* Paris: Honoré Champion, 2018.

Ba, M. Souley, René Hénane, Lilyan Kesteloot. *Introduction à* moi, laminaire. . . *d'Aimé Césaire: une édition critique.* Paris: L'Harmattan, 2011.

Basevich, Elvira. *W. E. B. Du Bois: The Lost and the Found.* Cambridge: Polity, 2021.

Bernabé, Jean, Patrick Chamoiseau and Raphaël Confiant. *Éloge de la Créolité.* Paris: Gallimard, 1989.

Bonner, Christopher T. 'The Ferrements of Poetry: The Geopolitical Vision of Aimé Césaire's Cold War Poems', *International Journal of Francophone Studies* 19.3–4 (2016): 275–300.

Bonner, Christopher T., *Cold War Negritude: Form and Alignment in French Caribbean Literature.* Liverpool: Liverpool University Press, 2023.

Bouteldja, Houari. *Les Blancs, les Juifs et nous: vers une politique de l'amour révolutionnaire.* Paris: La Fabrique, 2016.

Brathwaite, Kamau. *The Arrivants: A New World Trilogy.* Oxford: Oxford University Press, 1967.

Breton, André. 'Un grand poète noir', in Aimé Césaire, *Cahier d'un retour au pays natal.* Paris: Présence Africaine, 1971.

Britton, Celia. *Race and the Unconscious: Freudianism in French Caribbean Thought.* Oxford: Legenda, 2002.

Bona, Dénètem Touam. *Fugitif où cours-tu?* Paris: Presses Universitaires de France, 2016.

Cailler, Bernadette. *Proposition poétique: une lecture de l'œuvre d'Aimé Césaire.* Sherbrooke, Québec: Éditions Naaman de Sherbrooke, 1976.

Carpentier, Gilles. *Scandale de bronze: Lettre à Aimé Césaire.* Paris: Seuil, 1994.

Césaire, Suzanne. *Le Grand camouflage: Écrits de dissidence 1941–1945.* Paris: Seuil, 2009.

Césaire, Suzanne. *The Great Camouflage: Writings of Dissent 1941–1945.* Trans. Keith Walker. Middletown: Wesleyan University Press, 2012.

Bibliography

Chalaye, Sylvie. *Corps marron: les poétiques de marronnage des dramaturgies afro-contemporaines*. Paris: Passages, 2018.

Chalaye, Sylvie and Stéphanie Bérard (eds.). *Émergences Caraibe(s): une création théâtrale archipélique*. Paris: L'Harmattan, 2012.

Chamoiseau, Patrick. *Texaco*. Paris: Gallimard, 1992.

Childers, Kristen Stromberg. *Seeking Imperialism's Embrace: National Identity, Decolonization, and Assimilation in the French Caribbean*. Oxford: Oxford University Press, 2016.

Cogez, Gérard. *Aimé Césaire*. Lausanne. Ides et Calendes, 2018.

Condé, Maryse. *L'Héritage de Caliban*. Pointe-à-Pitre: Éditions Jasor, 1992.

Confiant, Raphaël. *Aimé Césaire: une traversée paradoxale du siècle*. Paris: Stock, 1993.

Corinus, Véronique. *Aimé Césaire*. Paris: Presses Universitaires de France, 2019.

Constant, Fred. 'Aimé Césaire et la politique: Sept leçons de leadership', *French Politics, Culture, and Society* 28.3 (2009): 34–43.

Davis, Gregson. *Aimé Césaire*. Cambridge: Cambridge University Press, 1997.

Depestre, René. 'Réponse à Aimé Césaire (Introduction à un art haïtien)', *Présence Africaine* 4 (1955): 42–62.

Depestre, René. *Bonjour et adieu à la Négritude*. Paris: Robert Laffont, 1980.

Edwards, Brent Hayes. 'Aimé Césaire and the Syntax of Influence', *Research in African Literatures* 36.2 (2005): 1–18.

Edwards, Brent Hayes. *The Practice of Diaspora: Literature, Translation, and the Rise of Black Internationalism*. Cambridge, Massachusetts: Harvard University Press, 2010.

Egger, Anne. *Césaire et Picasso: Corps perdu, Histoire d'une rencontre*. Paris: HC Editions, 2011.

Ekotto, Frieda. 'Aimé Césaire in the Era of Black Lives Matter', in Ken Seigneurie (ed.), *A Companion to World Literature*. Oxford: Wiley Blackwell, 2019.

Eshleman, Clayton. 'Aimé Césaire's Lost, Found, Scattered Body', *Callaloo* 31.4 (2008): 983–986.

Fanon, Frantz. *The Wretched of the Earth*. Trans. Richard Philcox. London: Grove Press, 2004.

Fanon, Frantz. *Œuvres*. Paris: La Découverte, 2011.

Fanon, Frantz. *Black Skin, White Masks*. Trans. Richard Philcox. London: Penguin, 2021.

Ferdinand, Malcom. *Decolonial Ecology: Thinking from the Caribbean World*. Trans. Anthony Paul Smith. Cambridge: Polity, 2022.

Fonkoua, Romuald. *Aimé Césaire*. Paris: Perrin, 2010.

Forsdick, Charles and Christian Hobsbjerg. *Toussaint Louverture: A Black Jacobin in the Age of Revolutions*. London: Pluto Press, 2017.

Frobenius, Léo. *Histoire de la civilisation africaine*, trans. D. H. Back and D. Ermont. Paris: Gallimard, 1936.

Frost, Jackqueline. '"The Red Hour": Poetic Violence and the Time of Transformation in Aimé Césaire's *Et les chiens se taisaient*', *The Global South* 11.1 (2017): 57–81.

Gibson, Nigel C. *Frantz Fanon: Combat Breathing*. Cambridge: Polity, 2024.

Glissant, Édouard. *Caribbean Discourse: Selected Essays*. Trans. J. Michael Dash. Charlottesville: University of Virginia Press, 1989.

Glissant, Édouard. *Le Discours Antillais*. Paris: Gallimard, 1997.

Gordon, Shane. '"It cancels the slave ship!" Africa, slavery, and the Haitian Revolution in Langston Hughes's *Emperor of Haiti* and Aimé Césaire's *Tragedy of King Christophe*', *Modern Drama* 62.4 (2019): 458–482.

Gratiant, Gilbert. 'Mulâtres: pour le bien et le mal', *L'Étudiant noir* 1 (1935): 5–7.

Hale, Thomas and Kora Véron. 'Is there unity in the writings of Aimé Césaire?', *Research in African Literatures* 41.1 (2010): 46–70 (p. 57).

Hale, Thomas and Kora Véron (eds.). *Les Écrits d'Aimé Césaire: Biobibliographie commentée*. Paris: Honoré Champion, 2013.

Harris, Rodney E. *L'Humanisme dans le théâtre d'Aimé Césaire*. Ottawa: Editions Naaman, 1973.

Hénane, René. *Les Armes miraculeuses d'Aimé Césaire*. Paris: L'Harmattan, 2008.

Hénane, René. *Ma conscience et son rythme de chair: Aimé Césaire, une poétique*. Paris: Orizons, 2018.

Irele, F. Abiola. 'Introduction', *Cahier d'un retour au pays natal/Journal of a Homecoming*, trans. Gregson Davis. Durham: Duke University Press, 2017.

James, C. L. R. *The Black Jacobins: Toussaint Louverture and the San Domingo Revolution*. London: Penguin, 1938.

Jennings, Eric T. *Escape from Vichy: The Refugee Exodus to the French Caribbean*. Cambridge, Massachusetts: Harvard University Press, 2018.

Jones, Donna V. *The Racial Discourses of Life Philosophy: Negritude, Vitalism, and Modernity*. New York: Columbia University Press, 2010.

Kalikoff, Hedy. 'Gender, Genre, and Geography in Aimé Césaire's *Cahier d'un retour au pays natal*', *Callaloo* 18.2 (1995): 492–505.

Kesteloot, Lilyan and Barthélemy Kotchy. *Aimé Césaire: l'homme et l'œuvre*. Paris: Présence Africaine, 1973.

Bibliography 281

Khalfa, Jean. *Poetics of the Antilles: Poetry, History and Philosophy in the Writings of Perse, Césaire, Fanon and Glissant*. Oxford: Peter Lang, 2017.

Laferrière, Dany. *L'Enigme du retour*. Paris: Grasset et Fasquelle, 2009.

Laforgue, Pierre. 'A l'Afrique d'Aimé Césaire: un poème dans l'histoire (variations génétiques)', *Présence Africaine* 184 (2011): 221–243.

Leiner, Jacqueline. *Aimé Césaire: le terreau primordial*. Tübingen: Gunter Narr Verlag, 1993.

Leiner, Jacqueline (ed.). *Soleil éclaté: Mélanges offerts à Aimé Césaire à l'occasion de son soixante-dixième anniversaire par une équipe internationale d'artistes et de chercheurs*. Tübingen: Gunter Narr Verlag, 1984.

Léro, Etienne. 'Misère d'une poésie', *Légitime Défense*. Paris: Jean-Michel Place, 1979.

Locke, Alain (ed.). *The New Negro: Voices of the Harlem Renaissance*. New York: Touchstone, 1999.

Maximin, Daniel. *Aimé Césaire: Frère Volcan*. Paris: Seuil, 2013.

McCarren, Felicia. *French Moves: The Cultural Politics of le Hip Hop*. Oxford: Oxford University Press, 2013.

Ménil, René. 'Pour une lecture critique de *Tropiques*', *Tropiques*. Paris: Jean-Michel Place, 1978, pp. xxv–xxxv.

Miller, Christopher L. *Nationalists and Nomads: Essays on Francophone African Literature and Culture*. Chicago: Chicago University Press, 1998.

Murdoch, H. Adlai. '*Ars poetica, ars politica*: The Double Life of Aimé Césaire', *Research in African Literatures* 41.1 (2010): 1–13.

Murdoch, H. Adlai (ed.) *The Struggle of Non-Sovereign Caribbean Territories: Neoliberalism since the French Antillean Uprisings of 2009*. New Brunswick, Newark and London: Rutgers, 2021.

Nardal, Paulette. 'Guignol Ouolof', *L'Étudiant noir* (1935): 4–5.

Nesbitt, Nick. *Voicing Memory: History and Subjectivity in French Caribbean Literature*. Charlottesville: University of Virginia Press, 2003.

Nesbitt, Nick. *Caribbean Critique: Antillean Theory from Toussaint to Glissant*. Liverpool: Liverpool University Press, 2013.

Nesbitt, Nick. *The Price of Slavery: Capitalism and Revolution in the Caribbean*. Charlottesville: University of Virginia Press, 2022.

Ngal, M. a M. *Aimé Césaire, un homme à la recherche d'une patrie*. Dakar: Les Nouvelles Éditions Africaines, 1975.

Nixon, Rob. 'Caribbean and African Appropriations of *The Tempest*', *Critical Inquiry* 13.3 (1987): 557–578.

Noland, Carrie. *Voices of Negritude in Modernist Print: Aesthetic Subjectivity, Diaspora, and the Lyric Regime*. New York: Columbia University Press, 2015.

Ojo-Ade, Femi. *Aimé Césaire's African Theater: Of Poets, Prophets and*

Politicians. Trenton, New Jersey and Asmara, Eritrea: Africa World Press, 2010.

Owasu-Sarpong, Albert. *Le temps historique dans l'œuvre théâtrale d'Aimé Césaire*. Sherbrooke: Éditions Naaman, 1986.

Palcy, Euzhan. *Aimé Césaire, une parole pour le XXIe siècle*. 2006.

Retamar, Roberto Fernandez. 'Caliban: Notes towards a Discussion of Culture in our America', *The Massachusetts Review* 15.1/2 (1974): 7–72.

Rimbaud, Arthur. 'Lettre à Paul Demeny'. *Poésies*. Paris: Gallimard, 1999.

Rosello, Mireille. 'The Césaire Effect: Or, How to Cultivate One's Nation', *Research in African Literatures* 32.4 (2001): 77–91.

Rothberg, Michael. *Multidirectional Memory: Remembering the Holocaust in the Age of Decolonization*. Stanford: Stanford University Press, 2009.

Sartre, Jean-Paul. 'Orphée noir', in Léopold Sédar Senghor (ed.), *Anthologie de la nouvelle poésie nègre et malgache de langue française*. Paris: Presses universitaires de France, 1948, pp. ix–xliv.

Sartre, Jean-Paul. 'Black Orpheus', *The Massachusetts Review* 6.1 (1964–5): 13–52.

Senghor, Léopold Sédar. 'L'Humanisme et nous: René Maran', *L'Étudiant noir* 1 (1935): 4.

Senghor, Léopold Sédar. 'Ce que l'homme noir apporte', *Liberté I: Négritude et humanisme*. Paris: Seuil, 1964.

Songolo, Aliko. *Aimé Césaire: une poétique de la découverte*. Paris: L'Harmattan, 1985.

Soyinka, Wolé. *The Burden of Memory, the Muse of Forgiveness*. Oxford: Oxford University Press, 1999.

Thébia-Melson, Annick (ed.). *Aimé Césaire, le legs: nous sommes de ceux qui disent non à l'ombre*. Paris: Argal Editions, 2009.

Tolliver, Julie-Françoise. 'Césaire/Lumumba: A Season of Solidarity', *Journal of Postcolonial Writing* 50.4 (2014): 398–409.

Toumson, Roger and Simonne Henry-Valmore. *Aimé Césaire: Le nègre inconsolé*. Paris: Syros, 1993.

Véron, Kora. 'Césaire at the Crossroads in Haiti: Correspondence with Henri Seyrig', *Comparative Literature Studies* 50.3 (2013): 430–444.

Véron, Kora. *Aimé Césaire: Configurations*. Paris: Seuil, 2021.

Véron, Kora. '*Corps perdu* d'Aimé Césaire et de Pablo Picasso, un recueil de guerres et de paix', *Continents manuscrits* 18 (2022): 1–13.

Watts, Richard. *Packing Postcoloniality: The Manufacture of Literary Identity in the Francophone World*. Lanham: Lexington, 2005.

Wilder, Gary. *Freedom Time: Negritude, Decolonization, and the Future of the World*. Durham and London: Duke University Press, 2015.

Index

Abel, Lionel 39, 97
Achille, Louis-Thomas 26, 29, 30, 154
Addis Ababa
  conference of African heads of state 175
Adotevi, Stanislas 55
Aeschylus 88
Africa
  Bantu culture 137, 184, 203
  and the *Cahier* 39, 40, 49, 97–8, 114
  and Caribbean identity 9
  in Césaire's thought 34, 35, 223
  in *Corps perdu* 128, 131
  decolonisation 6, 39, 133, 135, 140–1, 151–9, 169–70, 172, 174, 175, 202, 220
  Depestre and African poetry 143
  and *Et les chiens se taissaient* 89, 93
  in *Ferrements* 160, 165–7, 168–72
  and Haiti 187, 190–1
  independence movements 15, 134
  and *Les Armes miraculeuses* 83, 85
  and Martinique 146
  and negritude 13, 33, 34, 48, 49, 233
  pan-Africanism 10
  in *Soleil cou coupé* 122–3
  and *Tropiques* 62, 65–7, 68, 71–2

African art
  Festival mondial des arts nègres, Césaire's 'Discours sur l'art africain' 6, 14–15, 180–2
African culture
  and anticolonialism 152, 153–4
  and the *Cahier* 16
  and Césaire's plays 185
African poetry
  and *Ferrements* 165
African spirituality 110
  in *La Tragédie du Roi Christophe* 193, 197
  see also Voodoo spirituality; Yoruba spirituality
Algeria 20, 136, 141, 175
Aliker, André 36
Aliker, Pierre 30, 36, 149, 241
Almquist, Steven 207
anaphora
  in the *Cahier* 47–8, 49–50, 52–3, 69
  in *Corps perdu* 126
  in *Les Armes miraculeuses* 82
  in *moi, laminaire...* 228, 229
  in Péguy's poetry 69
  in *Soleil cou coupé* 119–20, 121, 131
Angola 158
Annonciation 225

284 INDEX

anticolonialism
  and African decolonisation 151–9
  Bandung Conference (1955) 141,
    152, 158
  and the *Cahier* 39, 41, 113, 134,
    155–9
  Césaire's *Discourse sur le colonialism*
    11–12, 54, 105, 106, 134–40,
    134–50, 151, 155, 206
  and Césaire's plays 186
  and communism 144–5
  and culture 180
  and ecology 110
  and *Ferrements* 160, 161
  and French capitalism 146
  in 'L'impossible contact' 105–6
  and Martinique departmentalisation
    101
  and *Soleil cou coupé* 116
  and *Une Tempête* 208–9
  see also decolonisation
antiracism
  and *Tropiques* 71, 73
  see also negritude
Anubis (dog-eared god) 89
Apollinaire, Guillaume 110, 112
  Alcools, 'Zone' 109
Aragon, Louis 141, 142, 145
  the 'Affaire Aragon' 31
  'Sur la poésie nationale' 142
Arnold, James
  and the *Cahier* 39–40, 48, 50,
    52, 54, 113, 155–6, 156–7,
    158
  and Césaire's legacy 248
  and Césaire's politicisation 152
  and *Comme un malentendu de salut*
    236
  and *Corps perdu* 124, 132
  and *Et les chiens se taissaient* 86–7,
    89–90
  and *Ferrements* 160
  and *moi, laminaire...* 235
  and *Soleil cou coupé* 118, 120,
    122
  on *La Tragédie du Roi Christophe*
    191, 192
Arthur H
  'L'Or noir' 245

assimilation
  cultural 25–6, 29, 32
  and departmentalisation 101
Asturias, Miguel Angel 223, 223–4
Avignon festival (1996) 191–2

Ba, M. Souley 226
Balzac, Honoré de 137
Bandung Conference (1955) 141,
  152, 158
Bantu culture 137, 184, 203
Barde, R.P. 136
Barnet, Rudi 200
Baudelaire, Charles 69, 74, 109, 137
  'L'Albatros' 47
  'L'Irrémédiable' 85
Bayle, Lieutenant de Vaisseau 10
Beauvoir, Simone de 20
Belgium
  and *Une Saison au Congo* 21, 200
Benin 131
Bergson, Henri 68
Bernabé, Jean 221
biblical imagery *see* Christian imagery
Biden, Joe 53
Bissol, Léopold 101, 147
black art 35
black consciousness 23, 24
  and Césaire's *Cahier* 38, 41–2,
    43–4
black culture/identity
  and anticolonialism 6, 153–4, 180
  black humanism 33, 50
  and the *Cahier* 40, 41, 49, 56–7
  and Césaire's plays 185
  cultural activism 125
  and negritude 13, 14, 15, 35,
    181–2
  and poetry 144
  and surrealism 72
  in *Tropiques* 62
  see also negritude
Black Hebdo 178
black internationalism in Paris 10,
  13, 24
'Black is Beautiful' movement 24–5
Black Lives Matter 104, 243
  and the *Cahier* 50–1, 98
  Cullors and leadership 22

INDEX

285

and negritude 12–13, 15, 25
and oppression and suffocation
60–1
Black Power movement 206, 207
black women 20, 55, 56, 247
Bona, Dénètem Touam 215
Bonner, Christopher 161
Boukman, Dutty 142
Bouteldja, Houria 243
Brathwaite, Kwame 24
'Caliban' 210
breath metaphor 59–61, 63, 181
Brecht, Berthold 89, 185
Breton, André 31, 72–3, 89, 108, 109,
110, 112, 145
and the *Cahier* 17, 38, 39, 54, 97,
113, 157
and Masson, André, *Martinique,
charmeuse de serpents* 72–3
and *Tropiques* 62, 69, 70, 72
'Un grand poète noir' 72
British Caribbean colonies 175–6
Brown, Sterling
'Strong Men' 33, 48

Cabrera, Lydia 74
Cadastre 172, 173
*Cahier d'un retour au pays natal
[Notebook of a Return to the
Native Land]* 6, 10, 23, 36–7,
75, 175, 221, 245, 246
1939 edition 16, 17, 35, 37–57, 59,
71
Arnold's work on 39–40
Bordas edition (1947) 39, 97, 108,
110, 112–15, 156, 157, 209
Brentano's edition (1947) 17, 39,
74, 97–9, 113, 114
and the Congo 114, 198
Cuban edition 74, 110
English translation 39
and *Et les chiens se taissaient* 87, 90,
91
and *Ferrements* 163, 171
Glissant on 223
and *Les Armes miraculeuses* 76, 79,
80, 81, 84, 85, 98, 115
and *moi, laminaire...* 226, 227, 229,
240

and negritude 13–14, 15–16, 37,
41, 42, 44, 45, 46–8
Présence Africaine edition (1956) 6,
39, 40, 56, 134, 155–9
and *La Tragédie du Roi Christophe*
198
and *Tropiques* 61, 63, 64
Volontés edition 6, 38–9, 110, 113
Caillois, Roger 134, 137
Camus, Albert 20
capitalism
and colonialism 136
Caribbean art, culture and history 16,
22, 110–11
and black culture 32
and Césaire's plays 186
in *Et les chiens se taissaient* 96, 98
and Glissant 222–3
and *Légitime Défense* 31, 37
and *Tropiques* 70, 75
writers 21
Caribbean decolonisation 175–6
censorship 6
Césaire, Aimé
and Communism 5, 17, 31, 100–1,
112, 114, 133, 134, 137,
145–8
and the Créolite movement 221–2
in Croatia 36–7
cultural legacy 244–8
death and commemoration 241–2
deaths of family and friends 223–4
dispute with Depestre 141–5, 155
divorce from Suzanne 133
family background 8–9
France and Martinique 19
in Haiti (1944) 74–5
and 'incandescent speech' 7
intellectual activism 20–1
and language 247–8
marriage to Suzanne Roussi 36
'nègre marron' identity 214–15,
242
and negritude 9, 12–16, 21
Nobel Peace Prize nomination 246
in Paris 9–10, 16, 24–36, 57
President of the Association des
Étudiants Martiniquais 32–3
political legacy 242–4

286 INDEX

Césaire, Aimé (*cont.*)
  politics 3, 7–8, 24, 54, 100–8, 172,
    173–80, 214–20, 223
    autonomy for Martinique 19,
      174–80, 184, 215–17
    as Deputy for Martinique 3, 7,
      10–11, 21, 22, 62, 100, 215,
      242
    and Martinique
      departmentalisation 5, 7–8,
      10–11, 101–5
    Mayor of Fort-de-France 10, 22,
      61, 100, 113, 215, 239
    and poetry 18–19, 21, 132, 214
    retirement from 219–20
  return to Martinique 57, 58–9
  and Schoelcher 2–3, 19, 73–4
  speeches 7, 106–8, 132, 138–41
    'Culture et colonisation' (Paris,
      1956) 6, 152–4, 156
    on decentralisation for
      Martinique 217–18
    'Discours sur la négritude' 220
    'Discours sur l'art africain'(Dakar,
      1966) 6, 14–15, 180–2
    'La mort aux colonies' 141
    'L'homme de culture et ses
      responsabilités' (Rome, 1959)
      5, 6, 154–5, 180
    on Martinique autonomy 177–8,
      178–9, 215–17
    'Poésie et connaissance' 74–5
    on Schoelcher 2
    on self-governance in Martinique
      175, 177
    'Société et littérature dans les
      Antilles' 182–3
    on Stalinism 147–8
  on writers and artists as 'inventors
    of souls' 5–6, 154–5
  see also Martinique; poetry; theatre;
    Tropiques
Césaire, Denise 224
Césaire, Fernand 8
Césaire, Francis 223–4
Césaire, Ina
  Mémoires d'isles 186
  Rosanie Soleil 186
Césaire, Jacques 58

Césaire, Jean-Paul 186
Césaire, Manuel 186
Césaire, Nicolas Fernand 8
Césaire, Suzanne 5–6, 10, 16, 36, 58,
  109, 133, 223, 224, 244, 247
  Tropiques articles 48, 61, 65, 66–7,
    70
Chalaye, Sylvie 215
Chamoiseau, Patrick 21, 221
Chauvin, Derek 60
Chemins du monde
  'L'impossible contract' in 11–12,
    111, 134, 135
chlordecone pesticide 224–5
Chraïbi, Khalid 180
Christian imagery
  in *Les Armes miraculeuses* 82
  and negritude 50
  in *Soleil cou coupé* 116, 118, 120
Christianity
  in *La Tragédie du Roi Christophe*
    197
Christophe, Henri 21
Claudel, Paul
  Livre de Christophe Colomb 89
climate crisis 16
Cold War 111
  in the *Cahier* 113–14
  and *Ferrements* 160
  and *Une Saison au Congo* 200
'Colombes et menfenil' 76, 110
'Simouns' 110
colonialism 5, 6, 29
  and art 181
  colonial oppression and the *Cahier*
    38
  and departmentalisation 103
  and Nazism 243
  neocolonialism 183
  and *Tropiques* 67–8
  see also anticolonialism; *Discours
    sur le colonialisme [Discourse on
    Colonialism]*
Columbus, Christopher 89
*Comme un malentendu de salut [Like a
  Misunderstanding of Salvation]*
  214, 235–40
'Configurations' 238–9
'Dérisoire' 237–8

INDEX

'Passage' 236–7
'Vertu des lucioles' 237
Communism
and anticolonialism 144–5
and Césaire 31, 100–1, 112, 114, 133, 134, 137, 145–8
Communist Party
Angola 158
French (the PCF) 5, 17, 112, 134, 145, 147–8, 155
Martinique 100, 101, 104–5, 134, 138, 147–8, 149, 178
Condé, Maryse 20, 56, 247
L'Héritage de Caliban 212
Confiant, Raphaël 20, 187, 218, 221
Aimé Césaire: une traversée paradoxale du siècle 221, 243–4
Congo, Democratic Republic of
in the *Cahier* 114, 198
decolonisation 12
Une Saison au Congo 12, 21, 174, 188, 198–205
Constant, Fred 21
Cook, Mercer 153
Corps perdu 101, 108, 112, 115, 124–32, 159, 172, 173, 224
and the *Cahier* 115
'Corps perdu' 123, 127–30
'Dit d'errance' 124, 130–2
and *Ferrements* 162
'Mot' 123, 124, 125–7, 130
Picasso's artworks 124–5, 127, 130
'Tête de nègre' 111–12
'Couteaux midi' 109
Creole culture 33, 179, 185, 221
in *Ferrements* 164–5
Creole language 144, 179, 221, 222, 243–4
in *Une Tempête* 210
in *La Tragédie du Roi Christophe* 193
Créolite movement 221–2, 244, 246
Cretinoir, Albert 167
Croatia 36–7
Cuba 74
Havana conference (1968) 176–7
Cullen, Countee 27
Cullors, Patrisse 22
cultural assimilation 25–6, 29, 32

Damas, Léon Gontran 9, 13, 26, 36, 107, 223, 234
Dante Alighieri 162–3
Darsières, Canille 217, 219
Davis, Gregson 88, 160, 162, 192, 199, 204–5, 233, 248
Davis, John 153
decolonisation 12, 17, 88
Africa 6, 39, 133, 135, 140–1, 151–9, 169–70, 172, 174, 175, 202, 220
Caribbean 175–6
culture of 5, 155
and *Ferrements* 160, 163, 165
Haiti 12, 190–1, 193, 195, 198
see also anticolonialism
Delafosse, Maurice 9, 34
Delgrès, Louis 1, 166–7, 170
Depestre, René 141–5, 155, 182, 245
Bonjour et adieu à la négritude 182
Végétations de clarté 141
Dessalines, Jean-Jacques 87, 142, 166, 189
Deveine, Michel 157
Diop, Alioune 134, 152, 236
Diop, Cheikh Anta 137
Nations nègres et culture 134
'Discours sur l'art africain' [discourse on African art] 6, 14–15, 180–2
Discours sur le colonialisme [Discourse on Colonialism] 11–12, 54, 105, 106, 134–40, 134–50, 151, 155, 181, 183, 206, 220, 242, 243
'Discourse sur la négritude' 220
Dobzynski, Charles 142
Drumont, Édouard 73
Du Bois, W.E.B. 27
Duvalier, François 187, 191

ecology
and anticolonialism 110
and Césaire's poetry 16, 17
in *Tropiques* 62, 66, 67–8
Edwards, Brent Hayes 27, 47, 48
Egypt 34
Egyptian mythology
and *Et les chiens se taissaient* 89
Ekotto, Frieda 243

288 INDEX

environmental issues 240
  in the Caribbean 16
  chlordecone pesticide 224–5
  in *Et les chiens se taissaient* 94
  in *Tropiques* 62, 68
equality
  and the *Cahier* 55
  Césaire's commitment to 151
  and Césaire'sm politics 141
Esclavage et colonisation 105
Eshleman, Clayton 39, 120, 127,
    160–1, 235, 236
*Et les chiens se taissaient [And the dogs
    were silent]* 12, 76, 86–96, 159,
    187
  and the *Cahier* 98
  and *Comme un malentendu de salut*
    237
  and *Ferrements* 167
  German edition 159
  in *Les Armes miraculeuses* (1956) 12,
    76, 86, 87, 90
  Présence Africaine edition 86, 87,
    92
  and *Soleil cou coupé* 119
  and *La Tragédie du Roi Christophe*
    195–6, 197
Ethiopian civilisation 16, 66–7
Études littéraires 182
Europe 27
European Economic Commission
    149–50, 217

Fanon, Franz 24, 59–60, 113, 137–8,
    183, 212, 220, 233, 234
  'Antillais et Africains' 28
  and decolonisation 154, 202
  Les Damnés de la Terre 138, 140
  Peau noire, masques blancs 138
fascism
  and surrealism 70
federalism
  and Martinique 18
Ferdinand, Malcom 224–5
Ferrements [Ferraments] 12, 17, 134,
    159–72, 173, 184, 225
  'A la mémoire d'un syndicaliste
    noir' 167
  'Afrique' 169

'Beau sang giclé' 164–5, 172
'Bucolique' 165, 172
'Ferrements' 161–2, 163, 171
'Le Temps de la liberté' 165–6
'mais il y a ce mal' 171
'Mémorial de Louis Delgrès'
    166–7, 170–1
'Pour saluer le tiers monde' 169–70
'Salut à la Guinée' 163–4, 165,
    168–9
'Spirales' 163–4, 173
'sur l'état de l'Union' 167–8, 170–1
Festival mondial des arts nègres
  Césaire's speech on African art 6,
    14–15, 180–2
First World War 28
Florenne, Yves 137
Floyd, George 60
Fonkoua, Romuald 21, 90, 134, 145,
    191, 246
Forsdick, Charles 190
Fort-de-France 107, 113, 138, 191,
    218, 219, 241
  Césaire as Mayor of 10–11, 22
  Festival Culturel de Fort-de-France
    186
  Lycée Schoelcher 10
  Schoelcher's statue in 4
France
  and Césaire's *Discours sur le
    colonialism* 134–6, 137–40, 151
  Communist Party 5, 17
  Constitution (1958) 150–1
  decolonisation 133
  and the departmentalisation of
    Martinique 5, 7–8, 10–11,
    101–5
  Indigènes de la République 243
  Nazi occupation of 20
  RPF (*Rassemblement du peuple
    français*) 104
  Vichy government 10, 58, 70
France-Observateur 145
Frazer, James
  The Golden Bough 89
freedom
  Césaire on autonomy for
    Martinique 179
  Césaire's commitment to 151

INDEX 289

in *Corps perdu* 126, 129, 131
and *Et les chiens se taissaient* 89, 96
in *Les Armes miraculeuses* 77, 78, 93
in *Soleil cou coupé* 119, 121
in *Une Tempête* 211
and *Tropiques* 73–4
French colonies
abolition of slavery 1–2, 12
and Republican ideology 8
French Empire 103
French Revolution 109
and *Toussaint Louverture: La Révolution française et le probleme colonial* (Césaire) 188–90
Freudian psychoanalysis
and *Légitime Défense* 31
Frobenius, Leo 9, 13, 30, 34, 49, 93, 183–4
Histoire de la civilisation africaine 66
'homme-plante' concept 16, 48–9, 66, 67, 79, 95, 98, 209, 224
and *Tropiques* 62, 65–6, 67, 68, 71
Frost, Jacqueline 92
Fuentes, Carlos 212

Gallimard
publication of *Les Armes miraculeuses* 75, 76, 77, 78, 80, 85
Garaudy, Roger 147
Garner, Eric 60
Gaulle, Charles de 104, 150
gender
in Césaire's *Cahier* 55–6
see also women
Ghana 169
Gilot, Françoise 112
Girard, Rosan 147
Giraudoux, Jean 74
Electre 86
La Guerre de Troie n'aura pas lieu 86
Giscard d'Estaing, Valéry 215
Glissant, Édouard 222–3, 230, 244, 245
Gobineau, Joseph Arthur 35, 51
Goll, Ivan 39, 76, 97
Gorman, Amanda
'The Hill We Climb' 53
Grandvorka 157
Gratiant, George 61, 65, 104, 144

Gratiant, Gilbert 223
'Mulâtres: pour le bien et le mal' 33
Greek reason
and negritude 14
Greek tragedy
and *Et les chiens se taissaient* 12, 86, 88, 89, 92–3
Grégoire, Abbé 138–9
Guadeloupe 150, 175, 218, 242
chlordecone pesticide 224, 225
Communist Federation 147
departmentalisation 11, 101, 102, 103, 107, 139
in *Ferrements* 166
Second World War 58
slave revolt 1
Guberina, Petar 36, 86, 157–8
Guérin, Daniel
Les Antilles décolonisées 149, 150
Guilloux, Louis and Renée 27
Guinea 151, 163, 169
Guiana 101, 103, 139, 150, 218

Haiti 21, 244–5
and Africa 187, 190–1
Césaire in (1944) 74–5, 87
decolonisation 12, 190–1, 193, 195, 198
Depestre on Haitian art 143–4
Duvalier dictatorship 187, 191
independence 166, 174, 187
in *La Tragédie du Roi Christophe* 174, 186–7, 190–8
Port-au-Prince, Congrès de Philosophie 74–5
Revolution 47, 86, 91, 185
Toussaint Louverture: La Révolution française et le probleme colonial (Césaire) 187–90
slave revolts 1, 13, 142, 187
and Césaire's *Cahier* 45–6
Hale, Thomas 8, 19
Harlem Renaissance 26, 30, 32
Harris, Kamala 21
Harris, Rodney 89, 90
Hartung, Hans 115
Hearn, Lafcadio 65
Hegel, G.W.F. 153

Hémisphères journal 72, 74, 76, 110
Hénane, René 77, 78, 82, 108, 109, 226
Henry-Valmore, Simonne 75, 116, 133, 145
Hermine, Eleanor 8
Hitler, Adolf 73, 106
Hogsbjerg, Christian 190
'homme-plante' concept (Frobenius) 16, 48–9, 66, 67, 79, 95, 98, 209
Hughes, Langston 10, 26, 27, 30, 73
humanism 33, 50, 106
  in Césaire's negritude 16
  and colonialism 135, 136
Hungary 145, 147
Hurston, Zora Neale 27

Ife 131
Indochina 134, 135
Irele, Francis Abiola 15
Ishtar, Babylonian Mother-Goddess 123

Jahn, Janheinz 159
Jamaica 176
James, C.L.R.
  The Black Jacobins 190
Jet magazine 168
Jones, Donna 67
Journal d'une poésie nationale 142
justice
  Césaire's commitment to 151
Justice (journal) 11, 104–5, 134, 138, 147

'K' (surrealist publishing house) 115
Kalikoff, Hedy 55–6
Kanor, Fabienne 245, 247
Kanor, Véronique 245
Kesteloot, Lilyan 18–19, 50, 226
Khalfa, Jean 16, 226
Khrushchev, Nikita 146, 148
King, Martin Luther 206, 209

la Brunelière, Monsignor Varin de, Bishop 73
La Dépêche Africaine 26
'La Martinique telle qu'elle est' 183–4

La Nouvelle critique 140
La Tragedie see Tragédie du Roi Christophe [The Tragedy of King Christophe]
La Voix des Nègres 28
Labéjof, Yvan 186
Laferrière, Dany
  L'Enigme de retour 244–5
Laforgue, Pierre 122
Lam, Wilfredo 70, 74, 97, 108, 109, 110–11, 112, 122, 169
  'La Jungle' 110
  and *moi, laminaire...* 223, 225, 226
Lamming, George 206, 212
Latin American cultures 154
Lautréamont, Comte de 137
'Le colonialisme n'est pas mort' 140
Le Progressiste 150, 175, 179, 182, 215
Le Sel noir 244
Légitime Défense 10, 30–1, 33, 37, 61, 70, 145
Leiner, Jacqueline 62, 63, 70, 75, 183, 238
Leiris, Michel 109, 148, 176
Lepervenche, Leon de 101
L'Époque 105
Léro, Étienne 30, 31
Les Armes miraculeuses [The Miraculous Weapons] 73, 75–86, 97, 110, 111, 124
  'Avis de tirs' 77–8
  'Batéké' 83, 84
  'Batouque' 83–4
  and the *Cahier* 76, 79, 80, 81, 84, 85, 98, 115
  'Conquête de l'aube' 80–1
  and *Et les chiens se taissaient* 12, 76, 86, 87, 89–90, 93
  and *Ferrements* 161–2, 165
  'La Forêt vierge' 84–5
  'Le Grand midi' 77, 79–80
  'Les Armes miraculeuses' 81–3
  'Les pur-sang' 69, 77, 78–9, 165, 224
  'L'Irrémédiable' 84, 85
  publication of 76
  and *Soleil cou coupé* 115, 116, 122
Les Chemins du monde (journal) 105–6
Letchimy, Serge 219

'Lettre á Maurice Thorez' 145–8, 151
L'Étudiant noir journal 10, 13, 32–3,
48, 83
articles 24
and Césaire's *Cahier* 41–2
as *L'Étudiant martiniquais* 32, 36
Nardal's article ('Guignol Ouolof')
26
'Nêgreries' articles (Césaire) 13,
26, 32, 33, 37, 41, 41–2, 43, 44,
45, 47, 49, 220–1
and *Tropiques* 61
L'Humanité 112, 147
'L'impossible contact' 105–6, 115,
134, 135, 136
Locke, Alain 26–7, 29
Locke, Alan 10
Loeb, Pierre 109
Louis-Philippe, French king 9
Louverture, Toussaint 1, 13, 73, 212
in the *Cahier* 45–6, 81, 114, 156
and *Et les chiens se taissaient* 86–7,
187
*Toussaint Louverture: La Révolution
française et le probleme colonial*
187–90
Lumumba, Patrice
in *Une Saison au Congo* 21, 199,
201–5
Lung Fou, Marie-Thérèse Julien 4

Mabille, Pierre 110
McKay, Claude 10, 26, 27, 30, 73
Banjo 29
Macni, Eugénie 8
Madagascar 134, 135, 136
Malcolm X 206
Mali 169
Mallarmé, Stéphane 69, 74
Malraux, André 20, 150–1, 181
Mandela, Nelson 138
Mannoni, Octave 137, 138, 206
Maran, René
Batouala 33
'marronage' poetry 142–3, 144
Marti, José 212
Martinique
abolition of slavery in 1–2
and Africa 146

Assembléé Nationale
Césaire as Deputy 3, 7, 10–11,
21, 22, 215
Césaire's speeches 106–8, 132,
138–41, 175
autonomy for 6, 19, 174–80, 184,
215–17
and the *Cahier* 40, 41, 42, 43–4, 45,
46–7, 54, 97
Centre Martiniquais d'Action
Culturelle 186
Césaire's return to 10, 37, 57,
58–9, 138
Communist Party 100, 101, 104–5,
134, 138, 147–8, 149, 178
culture 183–4
decentralization 217–18
departmentalisation 5, 7–8, 10–11,
101–5, 106–7, 108, 134, 135,
139–40, 148–9, 170, 172, 177,
179, 243
destruction of statues of Schoelcher
1–4
environmental devastation 224–5
and *Et les chiens se taissaient* 90
Free French in 10, 59
and French colonialism 138
and the French Constitution (1958)
150–1
and the Haitian Revolution 189
independence movement 19, 174,
176–80
inequality in 170
and *La Tragédie du Roi Christophe*
187
and *Les Armes miraculeuses* 84
Mount Pelée volcanic 7, 118
poverty in 43
PPM (Parti Progressiste
Martiniquais) 17–18, 149–50,
154, 162, 172, 173, 177–8,
179–80, 215, 216–17
regeneration projects 218–19
and the 'révolution refoulée'
['repressed revolution'] 59
Service Municipal d'Action
Culturelle 186, 218
slave revolt 1–2, 4
Socialist Federation 178

292 INDEX

Martinique (*cont.*)
 strikes 178, 242–3, 244
 and surrealism 72
 and *Une Tempête* 206, 207
 and *Tropiques* 63–5
 Trouillé administration 11
 Vichy regime 10, 11, 58–9, 63–4, 181
 see also Fort-de-France
Marxism 10, 145–6
 and development 177–8
 and *Discourse sur le colonialism* 137
 and *Légitime Défense* 30–1, 33, 145
 see also Communism
Masson, André 70, 72
Masurel, Laurence 179
Maugée, Aristide 61
Maximin, Daniel 7, 21, 185, 196, 225, 235–6, 244
 L'Isolé soleil 244
Mémoires d'isles (Ina Césaire) 186
Ménil, René 10, 30, 31, 33, 61, 63–4, 70, 147
 and *Ferrements* 161
 'Introduction au merveilleux' 70
 on *La Tragédie du Roi Christophe* 198
Miami conference on the black diaspora 220
Miller, Christopher 41
Mitterand, François 178, 215, 216, 217, 224
modernism
 French Caribbean culture 22
 and negritude 17
moi, laminaire...[i, laminaria...] 18, 110, 214, 223, 224, 225–35, 236, 239–40, 246
 'annonciations' 231
 'calendrier lagunaire' 228–9, 241–2
 'condition mangrove' 230
 'j'ai guidé du troupeau la longue transhumance' 229–30
 meaning of the title 226
 'nouvelle bonté' 235
 poem dedicated to Asturias 223–4
 poems dedicated to Wilfredo Lam 234–5
 'Rabordaille' 235

'Wilfredo Lam' 235
preface 227–8
'sentiments et ressentiments des mots' 231–3
'une belle parade de trochilidés' 230
Mollet, Guy 146
Monnerot, Jules 30
Monnerville, Gaston 101
Montesquieu 179
Muller, R.P. 136
Murdoch, Adlai 243
music 245

Nardal, Jane 10, 25, 27, 30
Nardal, Paulette 10, 25–6, 30
national culture, Césaire on 154–5, 182–3
Nazism 11–12, 106, 138
 and colonialism 243
'nègre', use of the term 23, 27–9
'Négreries' 13, 23, 26, 32, 33, 35, 37, 41, 41–2, 43, 44, 45, 47, 49
negritude 9, 12–16, 21, 62–3, 220–2, 245, 246
 and Africa 13, 33, 34, 48, 49, 233
 and 'Black is Beautiful' 24–5
 and Black Lives Matter 12–13, 15, 25
 and the *Cahier* 13–14, 15–16, 37, 41, 42, 44, 45, 46–8, 49–53, 54, 55, 56, 57, 62, 75, 187
 and Césaire on African art 181–2
 and *Comme un malentendu de salut* 236
 and *Corps perdu* 101, 127, 129–30, 131
 and the Créolité movement 222
 Depestre's criticism of 142
 'Discours sur la négritude' 220
 in *Et les chiens se taissaient* 87–8, 94, 187
 and Glissant 223
 and Haiti 187
 and *Les Armes miraculeuses* 75–6, 83, 101
 and *L'Étudiant noir* 32–3, 62, 83
 and *moi, laminaire...* 229
 'New Negro' concept 26–7, 29, 42

INDEX

in Paris 23–34, 35–6
and poetry 75
and *Une Saison au Congo* 201
and *Soleil cou coupé* 116, 120, 123–4
and surrealism 17
and *Une Tempête* 206, 207
and the term 'nègre' 23, 27–9, 33, 123, 124, 125, 129
and *Tropiques* 62–3
neocolonialism 183
Nesbitt, Nick 101, 160, 161, 192
Ngal, M. 34, 75
Nietzsche, Friedrich 68, 76, 96, 185
  The Birth of Tragedy 88
Nixon, Rob 212
Nkrumah, Kwame 175
Noland, Carrie 54, 94
'Noria' 225
Norland, Carrie 229

Obama, Barack 21
OJAM (Organisation de la jeunesse anticolonialiste de la Martinique) 176
Ojo-Ade, Femi 96, 211
Onan, biblical figure 51, 55, 157

Paley, Euzhan 19
pan-Africanism 10
Paris
  black internationalism 10, 13, 24, 57
  Césaire in 9–10, 16, 24–36
    address at the Sorbonne (1948) 105
  Comédie-Française 191
  Exposition coloniale internationale 29
  Exposition internationale du surréalisme 109
  fascism in 35–6
  Nardal salons 30
  plaque to Césaire at the Panthéon 241–2
  Premier Congrès des intellectuels et artistes noirs (1956) 6, 125, 152–4, 155
  staging of *Une Saison au Congo* 200
Péguy, Charles 48, 69
Pelorson, Georges 38

Perse, Saint-Jean 223
Pétain, Maréchal 58, 63–4
Pétion, Alexandre 192, 193, 195
Picasso, Pablo 108, 110, 111–12, 148
  artworks for *Corps Perdu* 112, 124–5, 127, 130
  'Tête de negre' 112, 125, 152
Pinto de Andrade, Mário 158
Piquine, Siméon 157
Place, Jean-Michel 183
plant-human concept 16, 48–9, 66, 67, 79, 95, 98, 209, 224
'Poésie et connaissance' 16, 68, 88
Poésie, Théâtre, Essais, et Discours 122, 158
poetry 108–15, 180, 247, 248
  Césaire and 'incandescent speech' 7
  Césaire on theatre and poetry 184–5
  and colonialism 181
  politicisation of 17
  and politics 18–19, 21, 132
  volcanic imagery in 7
  see also individual poetry volumes
Poland 145
  Congrès mondial pour la paix 111
police
  and Black Lives Matter 25, 60, 104
Pompidou, Georges 150
Ponton, Georges-Louis 73
Présence Africaine (journal and publications) 6, 11, 152, 236
  Cahier d'un retour au pays natal (1956 edition) 6, 39, 40, 56, 134, 155–9
  Césaire's article on Touré 151, 163
  'Décolonisation pour les Antilles' 148–9
  'Discours sur la négritude' 220
  Discours sur le colonialisme 134
  Et les chiens se taissaient 86, 87, 159
  'Réponse à Depestre poète haitien' 142–4
  'Sur la poésie nationale' 143–4
  Une Tempête 206

racial identity
  in *Une Tempête* 207–8

INDEX

racism 7
 and Césaire's *Cahier* 38, 55
 in France 243
 and negritude 13, 15, 75
 in *Tropiques* 62
racist stereotypes
 in the *Cahier* 46–7
rap music 245
Réclame 134
Renan, Ernest 106, 136, 211–12
Renard, Michel 179
René Corail, Khokho 4, 19
'Réponse à Depestre poète haitien
 (Éléments d'art poétique)'
 142–3
Retamar, Roberto Fernandez
 'Caliban: Notes towards a
 Discussion of Culture in Our
 America' 211–12
Réunion 101, 103, 107, 139
Revue de monde noir (journal) 10, 26,
 29–30, 32–3
Richepanse, French General 166
Rimbaud, Arthur 69, 74, 109
Robert, Admiral Georges 10, 58–9,
 61, 63, 73
Rome
 *Deuxième congrès des écrivains et
 artistes noir* (1959) 5, 6, 152,
 154–5, 180, 218
Rosanie Soleil (Ina Césaire) 186
Rosello, Mireille 56
 'The Césaire Effect' 18–19
Rothberg, Michael 136
Rouil, Marie-Thérèse 178
Roumain, Jacques
 Gouverneurs de la rosée 141
Rousseau, Henri 72–3
Roussi, Suzanne *see* Césaire,
 Suzanne

*Une Saison au Congo [A Season in
 the Congo]* 12, 21, 174, 188,
 198–205, 206
 and *Une Tempête* 210, 211, 212
 and *La Tragédie du Roi Christophe*
 200–1
Sarkozy, Nicolas 138, 241
Sarraut, Albert 136

Sartre, Jean-Paul 20, 113, 148, 158,
 176
 'Orphée noir' 38
Saurrat, Albert
 Grandeur et servitude coloniales 140
Schoelcher, Victor 2–3, 19, 73–4,
 102, 105
 destruction of statues of 1–4
 Esclavage et colonisation 2
Second World War 111
 in Martinique 58–9
 in Paris 35
Senegal
 Festival mondial des arts nègres
 (Dakar) 6, 14–15, 180–2, 191,
 220
 Théâtre National Daniel-Sorano
 191
Senghor, Lamine 28
Senghor, Léopold Sédar 9, 36, 70,
 125, 144, 175, 176, 236
 'Ce que l'homme noir apporte' 35
 and Césaire's *Cahier* 37
 and *Comme un malentendu de salut*
 236
 on cultural mixing 153–4
 and *Ferrements* 169
 and *L'Étudiant noir* 32, 33
 meeting with Césaire in Paris 33–4
 negritude 13, 14, 26, 33–5
 and *La Tragédie* 191
Serreau, Jean-Michel 191, 200, 206,
 207
sexuality
 in *Les Armes miraculeuses* 74, 83
Shakespeare, William 89, 185
 and Césaire's *La Tragédie* 192
 The Tempest 12, 52, 206, 207, 208,
 212
 see also Une Tempête
Sieger, Jacqueline 18
slavery/slave trade 1, 9, 102
 in the *Cahier* 40, 41, 44–5, 50–2,
 71, 77, 114, 115, 157, 175
 Code Noir 27–8, 50
 in *Corps perdu* 126–7, 128, 129, 130,
 131
 as a crime against humanity 219–20
 enslavement and *Tropiques* 63, 64–5

INDEX

295

and *Et les chiens se taissaient* 89,
    90–2, 93
and *Ferrements* 160, 161–2, 166
French abolition of 1–2, 12, 139
legacy of 105
and *Les Armes miraculeuses* 77–8,
    80, 81, 82–3, 84, 85
and *Soleil cou coupé* 116, 121
in *Une Tempête* 12
see also Haiti
Socé, Ousmane 9
Soleil cou coupé [Solar Throat Slashed]
    12, 101, 108, 112, 115–24, 172,
    173
'A l'Afrique' 110, 122–3, 169
'Barbare' 123–4
and the *Cahier* 115
'Chevelure' 247
'Couteaux midi' 109, 120–1
'Défaire et refaire le soleil' 119–20
'Demeure antipode' 120
'Demeure I' 119–20
and *Ferrements* 162, 163
'Jugement de lumière' 116
'Le coup de couteau du soleil dans
    le dos des villes surprises'
    118–19, 120
'Lynch' poems 116–18, 119, 130
'Magique' 116
and *moi, laminaire...* 230
'Ode à la Guinée' 163
publication 115–16
Songolo, Aliko 83–4, 160
South Africa 138
Soviet Union 107, 114
    Stalinism 5, 146, 147–8, 155
    Union of Soviet Writers 5
Soyinka, Wole 15, 55, 184
Spengler, Oswald 177
Stalinism 5, 146, 147–8, 155
suffocation imagery 59–61, 90–1, 98
the sun
    in *Corps perdu* 126–7
    in *Soleil cou coupé* 116, 118, 119,
        120–1
surrealism 10, 97, 112
    and Césaire's poetry 17, 73, 74,
        101, 108–9
    Cadastre 173

the *Cahier* 39, 71, 97, 156, 157–8
Ferrements 161, 162
Les Armes miraculeuses 75–6, 84
Soleil cou coupé 116, 120, 121
and *Légitime Défense* 30–1, 70
and *Tropiques* 61–2, 70–3

Tempels, Placide 137
Une Tempête [A Tempest] 12, 186,
    206–13, 247
theatre 86, 172, 173, 180, 184–98
    and anticolonialism 186
    *La Tragédie du Roi Christophe [The
        Tragedy of King Christophe]* 12,
        21, 174, 185, 186–7, 190–8
    language of Césaire's plays 185–6
    *Une Saison au Congo [A Season in the
        Congo]* 12, 174, 188
    Une Tempête [A Tempest] 12, 186,
        206–13, 247
Thorez, Maurice 145, 147–8
Till, Emmett 167–8
Tolliver, Julie-Françoise 200
'Tombeau du soleil' 76
Toumson, Roger 75, 116, 133, 145
Touré, Sékou 151, 163, 175
*Toussaint Louverture: La Révolution
    française et le problème colonial*
    187–90
*La Tragédie du Roi Christophe [The
    Tragedy of King Christophe]* 12,
    21, 174, 185, 186–7, 190–8,
    206
    and Césaire's *Toussaint Louverture*
        187–90
    critical reception of 191–2
    and *Une Tempête* 206, 207, 210,
        211, 212
    and *Une Saison au Congo* 200–1
Trinidad and Tobago 175–6
Tropiques 6, 16, 37, 48, 61–74, 75, 97,
    100, 101, 110, 155, 203, 223,
    224, 244, 246
    'André Breton, poète' (Suzanne
        Césaire) 70
    and antiracism 71, 73
    and the *Cahier* 39, 48, 98
    'En guise de manifeste littéraire' 71
    and *Ferrements* 170

Tropiques (cont.)
 final issue of 108
 founding of 10
 and French poetry 68–70
 'Introduction au folklore
  martiniquais' (Césaire and
  Ménil) 64–5
 'Introduction au merveilleux'
  (Ménil) 70
 'Le Grand camouflage' (Suzanne
  Césaire) 65
 'Léo Frobénius et le problème des
  civilisations' (Suzanne Césaire)
  66–7
 and *Les Armes miraculeuses* 69, 75,
  78, 79, 80
 'Maintenir la poésie' 69
 'Malaise d'une civilisation' (Suzanne
  Césaire) 67
 'Panorama' 181, 248
 'Poésie et connaissance' 16, 68
 republication (1978) 183
 'Un grand poète noir' (Breton) 72
Trouillé, Pierre, Préfet 11, 104–5,
 107
Truman, Harry 138
Tyrtaeus (poet of Sparta) 166
Tzara, Tristan 109

Ulysses 162
United States
 Black Power movement 206, 207
 Black Renaissance 220
 and the *Cahier* 40, 45
 and Césaire's 'sur l'état de l'Union'
  167–8
 police and Black Lives Matter 25,
  60
 slave revolts 45
 and wartime Martinique 58–9

Vaisseau Baylé, Lieutenant de 73
Valéry, Paul 69

'Varsovie' (poem) 111
Vasselot, Anatole Marquet de 4
Vergès, Françoise 30
Vergès, Raymond 101
Véron, Kora 8, 19, 29, 30, 34, 36, 72,
 100, 105, 109, 112, 177, 179,
 222, 238, 248
Vigne d'Octon, Paul
 A la gloire du sabre 140
violence
 in *Corps perdu* 126–7, 129, 130–1
 in *Ferrements* 167–8
 police and Black Lives Matter 25,
  60, 104
 and protest in Martinique 104
 in *Soleil cou coupé* 116–18, 119
Volontés (journal) 6, 17
 publication of Césaire's *Cahier* 6,
  38–9, 110, 113
Voodoo spirituality 110, 185
 in *Soleil cou coupé* 119
 in *Une Tempête* 206
 in *La Tragédie du Roi Christophe*
  193, 197
VVV journal 74

Wilberforce, William
 in *La Tragédie du Roi Christophe* 174
Wilder, Gary 149, 176
Wilson, Mantonica 235
women
 Césaire and black women 20, 55,
  56, 247
 Césaire and female characters 196,
  204, 212–13, 247
Wright, Richard 145, 153
 'I have seen Black Hands' 33

Yoruba spirituality
 in *Une Tempête* 206, 209–10
 in *La Tragédie du Roi Christophe* 197
Youssoupha
 'Rendons à Césaire' 245